Plant-Based Cookbook for Beginners

600 Quick & Delicious Vegan Recipes
For Busy People on the Plant Based Diet

Jackie Collins

Copyright © 2020 by Jackie Collins

All Right Reserved.

ISBN: 979-8621451226

Under no circumstances, no part of this publication may be reproduced, distributed, or transmitted in any form or by any means, including photocopying, recording, or other electronic or mechanical methods, or by any information storage and retrieval system without the prior written permission of the copyright holder.

The information in this book is accurate and complete, however, the author and the publisher do not warrant the accuracy of the information, text and graphics contained within the book due to the rapidly changing nature of science, research, known and unknown facts and internet. The author and the publisher do not hold any responsibility for errors, omissions or contrary interpretation of the subject matter herein. This book is presented solely for motivational and informational purposes only.

CONTENTS

INTRODUCTION 9

BASIC INGREDIENTS FOR PLANT-BASED RECIPES 11

1. Simple Vegetable Broth 11
2. Parsley Veggie Broth 11
3. Turnip & Parsnip Broth 11
4. Plant-Based Cheddar Cheese 12
5. Plant-Based Mozzarella Cheese 12
6. Plant-Based Parmesan Cheese 13
7. Cashew Cream Cheese 13
8. Tofu Mayonnaise 13
9. Plant-Based Cashew Cheese 13

BREAKFAST & SMOOTHIES 14

10. Coconut Porridge with Strawberries 14
11. Broccoli Hash Browns 14
12. Pesto Bread Twists 14
13. Classic French Toasts 15
14. Creamy Sesame Bread 15
15. Mexican Tofu Scramble 16
16. Mixed Seeds Bread 16
17. No-Bread Avocado Sandwich 16
18. Almond Flour English Muffins 17
19. Breakfast Naan Bread 17
20. Lemon-Almond Waffles 17
21. Mushroom & Spinach Chickpea Omelet 18
22. Coconut & Raspberry Pancakes 18
23. Blueberry Chia Pudding 18
24. Pumpkin Cake with Pistachios 19
25. Scrambled Tofu with Bell Pepper 19
26. Coconut Chia Pudding 19
27. Veggie Panini 20
28. Potato & Cauliflower Hash Browns 20
29. Chocolate & Carrot Bread with Raisins 20
30. Tropical French Toasts 21
31. Cashew Cheese Pimiento Biscuits 21
32. Vanilla Crepes with Berry Cream Compote Topping 22
33. Morning Naan Bread with Mango Jam 22
34. Sweet Orange Crepes 23
35. Cheddar Grits with Soy Chorizo 23
36. Pecan & Pumpkin Seed Oat Jars 23
37. Simple Apple Muffins 24
38. Orange-Glazed Raspberry Muffins 24
39. Almond Yogurt with Berries & Walnuts 24
40. Crispy Corn Cakes 25
41. Coconut Oat Bread 25
42. Banana French Toast with Strawberry Syrup 25
43. Spicy Quinoa Bowl with Black Beans 26
44. Orange Granola with Hazelnuts 26
45. Almond & Raisin Granola 26
46. Blueberry Muesli Breakfast 26
47. Chocolate-Mango Quinoa Bowl 27
48. Orange-Carrot Muffins with Cherries 27
49. Morning Pecan & Pear Farro 27
50. Almond Oatmeal Porridge 28
51. Classic Walnut Waffles with Maple Syrup 28
52. Orange-Bran Cups with Dates 28
53. Maple Banana Oats 28
54. Mushroom Crepes 29
55. Coconut Blueberry Muffins 29
56. Lemony Quinoa Muffins 29
57. Blackberry Waffles 30
58. Sweet Kiwi Oatmeal Bars 30
59. Scrambled Tofu with Swiss Chard 30
60. Tangerine Banana Toast 30
61. Spicy Apple Pancakes 31
62. Almond & Coconut Granola with Cherries ... 31
63. Cranberry Oat Cookies 31
64. Cinnamon Buckwheat with Almonds 32
65. Berry Quinoa Bowl 32
66. Mango Rice Pudding 32
67. Strawberry & Pecan Breakfast 32
68. Simple Pear Oatmeal 32
69. Fresh Peach Smoothie 33
70. Apple-Date Couscous with Macadamia Nuts 33
71. Thyme Pumpkin Stir-Fry 33
72. Choco-Berry Smoothie 33
73. Raspberry Almond Smoothie 34
74. Banana-Strawberry Smoothie 34
75. Tropical Smoothie Bowl 34
76. Coconut Fruit Smoothie 34
77. Amazing Yellow Smoothie 34
78. Delicious Matcha Smoothie 35
79. Hearty Smoothie 35
80. Apple Chocolate Smoothie 35
81. Carrot-Strawberry Smoothie 35
82. Power Green Smoothie 36
83. Maple Blueberry Smoothie 36
84. Energy Chia-Peach Smoothie 36
85. Morning Green Smoothie 36

SOUPS & STEWS 37

86. Spinach & Kale Soup with Fried Collards 37
87. Tofu Goulash Soup 37
88. Coconut Cream Pumpkin Soup 37
89. Celery Dill Soup 38

#	Recipe	Page
90.	Broccoli Fennel Soup	38
91.	Medley of Mushroom Soup	38
92.	Asian-Style Bean Soup	39
93.	Carrot & Mushroom Broth	39
94.	Mexican Tortilla Soup	39
95.	Spicy Bean Soup	40
96.	Celery & Potato Soup	40
97.	Cabbage & Red Bean Chili	40
98.	Rice Wine Mushroom Soup	40
99.	Tangy Bean Tomato Soup	41
100.	Vegetable Chili	41
101.	Turmeric Bean Soup	41
102.	Spinach & Potato Soup	42
103.	Arugula Coconut Soup	42
104.	Cayenne Pumpkin Soup	42
105.	Bell Pepper & Mushroom Soup	43
106.	Pumpkin & Garbanzo Chili with Kale	43
107.	Cream Soup of Zucchini with Walnuts	43
108.	Homemade Ramen Soup	43
109.	Vegetable & Rice Soup	44
110.	Daikon & Sweet Potato Soup	44
111.	Pressure Cooker Green Onion & Potato Soup	44
112.	Black-Eyed Pea Soup	44
113.	Chickpea & Vegetable Soup	45
114.	Italian Bean Soups	45
115.	Brussels Sprouts & Tofu Soup	45
116.	Roasted Basil & Tomato Soup	46
117.	Pasta & Tomato Soup	46
118.	Rosemary White Bean Soup	46
119.	Mushroom & Tofu Soup	46
120.	Rice Noodle Soup with Beans	47
121.	Brown Rice & Bean Chili	47
122.	Butternut Squash Coconut Cream Soup	47
123.	Cauliflower Soup with Leeks	47
124.	Lime Lentil Soup	48
125.	Spinach, Rice & Bean Soup	48
126.	Ginger Broccoli Soup	48
127.	Coconut Mushroom Soup	48
128.	Mustard Green & Potato Soup	49
129.	Sunday Soup	49
130.	Pumpkin Soup with Apples	49
131.	Pomodoro Cream Soup	49
132.	Potato Soup with Kale	50
133.	Mediterranean Soup	50
134.	Hot Bean & Corn Soup	50
135.	Vegetable Soup with Vermicelli	50
136.	Mushroom Curry Soup	51
137.	Garlicky Broccoli Soup	51
138.	Spanish Gazpacho	51
139.	Celery Butternut Squash Soup	51
140.	Vegetable & Black Bean Soup	52
141.	Basil Coconut Soup	52
142.	Habanero Bean Soup with Brown Rice	52
143.	Classic Minestrone Soup	52
144.	Turnip & Rutabaga Soup	53
145.	Green Onion Corn & Bean Soup	53
146.	Mushroom, Chickpea & Eggplant Stew	53
147.	Sweet African Soup	54
148.	Cold Vegetable Soup	54
149.	Lime Pumpkin Soup	54
150.	Easy Garbanzo Soup	54
151.	Garlic Veggie Bisque	55
152.	Coconut Artichoke Soup with Almonds	55
153.	Noodle Soup	55
154.	Coconut & Tofu Soup	56
155.	Hot Lentil Soup with Zucchini	56
156.	Shallot Lentil Soup with Walnuts	56
157.	Fennel & Corn Chowder	56
158.	Ginger Squash Soup	57
159.	Fennel & Parsnip Bisque	57
160.	Spicy Potato Soup	57
161.	Spinach Soup with Gnocchi	58
162.	Mushroom Rice Soup	58
163.	Chili Gazpacho	58
164.	Butternut Squash Soup	58
165.	Green Bean & Rice Soup	59
166.	Celery & Potato Rice Soup	59
167.	Rotini & Tomato Soup	59
168.	Green Bean & Zucchini Velouté	59
169.	Kale & Potato Stew	60
170.	Caribbean Lentil Stew	60
171.	Moroccan Bean Stew	60
172.	Pearl Barley & Vegetable Stew	60
173.	Chicago-Style Vegetable Stew	61
174.	Mushroom & Bean Stew	61
175.	Asian Veggie Stew	61
176.	Mediterranean Vegetable Stew	62
177.	Tomato Lentil Stew	62
178.	Sudanese Veggie Stew	62
179.	Fall Medley Stew	62
180.	Homemade Succotash Stew	63
181.	Balsamic Veggie & Rice Stew	63
182.	Chili Cannellini Bean Stew	63

SALADS & ENTRÉES 64

#	Recipe	Page
183.	Greek Salad	64
184.	Squash Salad	64
185.	Beet Tofu Salad	64
186.	African Zucchini Salad	64
187.	Tangy Nutty Brussel Sprout Salad	65
188.	Roasted Mushrooms and Green Beans Salad	65
189.	Seitan & Spinach Salad a la Puttanesca	65
190.	Bean & Farro Salad	66
191.	Warm Collard Salad	66
192.	Fried Broccoli Salad with Tempeh & Cranberries	66

#	Title	Page
193.	Savory Pasta Salad with Cannellini Beans	66
194.	Bean & Couscous Salad	67
195.	Tomato & Avocado Lettuce Salad	67
196.	Balsamic Lentil Salad	67
197.	Warm Green Bean & Potato Salad	68
198.	Mango Rice Salad with Lime Dressing	68
199.	Orange & Kale Salad	68
200.	Millet Salad with Olives & Cherries	68
201.	Daikon Salad with Caramelized Onion	69
202.	Cucumber, Lettuce & Tomato Salad	69
203.	Quick Fresh Salad	69
204.	Radish & Tomato Salad	69
205.	Carrot & Cabbage Salad with Avocado & Capers	70
206.	Chickpea & Celery Salad	70
207.	Tropical Salad	70
208.	Traditional Lebanese Salad	70
209.	Mediterranean Pasta Salad	71
210.	Mexican Bean Salad	71
211.	Zucchini & Bell Pepper Salad with Beans	71
212.	Cashew & Raisin Salad with & Haricots Verts	71
213.	Lettuce & Tomato Salad with Quinoa	72
214.	Minty Eggplant Salad	72
215.	Artichoke & Potato Salad	72
216.	Lemon Potato Salad with Kalamata Olives	72
217.	Italian Vegetable Relish	73
218.	Bulgur & Kale Salad	73
219.	Potato & Green Bean Salad	73
220.	Beet & Cucumber Salad with Balsamic Dressing	74
221.	Colorful Quinoa Salad	74
222.	Chinese-Style Cabbage Salad	74
223.	Radicchio & Cabbage Coleslaw	74
224.	Avocado Salad with Sesame Seeds	75
225.	Cilantro Chickpea & Corn Salad	75
226.	Radish & Cabbage Ginger Salad	75
227.	Coleslaw & Spinach Salad with Grapefruit	75
228.	Easy Pineapple & Jicama Salad	76
229.	Broccoli & Mango Rice Salad	76
230.	Mom´s Caesar Salad	76
231.	Fantastic Green Salad	76
232.	Carrot Salad with Cherries & Pecans	77
233.	Apple & Spinach Salad with Walnut Crunch	77
234.	Apple & Kale Salad with Raspberry Vinaigrette	77
235.	Dijon Potato Salad	77
236.	Baked Potato & Black-Eyed Pea Salad	78
237.	Bean & Roasted Parsnip Salad	78
238.	Beet Slaw with Apples	78
239.	Spinach Salad with Blackberries & Pecans	78
240.	Festive Nicoise Salad Potato Salad	79
241.	Cowboy Salad	79
242.	Christmas Potato Salad	79
243.	Dijon Potato & Carrot Salad	79
244.	Chickpea & Quinoa Salad with Capers	80
245.	Cucumber & Pear Rice Salad	80
246.	Apple & Arugula Salad with Walnuts	80
247.	Lemony Ditalini Salad with Chickpeas	80
248.	Tomato Bean & Bulgur Salad	81
249.	Bell Pepper & Quinoa Salad	81
250.	Apple & Spinach Salad with Nuts & Cranberries	81
251.	Chickpea & Faro Entrée	81

LUNCH 82

#	Title	Page
252.	Tofu Cabbage Stir-Fry	82
253.	Smoked Tempeh with Broccoli Fritters	82
254.	Cheesy Cauliflower Casserole	82
255.	Spicy Veggie Steaks with Green Salad	83
256.	Mushroom Curry Pie	83
257.	Vegan Mushroom Pizza	83
258.	Avocado Coconut Pie	84
259.	Tofu & Spinach Lasagna with Red Sauce	84
260.	Curried Tofu with Buttery Cabbage	85
261.	Green Avocado Carbonara	85
262.	Mushroom Lettuce Wraps	85
263.	Kale & Mushroom Pierogis	86
264.	Cashew Buttered Quesadillas with Leafy Greens	86
265.	Grilled Zucchini with Spinach Avocado Pesto	87
266.	Baked Cheesy Spaghetti Squash	87
267.	Baked Tofu with Roasted Pepper	87
268.	Zoodle Bolognese	88
269.	Tofu Skewers with Salsa Verde & Squash Mash	88
270.	Zucchini Boats with Vegan Cheese	88
271.	Asparagus with Creamy Puree	89
272.	Roasted Butternut Squash with Chimichurri	89
273.	Sweet and Spicy Brussel Sprout Stir-Fry	89
274.	Spicy Cheese with Tofu Balls	90
275.	Seitan Cakes with Broccoli Mash	90
276.	White Pizza with Mixed Mushrooms	90
277.	Eggplant Fries with Chili Aioli & Beet Salad	91
278.	Chili Bean & Brown Rice Tortillas	91
279.	Mushroom & Green Bean Biryani	92
280.	Quinoa & Veggie Burgers	92
281.	Black Bean Burgers with BBQ Sauce	92
282.	Kale Mushroom Galette	93
283.	Jalapeño Quinoa Bowl with Lima Beans	93
284.	Seitan Cauliflower Gratin	94
285.	Tempeh Coconut Curry Bake	94
286.	Caprese Casserole	94
287.	Tempeh Garam Masala Bake	95
288.	Vegan Cordon Bleu Casserole	95
289.	Creamy Brussels Sprouts Bake	95
290.	Tomato Artichoke Pizza	96
291.	Basil Pesto Seitan Panini	96
292.	American-Style Tempeh Bake with Garden Peas	96
293.	Savoy Cabbage Rolls with Tofu & Buckwheat	97
294.	Green Beans & Grilled Tempeh	97
295.	Zesty Rice Bowls with Tempeh	98

#	Recipe	Page
296.	Pea & Basil Fettuccine	98
297.	Tofu Loaf with Nuts	98
298.	Mexican-Style Soy Chorizo & Rice Bowls	99
299.	Pesto Mushroom Pizza	99
300.	Scallion Sweet Potatoes with Chili Corn Salad	99
301.	Plant-Based Cheddar Broccoli Gratin	100
302.	Oat & Chickpea Burgers with Avocado Dip	100
303.	Chickpea & Bean Patties	100
304.	Corn & Bean Quesadillas	101
305.	Hot Seitan with Rice	101
306.	Tomato & Alfredo Fettuccine	101
307.	Vegetable & Hummus Pizza	102
308.	Stuffed Zucchini Rolls with Tempeh & Tofu	102
309.	Basil & Tofu Stuffed Portobello Mushrooms	102
310.	Kale Pizza with Grilled Zucchini	103
311.	Amazing Tofu Burgers	103
312.	Bell Pepper & Tempeh Balls with Asparagus	103
313.	Black Olive & Chickpea Lunch	104
314.	Gingery Pea & Potato Skillet	104
315.	Broccoli Stuffed Cremini Mushrooms	104
316.	Saucy Seitan with Sesame Seeds	104
317.	Tempeh & Vegetable Stir-Fry	105
318.	Watercress & Mushroom Spaghetti	105
319.	Pasta Primavera with Cherry Tomatoes	105
320.	Rice with Green Lentil & Celery	106
321.	Quinoa a la Puttanesca	106
322.	Cherry & Quinoa Tacos	106
323.	Herby Quinoa with Walnuts	106
324.	Spinach & Chickpea Pizza with Avocado	107
325.	Acorn Squash Stuffed with Beans & Spinach	107
326.	Cabbage & Bean Stir-Fry	107
327.	Lemony Green Bean Risotto	108
328.	Chipotle Kidney Bean Chili	108
329.	Carrot & Black Bean Chili	108
330.	Special Butternut Squash Chili	108
331.	Bean Gyros	109
332.	Mediterranean Chickpeas with Vegetables	109
333.	Bean & Spinach Casserole	109
334.	Southern Bean Salad	110
335.	Hot Coconut Beans with Vegetables	110
336.	Hot Bean Salad	110
337.	Seitan & Lentil Chili	110
338.	White Salad with Walnut Pesto	111
339.	Hot Lentil Tacos with Guacamole	111
340.	Curried Indian Rolls	111
341.	Rice, Lentil & Spinach Pilaf	112
342.	Dijon Faro & Walnut Salad	112
343.	Awesome Barley Jambalaya	112
344.	Parsley Bean & Olives Salad	112
345.	Habanero Pinto Beans with Bell Pepper Pot	113
346.	Baked Mustard Beans	113
347.	Cucumber & Carrot Pizza with Pesto	113
348.	Hot Paprika Lentils	113

DINNER 114

#	Recipe	Page
349.	Black-Eyed Pea Oat Bake	114
350.	Paprika Fava Bean Patties	114
351.	Walnut Lentil Burgers	114
352.	Bean & Pecan Sandwiches	115
353.	Homemade Kitchari	115
354.	Faro & Black Bean Loaf	115
355.	Cuban-Style Millet	116
356.	Traditional Cilantro Pilaf	116
357.	Oriental Bulgur & White Beans	116
358.	One-Pot Red Lentils with Mushrooms	116
359.	Picante Green Rice	117
360.	Sherry Shallot Beans	117
361.	Celery Buckwheat Croquettes	117
362.	Oregano Chickpeas	117
363.	Matcha-Infused Tofu Rice	118
364.	Chinese Fried Rice	118
365.	Green Pea & Lemon Couscous	118
366.	Chimichurri Fusili with Navy Beans	118
367.	Buckwheat Pilaf with Pine Nuts	119
368.	Korean-Style Millet	119
369.	Savory Seitan & Bell Pepper Rice	119
370.	Mushroom Fried Rice	119
371.	Veggie Paella with Lentils	120
372.	Bean & Brown Rice with Artichokes	120
373.	Cherry & Pistachio Bulgur	120
374.	Quinoa & Chickpea Pot	120
375.	Italian Holiday Stuffing	121
376.	Curry Bean with Artichokes	121
377.	Pressure Cooker Green Lentils	121
378.	Simple Pesto Millet	121
379.	Peppered Pinto Beans	122
380.	Black-Eyed Peas with Sun-Dried Tomatoes	122
381.	Pressure Cooker Celery & Spinach Chickpeas	122
382.	Vegetarian Quinoa Curry	122
383.	Alfredo Rice with Green Beans	123
384.	Couscous & Quinoa Burgers	123
385.	Lemony Chickpeas with Kale	123
386.	Endive Slaw with Olives	123
387.	Dinner Rice & Lentils	124
388.	Asparagus & Mushrooms with Mashed Potatoes	124
389.	Sesame Kale Slaw	124
390.	Spicy Steamed Broccoli	124
391.	Paprika Cauliflower Tacos	125
392.	Garlic Roasted Carrots	125
393.	Asian Quinoa Sauté	125
394.	Eggplant & Hummus Pizza	126
395.	Miso Green Cabbage	126
396.	Cilantro Okra	126
397.	Citrus Asparagus	126
398.	Japanese-Style Tofu with Haricots Vert	127

#	Recipe	Page
399.	Raisin & Orzo Stuffed Tomatoes	127
400.	Rosemary Baked Potatoes with Cherry Tomatoes	127
401.	Squash & Zucchini Stir-Fry	127
402.	Steamed Broccoli with Hazelnuts	128
403.	Sweet Potatoes with Curry Glaze	128
404.	Spaghetti Squash in Tahini Sauce	128
405.	Cumin Red & White Cabbage with Apples	128
406.	Parsley Carrots & Parsnips	129
407.	Basil Beet Pasta	129
408.	Sherry Eggplants with Cherry Tomatoes	129
409.	Date Caramelized Vegetables	129
410.	Sesame Roasted Broccoli with Brown Rice	130
411.	Tofu Eggplant Pizza	130
412.	Raisin & Pine Nut Zucchini Rolls	130
413.	Almond & Chickpea Patties	131
414.	Korean-Style Buckwheat	131
415.	Basil Bell Pepper & Mushroom Medley	131
416.	Peanut Quinoa & Chickpea Pilaf	131
417.	Spicy Vegetable Paella	132
418.	Baked Potatoes & Asparagus & Pine Nuts	132
419.	Italian Potato & Swiss Chard Au Gratin	132
420.	French Vegetable Byaldi	133
421.	Sautéed Veggies with Rice	133
422.	Melon & Cucumber Gazpacho	133
423.	Artichoke & Tomato Tart with Peanuts	134
424.	Chili Broccoli & Beans with Almonds	134
425.	Bean & Pecan Stuffed Mushrooms	134
426.	Dilly Potatoes	135
427.	Balsamic Artichoke Hearts	135
428.	Roasted Sweet Potato Porridge	135
429.	Orange Kale Stir-Fry	135
430.	Parsley Faro & Bean Casserole	136
431.	Creamy Bell Pepper Goulash	136
432.	Pomegranate Bell Peppers & Eggplants	136
433.	Thyme Black Bean Loaf with Artichokes	137
434.	Leek & Mushroom Stroganoff	137
435.	Couscous & Lentil Curry	137
436.	Sicilian Spaghetti Squash	138
437.	Sesame Tempeh Sauté	138
438.	Cayenne Kale	138
439.	Parsley Pumpkin Noodles	139
440.	Cinnamon-Brandy Acorn Squash	139
441.	Maple Green Cabbage Hash	139
442.	Eggplant with Tofu	139
443.	Lemony Arugula with Pine Nuts	140
444.	Bell Pepper & Spinach with Walnuts	140
445.	Mustard Tofu & Cauliflower	140
446.	Lentil Stuffed Avocados	140
447.	Lentil & Sweet Potato Tortillas	141
448.	Spicy Broccoli in Pecan Pesto	141
449.	Grilled Tofu Mayo Sandwiches	141
450.	Bulgur & Bean Bowls with Tortilla Chips	141

SNAKS AND SIDES 142

#	Recipe	Page
451.	Kentucky Cauliflower with Mashed Parsnips	142
452.	Spinach Chips with Guacamole Hummus	142
453.	Parmesan Croutons with Rosemary Tomato Soup	142
454.	Buttered Carrot Noodles with Kale	143
455.	Baked Spicy Eggplant	143
456.	Mashed Broccoli with Roasted Garlic	144
457.	Spicy Pistachio Dip	144
458.	Paprika Roasted Nuts	144
459.	Onion Rings & Kale Dip	144
460.	Soy Chorizo Stuffed Cabbage Rolls	145
461.	Tofu Stuffed Peppers	145
462.	Curry Cauli Rice with Mushrooms	146
463.	Mushroom Broccoli Faux Risotto	146
464.	Crispy Squash Nacho Chips	146
465.	Pepita Cheese Tomato Chips	147
466.	Mixed Seed Crackers	147
467.	Mixed Vegetables with Basil	147
468.	Four-Seed Crackers	148
469.	Bell Pepper & Seitan Balls	148
470.	Chocolate Bars with Walnuts	148
471.	Baked Brussels Sprouts with Cranberries	148
472.	Dijon Roasted Asparagus	149
473.	Paprika Tofu & Zucchini Skewers	149
474.	Sesame Cabbage Sauté	149
475.	Parmesan Broccoli Tots	150
476.	Tomatoes Stuffed with Chickpeas & Quinoa	150
477.	Herbed Vegetable Traybake	150
478.	Louisiana-Style Sweet Potato Chips	151
479.	Cinnamon-Maple Popcorn	151
480.	Strawberries Stuffed with Banana Cream	151
481.	Mediterranean Tahini Beans	151
482.	Hot Crunchy Nuts	152
483.	Maple-Glazed Butternut Squash	152
484.	Beet & Carrot Stir-Fry	152
485.	Parmesan Baby Potatoes	152
486.	Lemon-Maple Glazed Carrots	153
487.	Carrot Nori Rolls	153
488.	Guacamole with Daikon	153
489.	Tofu & Tomato Sandwiches	153
490.	Mustard Tofu-Avocado Wraps	154
491.	Walnut & Tempeh Ball	154
492.	Yummy Vegetarian Burritos	154
493.	Paprika Baked Beans	154
494.	Pecan Tempeh Cakes	155
495.	Homemade Seedy Bars	155
496.	Curry Mango-Tofu Pitas	155
497.	Spicy Nut Burgers	156
498.	Soy Chorizo & Avocado Tacos	156
499.	Paprika Hummus with Mushrooms	156
500.	Hazelnut Snack	156
501.	Crispy Mushroom Wontons	157
502.	French Mushroom Tarts	157

#	Title	Page
503.	Maple-Pumpkin Cookies	157
504.	Middle Eastern Onion Phyllo	158
505.	Arugula & Hummus Pitas	158
506.	Roman Balsamic Tomato Bruschetta	158
507.	Authentic Guacamole	158
508.	Cucumber Stuffed Tomatoes	159
509.	Garbanzo Quesadillas with Salsa	159
510.	Coconut & Parsley Wraps	159
511.	Tamari Lentil Dip	159
512.	Chili Roasted Hazelnuts	160
513.	Balsamic Roasted Red Pepper & Pecan Crostini	160
514.	Tarragon Potato Chips	160
515.	Kale & Hummus Pinwheels	160
516.	Chickpea & Pecan Balls	161
517.	Swiss Chard & Pecan Stuffed Mushrooms	161
518.	Vegetable & Rice Vermicelli Lettuce Rolls	161
519.	Green Salsa	162
520.	Primavera Lettuce Rolls	162
521.	Citrus-Parsley Mushrooms	162
522.	Minty Berry Cocktail	162
523.	Bell Peppers Stuffed with Spinach & Tofu	163
524.	Mustard Mac & Cheese	163
525.	Grilled Vegetables with Romesco Dip	163

DESSERTS & SWEET TREATS 164

#	Title	Page
526.	Vanilla Brownies	164
527.	Vegan Cheesecake with Blueberries	164
528.	Lime Avocado Ice Cream	164
529.	Berries, Nuts & Cream Bowl	165
530.	Vanilla White Chocolate Pudding	165
531.	Mint Ice Cream	166
532.	Cardamom Coconut Fat Bombs	166
533.	Chocolate Peppermint Mousse	166
534.	Walnut Chocolate Squares	166
535.	Raspberries Turmeric Panna Cotta	167
536.	Cinnamon Faux Rice Pudding	167
537.	White Chocolate Fudge	167
538.	Macedonia Salad with Coconut & Pecans	167
539.	Berry Hazelnut Trifle	168
540.	Cacao Nut Bites	168
541.	Avocado Truffles with Chocolate Coating	168
542.	Summer Banana Pudding	168
543.	Vanilla Berry Tarts	169
544.	Southern Apple Cobbler with Raspberries	169
545.	Chocolate Fudge with Nuts	169
546.	Aunt´s Apricot Tarte Tatin	170
547.	Chocolate & Peanut Butter Cookies	170
548.	Mixed Berry Yogurt Ice Pops	170
549.	Coconut Chocolate Barks	171
550.	Nutty Date Cake	171
551.	Baked Apples Filled with Nuts	171
552.	Coconut & Chocolate Cake	172
553.	Berry Macedonia with Mint	172
554.	Berry Cupcakes with Cashew Cheese Icing	172
555.	Holiday Pecan Tart	173
556.	Cinnamon Pumpkin Pie	173
557.	Cashew & Cranberry Truffles	174
558.	Tropical Cheesecake	174
559.	Raisin Oatmeal Biscuits	174
560.	Pistachios & Chocolate Popsicles	175
561.	Cashew & Plum Cheesecake	175
562.	Party Matcha & Hazelnut Cheesecake	175
563.	Oatmeal Cookies with Hazelnuts	176
564.	Coconut Chocolate Truffles	176
565.	Coconut Peach Tart	176
566.	Layered Raspberry & Tofu Cups	176
567.	Mango Muffins with Chocolate Chips	177
568.	Vanilla Cookies with Poppy Seeds	177
569.	Kiwi & Peanut Bars	177
570.	Easy Maple Rice Pudding	178
571.	Coconut & Chocolate Brownies	178
572.	Coconut Chia Pudding	178
573.	Homemade Goji Berry Chocolate Granita	178
574.	Maple Fruit Crumble	179
575.	Peanut Chocolate Brownies	179
576.	Sherry-Lime Mango Dessert	179
577.	Almond & Chia Bites with Cherries	179
578.	Vanilla Cranberry & Almond Balls	180
579.	Chocolate Campanelle with Hazelnuts	180
580.	Pressure Cooker Apple Cupcakes	180
581.	Coconut & Date Truffles with Walnuts	180
582.	Roasted Apples Stuffed with Pecans & Dates	181
583.	Pumpkin Brownie	181
584.	Mango Chocolate Fudge	181
585.	Coconut & Chocolate Macaroons	181
586.	Melon Chocolate Pudding	182
587.	Sicilian Papaya Sorbet	182
588.	Poppy-Granola Balls with Chocolate	182
589.	Caribbean Pudding	182
590.	Balsamic Glazed Caramelized Quinces	183
591.	Glazed Chili Chocolate Cake	183
592.	Cinnamon Tropical Cobbler	183
593.	Lemon Blackberry Cake	184
594.	Hazelnut Topped Coconut Caramelized Bananas	184
595.	Apple & Cashew Quiche	184
596.	Tofu & Almond Pancakes	184
597.	Almond Berry Cream	185
598.	Pumpkin & Mango Lemon Cake	185
599.	Blueberry Lime Granizado	185
600.	Coconut Bars with Chocolate Chips	185

INTRODUCTION

When I was growing up, I had to learn fast the rules for keeping my body in the best shape and excellent health, and going on plant-based lifestyle was my secret.

I have been dieting primarily on plant-based foods for the last couple of years and I feel happy, energetic and full of life. That's why I take this opportunity to share my experiences with you through this cookbook.

This Plant-Based cookbook is one stemmed from a deep place of passion and lessons where I guide regular dieters and beginners who want to make the switch to the plant-based lifestyle on its importance in the current age. It takes into consideration a trendy style of eating, busy schedules, and tasty ideas to ensure that each recipe produced isn't boring but delicious enough to make enjoy the cooking and eating.

My suggestion for you is to give the recipes a straight dive in and enjoy all the scrumptious goodness that awaits you.

What is the Plant-Based Diet?

While the plant-based diet may seem to be torn between the vegetarian and vegan diet, it is not any of them. In fant, it's not a diet but a healthy lifestyle.

It is no surprise that there are vast argument claiming that the plant-based diet is either a vegan one (which is plant focused) or vegetarian (which accommodates some amount of animal foods). Both cases are still incorrect. The plant-based diet uses food from plants, and it strongly rejects processed foods like white rice and added sugars. On the other hand, the vegan and vegetarian diets allow some processed foods.

In this book, my goal is to present you with plant-based recipes in its most wholesome forms. The cookbook seeks to guide you. especially the beginners on the plant-based diet, to appreciate the essentials of whole-based plant foods, giving you flexible options and various cooking combinations.

Benefits of the Plant-Based diet

Plant foods are an excellent source for many nutrients that boost the body's metabolism in many ways. They are easy to digest thanks to thier rich content of antioxidants.

- **Reduced Risk of Heart Diseases**

Processed and animal foods are culprits for many heart diseases. Whole foods plant based diet is better at nourishing the body with essential nutrients while improving the heart's function to produce and transport blood to and from the various body parts.

- **Prevents and Heals Diabetes**

Plant-based foods are excellent at reducing high blood sugars. Many studies comparing vegetarian and vegan diet to a regular meat filled diet proved that dieting with more plant foods reduced the risk of diabetes by 50%.

- **Improved Cognitive Incline**

Fruits and vegetables are excellent for cleansing and boosting metabolism. They release high numbers of plant compounds and antioxidants that slow or prevent cognitive decline. On a plant-based diet, the brain is boosted with sustainable energy, which promotes sharp memory, language, thinking, and judgement abilities.

- **Quick Weight Loss**

A high animal food diet is known to drive weight gain. Switching to a plant-based diet helps the body shed fat walls easily, which quickly drives weight loss.

What to eat on the Plant-Based lifestyle and PB Swaps

- **Fruits** - consume wide range of fruits either fresh, dried, boiled, pureed, etc.
- **Vegetables** - all vegetables are permissible on the plant-based diet, and they also provide lots of essential vitamins and minerals for the body.
- **Legumes** are an excellent source for plant-based protein and fiber. Fiber is one nutrient that many people lack; and it's important to boost its content in the body.
- **Whole Grains** provide nutrients like selenium, copper, and magnesium to the body. Meanwhile, they are rich in fiber when consumed in their whole forms. Avoid processed flours, rice, pasta, and breads on the plant-based diet but consume brown rice, whole-wheat pasta, whole-grain bread, oats, barley, buckwheat, rye, quinoa, spelt.
- **Nuts and Nut Butters** - Nuts are an essential source of selenium, vitamin E, and plant-based protein. They are excellent additions to desserts, smoothies, and snacks.
- **Seeds** are rich in calcium, vimatins, and healthy fats. Consume chia seeds, hemp seeds, flaxseeds, pumpkin seeds, sunflower seeds, sesame seeds, etc.
- **Healthy Oils and Fats** - Plants offer some sweet-smelling, healthy oils and fats options, which are perfect for baking, frying, sautéing, etc. They serve as excellent dairy replacement and are rich in omega-3 fatty acids. Use olive oil, avocados, canola oil, walnuts, peanuts, hemp seeds, flaxseeds, chia seeds, cashew nuts, coconut oil.
- **Plant-Based Milk, Cream, and Cheeses** - going plant-based doesn't mean staying away from creamy, milky, cheesy foods. You can enjoy plant-based alternatives using almond milk, soy milk, rice milk, cashew milk, coconut milk, coconut cream, cashew cream, hemp milk, oats milk.
- **Plant-Based Meats** - Have tofu, tempeh, seitan.
- **Spices, Herbs, and Condiments** - all spices, herbs, and plant-based condiments are permissible on the plant-based diet. Use basil, parsley, turmeric, curry, black pepper, rosemary, oregano, thyme, sage, marjoram, salt, salsa, soy sauce, nutritional yeast, vinegar, homemade BBQ sauce, homemade plant-based mayonnaise, etc.
- **Beverages** - You can drink coffee, sparking water, tea, smoothies, etc.

BASIC INGREDIENTS FOR PLANT-BASED RECIPES

Simple Vegetable Broth

Ingredients for 4 servings

3 tbsp olive oil
2 onions, quartered
2 carrots, chopped
1 cup celeriac, chopped
2 garlic cloves, unpeeled and crushed
6 cups water
2 tsp soy sauce
⅓ cup chopped fresh cilantro
1 bay leaf
Salt to taste
½ tsp black peppercorns

Directions and Total Time: 45 minutes

Warm the oil in a pot over medium heat. Place in onions, carrots, celeriac, and garlic. Cook for 5 minutes until softened. Pour in water, soy sauce, cilantro, bay leaf, and peppercorns. Bring to a boil, lower the heat and simmer uncovered for 30 minutes.

Let cool for a few minutes, then pour over a strainer into a pot. Divide between glass mason jars and allow to cool completely. Seal and store in the fridge up to 5 days or 1 month in the freezer.

Parsley Veggie Broth

Ingredients for 4 servings

1 onion, sliced
1 parsnip, chopped
1 celery stalk, chopped
1 potato, unpeeled and chopped
3 garlic cloves, minced
2 tbsp olive oil
Salt and black pepper to taste
6 cups water
⅓ cup chopped fresh parsley

Directions and Total Time: 1 hour 25 minutes

Preheat oven to 425 F. Grease a baking dish with cooking spray. Put in the onion, parsnip, celery, potato, and garlic and spread them in a single layer. Sprinkle with oil, salt and pepper. Roast the veggies for 30 minutes, turning once by half. Let cool for 10 minutes.

Transfer the vegetables to a pot over medium heat. Add in water, parsley and salt. Bring to a boil, then lower the heat and simmer uncovered for 45 minutes until the broth has reduced slightly.

Let cool for a few minutes, then pour over a strainer into a pot. Divide between glass mason jars and allow to cool completely. Seal and store in the fridge up to 5 days or 1 month in the freezer.

Turnip & Parsnip Broth

Ingredients for 4 servings

1 tbsp olive oil
1 onion, chopped
2 carrots, chopped
2 parsnips, coarsely chopped
1 turnip, coarsely chopped
6 cups water
1 beet, quartered
3 garlic cloves, sliced
¾ cup chives, chopped
2 bay leaves
Salt and black pepper to taste

Directions and Total Time: 1 hour 45 minutes

Warm oil in a pot and place onion, carrots, parsnips, and turnip. Cook for 10 minutes. Pour in water, beet, garlic, chives, bay leaves, salt, and pepper. Bring to a boil, then lower the heat and simmer for 1 ½ hours. Let cool for a few minutes, then pour over a strainer into a pot. Divide between glass mason jars and allow to cool completely. Seal and store in the fridge up to 5 days.

Plant-Based Cheddar Cheese

Ingredients for 4 servings

1 cup raw cashew nuts
1 red bell pepper, chopped
¼ cup tahini
1 tbsp tamarind sauce
1 lemon, juiced

2 tbsp coconut oil
1 tsp garlic powder
2 tsp onion powder
1 tbsp tomato paste
2 tsp apple cider vinegar

1 tbsp Dijon mustard
¼ cup nutritional yeast
½ tsp smoked paprika
1/8 tsp cayenne pepper
1 tbsp xanthan gum

Directions and Total Time: 10 minutes + chilling time

Grease a round dish with cooking spray and set aside.

Pour 1 cup of water into a pot and mix in xanthan gum. Bring to a boil for 1 minute with continuous stirring. Pour the mixture into a food processor.

Add in cashew nuts, red bell pepper, salt, 1/3 cup of water, tahini, tamarind sauce, lemon juice, coconut oil, garlic powder, onion powder, tomato paste, apple cider vinegar, Dijon mustard, nutritional yeast, smoked paprika, and cayenne pepper and blend the ingredients until smooth.

Quickly pour the mixture into the round dish and spread around well. Place in the fridge to set, 45 minutes to 1 hour. Remove the bowl from the fridge and invert the cheese onto a plate. Use as the recipe requires.

Plant-Based Mozzarella Cheese

Ingredients for 4 servings

1 cup raw cashew nuts
¼ cup plant-based yogurt

1 ½ tbsp freshly juiced lemon
2 tbsp nutritional yeast

½ cup unsweetened almond milk
4 tbsp tapioca starch

Directions and Total Time: 10 minutes + chilling time

Soak the cashews in hot water for 1 hour or overnight. Drain well.

Pour the cashews into a food processor and add the yogurt, lemon juice, salt, nutritional yeast, almond milk, tapioca, and process until smooth and creamy while scraping the sides into the mixture.

Adjust the taste as needed with more salt for saltiness, nutritional yeast for cheesiness, yogurt for creaminess, and lemon juice for acidity. The texture should be smooth, creamy, and pourable.

Add the mix to a medium skillet and cook over medium heat while whisking until thickened and ball-like shape forms, 4-5 minutes. Reduce the heat to low, then use a wooden spoon to mix the mixture until loose ball forms. Transfer the mixture to a small mixing bowl.

Cover the bowl with plastic wrap, refrigerate for 1 hour, and then scoop 1 tbsp pieces and form into mozzarella-like balls. Use as the recipe requires.

Plant-Based Parmesan Cheese

Ingredients for 4 servings

1 cup of raw cashews　　　1 tbsp Italian seasoning　　　½ cup nutritional yeast

Directions and Total Time: 5 minutes

In a blender, pour in the cashew nuts, Italian seasoning, nutritional yeast, and salt. Process the ingredients until smooth. Use as the recipe requires.

Cashew Cream Cheese

Ingredients for 4 servings

1 cup cashew nuts, soaked　　　½ cup water　　　¼ tsp salt

Directions and Total Time: 5 minutes

Blend the cashew nuts, water, and salt in a blender until smooth. To lighten the cream, add some water until your desired thickness is achieved.

Tofu Mayonnaise

Ingredients for 4 servings

8 oz silken tofu, cubed　　　1 tsp distilled white vinegar　　　¼ tsp Dijon mustard
1 tsp freshly squeezed lemon juice　　　½ tsp nutritional yeast　　　¼ tsp pure maple syrup

Directions and Total Time: 5 minutes

In a blender, process tofu, lemon juice, white vinegar, nutritional yeast, Dijon mustard, salt, and maple syrup until smooth.

Plant-Based Cashew Cheese

Ingredients for 4 servings

1 cup raw cashew nuts　　　2 tablespoons nutritional yeast　　　Salt and black pepper to taste
2 tbsp freshly squeezed lemon juice　　　¼ tsp garlic powder　　　¼ cup water or as needed

Directions and Total Time: 10 minutes

In a blender, process the cashew nuts, lemon juice, nutritional yeast, garlic powder, salt, black pepper, and water until smooth. Adjust the taste with more lemon juice, salt, and black pepper as desired and blend again. Pour the mixture into an airtight container and use it as the recipe desires.

BREAKFAST & SMOOTHIES

Coconut Porridge with Strawberries

Ingredients for 2 servings

1 tbsp flax seed powder
1 oz olive oil

1 tbsp coconut flour
1 pinch ground chia seeds

5 tbsp coconut cream
Thawed frozen strawberries

Directions and Total Time: 12 minutes

In a small bowl, mix the flax seed powder with the 3 tbsp water, and allow soaking for 5 minutes.

Place a non-stick saucepan over low heat and pour in the olive oil, flax egg, coconut flour, chia seeds, and coconut cream. Cook the mixture while stirring continuously until your desired consistency is achieved. Turn the heat off and spoon the porridge into serving bowls. Top with 4 to 6 strawberries desired and serve immediately.

Broccoli Hash Browns

Ingredients for 4 servings

3 tbsp flax seed powder
1 head broccoli, cut into florets

½ white onion, grated
1 tsp salt

1 tbsp freshly ground black pepper
5 tbsp plant butter, for frying

Directions and Total Time: 35 minutes

In a small bowl, mix the flax seed powder with 9 tbsp water, and allow soaking for 5 minutes. Pour the broccoli into a food processor and pulse a few times until smoothly grated.

Transfer the broccoli into a bowl, add the flax egg, white onion, salt, and black pepper. Use a spoon to mix the ingredients evenly, and set aside for 5 to 10 minutes to firm up a bit. Place a large non-stick skillet over medium heat and drop 1/3 of the plant butter to melt until no longer shimmering.

Ladle scoops of the broccoli mixture into the skillet (about 3 to 4 hash browns per batch), flatten the pancakes to measure 3 to 4 inches in diameter and fry until golden brown on one side, 4 minutes. Turn the pancakes with a spatula and cook the other side to brown too, another 5 minutes.

Transfer the hash browns to a serving plate and repeat the frying process for the remaining broccoli mixture. Serve the hash browns warm with fresh garden green salad.

Pesto Bread Twists

Ingredients for 6 servings

1 ½ cups grated plant-based mozzarella cheese
1 tbsp flax seed powder
4 tbsp coconut flour

½ cup almond flour
½ tsp salt
1 tsp baking powder
5 tbsp plant butter

2 oz pesto
Olive oil for brushing

Directions and Total Time: 35 minutes

First, mix the flax seed powder with 3 tbsp water in a bowl, and set aside to soak for 5 minutes.

Preheat oven to 350 F and line a baking sheet with parchment paper. In a bowl, evenly combine the coconut flour, almond flour, salt, and baking powder. Melt the plant butter and cheese in a deep skillet over medium heat and stir in the flax egg. Mix in the flour mixture until a firm dough forms.

Turn the heat off and transfer the mixture in between two parchment papers, then use a rolling pin to flatten out the dough of about an inch's thickness.

Remove the parchment paper on top and spread the pesto all over the dough. Now, use a knife to cut the dough into strips, twist each piece, and place on the baking sheet.

Brush with olive oil and bake for 15 to 20 minutes until golden brown.

Remove the bread twist; allow cooling for a few minutes, and serve with warm almond milk.

Classic French Toasts

Ingredients for 2 servings

- 4 tbsp flax seed meal
- 1 tsp plant butter
- 2 tbsp coconut flour
- 2 tbsp almond flour
- 1 ½ tsp baking powder
- A pinch salt
- 2 tbsp coconut cream
- 2 tbsp coconut milk whipping cream
- ½ tsp cinnamon powder
- 2 tbsp plant butter

Directions and Total Time: 16 minutes

For the flax egg, whisk flax seed powder and 12 tbsp water in two separate bowls and leave to soak for 5 minutes.

Grease a glass dish (for the microwave) with the plant butter. In another bowl, mix coconut flour, almond flour, baking powder, and a pinch of salt.

When the flax seed egg is ready, whisk one portion with the coconut cream and add the mixture to the dry ingredients. Continue whisking until the mixture is smooth with no lumps. Pour the dough into the glass dish and microwave for 2 minutes or until the middle part of the bread is done. Take out and allow the bread to cool. Remove the bread and slice in half. Return to the glass dish.

Whisk the remaining flax egg with the coconut milk whipping cream until well combined. Pour the mixture over the bread slices and leave to soak. Turn the bread a few times to soak in as much of the batter. Melt the plant butter in a frying pan and fry the bread slices on both sides. Transfer to a serving plate, sprinkle with cinnamon powder, and serve immediately.

Creamy Sesame Bread

Ingredients for 6 servings

- 4 tbsp flax seed powder
- 2/3 cup cashew cream cheese
- 4 tbsp sesame oil + for brushing
- 1 cup coconut flour
- 2 tbsp psyllium husk powder
- 1 tsp salt
- 1 tsp baking powder
- 1 tbsp sesame seeds

Directions and Total Time: 40 minutes

In a medium bowl, mix the flax seed powder with 1 ½ cups water until smoothly combined and set aside to soak for 5 minutes. Preheat oven to 400 F. When the flax egg is ready, beat in the cream cheese and sesame oil until well mixed.

Whisk in the coconut flour, psyllium husk powder, salt, and baking powder until adequately blended.

Grease a 9 x 5 inches baking tray with cooking spray, and spread the dough in the tray. Allow the mixture to stand for 5 minutes and then brush with some sesame oil.

Sprinkle with the sesame seeds and bake the dough for 30 minutes or until golden brown on top and set within. Take out the bread and allow cooling for a few minutes. Slice and serve.

Mexican Tofu Scramble

Ingredients for 4 servings

8 oz water-packed extra firm tofu	1 tomato, finely chopped	1 tsp Mexican-style chili powder
2 tbsp plant butter, for frying	2 tbsp freshly chopped scallions	3 oz grated plant-based Parmesan
1 green bell pepper, finely chopped	Salt and black pepper to taste	

Directions and Total Time: 46 minutes

Place the tofu in between two parchment papers to drain liquid for about 30 minutes.

Melt the plant butter in a large non-stick skillet until no longer foaming. Crumble the tofu into the plant butter and fry until golden brown, stirring occasionally and making sure not to break up the tofu into tiny pieces. The goal is to have the tofu like scrambled eggs, about 4 to 6 minutes.

Stir in the bell pepper, tomato, scallions, and cook until the vegetables are soft, about 4 minutes. Then, season with salt, black pepper, chili powder, and stir in the cheese to incorporate and beginning to melt about 2 minutes. Spoon the scramble into a serving platter and serve warm.

Mixed Seeds Bread

Ingredients for 6 servings

3 tbsp ground flax seeds	½ cup chia seeds	2/3 cup cashew cream cheese
¾ cup coconut flour	1 tsp ground caraway seeds	½ cup melted coconut oil
1 cup almond flour	1 tsp hemp seeds	¾ cup coconut cream
3 tsp baking powder	¼ cup psyllium husk powder	1 tbsp poppy seeds
5 tbsp sesame seeds	1 tsp salt	

Directions and Total Time: 55 minutes

Preheat oven to 350 F and line a loaf pan with parchment paper.

For the flax eggs, whisk flax seed powder with ½ cup water, and let the mixture sit to soak for 5 minutes. In a bowl, evenly combine the coconut flour, almond flour, baking powder, sesame seeds, chia seeds, ground caraway seeds, hemp seeds, psyllium husk powder, and salt.

In another bowl, use an electric hand mixer to whisk the cream cheese, coconut oil, coconut whipping cream, and flax egg. Pour the liquid ingredients into the dry ingredients, and continue whisking with the hand mixer until a dough forms. Transfer the dough to the loaf pan, sprinkle with poppy seeds, and bake in the oven for 45 minutes or until a knife inserted into the bread comes out clean. Remove the parchment paper with the bread, and allow cooling on a rack.

No-Bread Avocado Sandwich

Ingredients for 2 servings

1 avocado, sliced	2 oz little gem lettuce	1 oz tofu, sliced
1 large red tomato, sliced	½ oz plant butter	Freshly chopped parsley to garnish

Directions and Total Time: 10 minutes

Put avocado in a plate and place the tomato slices by the avocado. Arrange the lettuce (with the inner side facing you) on a flat plate to serve as the base of the sandwich.

To assemble the sandwich, smear each leave with plant butter, and arrange some tofu slices in the leaves. Then, share the avocado and tomato slices on each cheese. Garnish with parsley and serve.

Almond Flour English Muffins

Ingredients for 4 servings

2 tbsp flax seed powder
2 tbsp almond flour
½ tsp baking powder
1 pinch salt
3 tbsp plant butter

Directions and Total Time: 20 minutes

In a small bowl, mix the flax seed with 6 tbsp water until evenly combined, and leave to soak for 5 minutes. In another bowl, evenly combine the almond flour, baking powder, and salt. Then, pour in the flax egg and whisk again. Let the batter sit for 5 minutes to set.

Melt plant butter in a frying pan and add the mixture in four dollops. Fry until golden brown on one side, then, flip the bread with a spatula and fry further until golden brown. Serve.

Breakfast Naan Bread

Ingredients for 6 servings

¾ cup almond flour
2 tbsp psyllium husk powder
½ tsp salt
½ tsp baking powder
1/3 cup olive oil
Plant butter, for frying
4 oz plant butter
2 garlic cloves, minced

Directions and Total Time: 25 minutes

In a bowl, mix the almond flour, psyllium husk powder, salt, and baking powder.

Mix in some olive oil and 2 cups of boiling water to combine the ingredients, like a thick porridge. Stir thoroughly and allow the dough rise for 5 minutes.

Divide the dough into 6 to 8 pieces and mold into balls. Place the balls on a parchment paper and flatten with your hands.

Melt the plant butter in a frying pan and fry the naan on both sides to have a beautiful, golden color. Transfer the naan to a plate and keep warm in the oven. For the garlic butter, add the remaining plant butter to the frying pan and sauté the garlic until fragrant, about 3 minutes. Pour the garlic butter into a bowl and serve as a dip along with the naan.

Lemon-Almond Waffles

Ingredients for 4 servings

2 tbsp flax seed powder
2/3 cup almond flour
2 ½ tsp baking powder
A pinch salt
1 ½ cups almond milk
2 tbsp plant butter
1 cup fresh almond butter
2 tbsp pure maple syrup
1 tsp fresh lemon juice

Directions and Total Time: 20 minutes

In a medium bowl, mix the flax seed powder with 6 tbsp water and allow soaking for 5 minutes. Add the almond flour, baking powder, salt, and almond milk. Mix until well combined. Preheat a waffle iron and brush with some plant butter. Pour in a quarter cup of the batter, close the iron and cook until the waffles are golden and crisp, 2-3 minutes.

Transfer the waffles to a plate and make more waffles using the same process and ingredient proportions. In a medium bowl, mix the almond butter with the maple syrup and lemon juice. Spread the top with the almond-lemon mixture and serve.

Mushroom & Spinach Chickpea Omelet

Ingredients for 4 servings

1 cup chickpea flour	1/3 cup nutritional yeast	1 cup sautéed button mushrooms
½ tsp onion powder	½ tsp baking soda	½ cup chopped fresh spinach
½ tsp garlic powder	1 green bell pepper, chopped	1 cup halved cherry tomatoes
¼ tsp white pepper	3 scallions, chopped	1 tbsp fresh parsley leaves

Directions and Total Time: 25 minutes

In a medium bowl, mix the chickpea flour, onion powder, garlic powder, white pepper, nutritional yeast, and baking soda until well combined. Heat a medium skillet over medium heat and add a quarter of the batter. Swirl the pan to spread the batter across the pan. Scatter a quarter each of the bell pepper, scallions, mushrooms, and spinach on top, and cook until the bottom part of the omelet sets, 1-2 minutes.

Carefully, flip the omelet and cook the other side until set and golden brown. Transfer the omelet to a plate and make the remaining omelets. Serve the omelet with the tomatoes and garnish with the parsley leaves.

Coconut & Raspberry Pancakes

Ingredients for 4 servings

2 tbsp flax seed powder	1 tsp baking soda	½ tsp cinnamon powder
½ cup coconut milk	A pinch salt	2 tbsp unsweetened coconut flakes
¼ cup fresh raspberries, mashed	1 tbsp coconut sugar	2 tsp plant butter
½ cup oat flour	2 tbsp pure date syrup	Fresh raspberries for garnishing

Directions and Total Time: 25 minutes

In medium bowl, mix the flax seed powder with the 6 tbsp water and allow thickening for 5 minutes. Mix in coconut milk and raspberries. Add the oat flour, baking soda, salt, coconut sugar, date syrup, and cinnamon powder. Fold in the coconut flakes until well combined.

Working in batches, melt a quarter of the butter in a non-stick skillet and add ¼ cup of the batter. Cook until set beneath and golden brown, 2 minutes. Flip the pancake and cook on the other side until set and golden brown, 2 minutes. Transfer to a plate and make the remaining pancakes using the rest of the ingredients in the same proportions. Garnish the pancakes with some raspberries and serve warm!

Blueberry Chia Pudding

Ingredients for 2 servings

¾ cup coconut milk	½ cup blueberries	Chopped walnuts to garnish
½ tsp vanilla extract	2 tbsp chia seeds	

Directions and Total Time: 5 minutes + chilling time

In a blender, pour the coconut milk, vanilla extract, and half of the blueberries. Process the ingredients in high speed until the blueberries have incorporated into the liquid. Open the blender and mix in the chia seeds. Share the mixture into two breakfast jars, cover, and refrigerate for 4 hours to allow the mixture gel. Garnish the pudding with the remaining blueberries and walnuts. Serve immediately.

Pumpkin Cake with Pistachios

Ingredients for 4 servings

2 tbsp flaxseed powder
3 tbsp vegetable oil
¾ cup canned pumpkin puree
½ cup pure corn syrup

3 tbsp pure date sugar
1 ½ cups whole-wheat flour
½ tsp cinnamon powder
½ tsp baking powder

¼ tsp cloves powder
½ tsp allspice powder
½ tsp nutmeg powder
2 tbsp chopped pistachios

Directions and Total Time: 70 minutes

Preheat the oven to 350 F and lightly coat an 8 x 4-inch loaf pan with cooking spray. In a medium bowl, mix the flax seed powder with 6 tbsp water and allow thickening for 5 minutes to make the flax egg.

In a bowl, whisk the vegetable oil, pumpkin puree, corn syrup, date sugar, and flax egg. In another bowl, mix the flour, cinnamon powder, baking powder, cloves powder, allspice powder, and nutmeg powder. Add this mixture to the wet batter and mix until well combined. Pour the batter into the loaf pan, sprinkle the pistachios on top, and gently press the nuts onto the batter to stick.

Bake in the oven for 50-55 minutes or until a toothpick inserted into the cake comes out clean. Remove the cake onto a wire rack, allow cooling, slice, and serve.

Scrambled Tofu with Bell Pepper

Ingredients for 4 servings

2 tbsp plant butter, for frying
1 (14 oz) pack firm tofu, crumbled
1 red bell pepper, chopped
1 green bell pepper, chopped

1 tomato, finely chopped
2 tbsp chopped fresh green onions
Salt and black pepper to taste
1 tsp turmeric powder

1 tsp Creole seasoning
½ cup chopped baby kale
¼ cup grated plant-based Parmesan

Directions and Total Time: 20 minutes

Melt the plant butter in a large skillet over medium heat and add the tofu. Cook with occasional stirring until the tofu is light golden brown while making sure not to break the tofu into tiny bits but to have scrambled egg resemblance, 5 minutes.

Stir in the bell peppers, tomato, green onions, salt, black pepper, turmeric powder, and Creole seasoning. Sauté until the vegetables soften, 5 minutes. Mix in the kale to wilt, 3 minutes and then, half of the plant-based Parmesan cheese. Allow melting for 1 to 2 minutes and then turn the heat off. Top with the remaining cheese and serve warm.

Coconut Chia Pudding

Ingredients for 4 servings

1 cup coconut milk
½ tsp vanilla extract

3 tbsp chia seeds
½ cup granola

2/3 cup chopped sweet nectarine

Directions and Total Time: 5 minutes+ cooling time

In a medium bowl, mix the coconut milk, vanilla, and chia seeds until well combined. Divide the mixture between 4 breakfast cups and refrigerate for at least 4 hours to allow the mixture to gel. Top with the granola and nectarine. Enjoy immediately.

Veggie Panini

Ingredients for 4 servings

1 tbsp olive oil
1 cup sliced button mushrooms
Salt and black pepper to taste
1 ripe avocado, sliced
2 tbsp freshly squeezed lemon juice
1 tbsp chopped parsley
½ tsp pure maple syrup
8 slices whole-wheat ciabatta
4 oz sliced plant-based Parmesan

Directions and Total Time: 30 minutes

Heat the olive oil in a medium skillet over medium heat and sauté the mushrooms until softened, 5 minutes. Season with salt and black pepper. Turn the heat off.

Preheat a panini press to medium heat, 3 to 5 minutes. Mash the avocado in a medium bowl and mix in the lemon juice, parsley, and maple syrup. Spread the mixture on 4 bread slices, divide the mushrooms and plant-based Parmesan cheese on top. Cover with the other bread slices and brush the top with olive oil. Grill the sandwiches one after another in the heated press until golden brown and the cheese melted. Serve.

Potato & Cauliflower Hash Browns

Ingredients for 4 servings

3 tbsp flax seed powder
2 large potatoes, shredded
1 big head cauliflower, riced
½ white onion, grated
Salt and black pepper to taste
4 tbsp plant butter

Directions and Total Time: 35 minutes

In a medium bowl, mix the flaxseed powder and 9 tbsp water. Allow thickening for 5 minutes for the flax egg. Add the potatoes, cauliflower, onion, salt, and black pepper to the flax egg and mix until well combined. Allow sitting for 5 minutes to thicken.

Working in batches, melt 1 tbsp of plant butter in a non-stick skillet and add 4 scoops of the hashbrown mixture to the skillet. Make sure to have 1 to 2-inch intervals between each scoop.

Use the spoon to flatten the batter and cook until compacted and golden brown on the bottom part, 2 minutes. Flip the hashbrowns and cook further for 2 minutes or until the vegetable cook and is golden brown. Transfer to a paper-towel-lined plate to drain grease. Make the remaining hashbrowns using the remaining ingredients. Serve warm.

Chocolate & Carrot Bread with Raisins

Ingredients for 4 servings

1 ½ cup whole-wheat flour
¼ cup almond flour
¼ tsp salt
¼ tsp cloves powder
¼ tsp cayenne pepper
1 tbsp cinnamon powder
½ tsp nutmeg powder
1 ½ tsp baking powder
2 tbsp flax seed powder
½ cup pure date sugar
¼ cup pure maple syrup
¾ tsp almond extract
1 tbsp grated lemon zest
½ cup unsweetened applesauce
¼ cup olive oil
4 carrots, shredded
3 tbsp unsweetened chocolate chips
2/3 cup black raisins

Directions and Total Time: 75 minutes

Preheat oven to 375 F and line a loaf tin with baking paper. In a bowl, mix all the flours, salt, cloves powder, cayenne pepper, cinnamon powder, nutmeg powder, and baking powder.

In another bowl, mix the flax seed powder, 6 tbsp water, and allow thickening for 5 minutes. Mix in the date sugar, maple syrup, almond extract, lemon zest, applesauce, and olive oil. Combine both mixtures until smooth and fold in the carrots, chocolate chips, and raisins.

Pour the mixture into a loaf pan and bake in the oven until golden brown on top or a toothpick inserted into the bread comes out clean, 45-50 minutes. Remove from the oven, transfer the bread onto wire rack to cool, slice, and serve.

Tropical French Toasts

Ingredients for 4 servings

2 tbsp flax seed powder
1 ½ cups unsweetened almond milk
½ cup almond flour
2 tbsp maple syrup + extra for drizzling
2 pinches of salt
½ tbsp cinnamon powder
½ tsp fresh lemon zest
1 tbsp fresh pineapple juice
8 whole-grain bread slices

Directions and Total Time: 55 minutes

Preheat the oven to 400 F and lightly grease a roasting rack with olive oil. Set aside.

In a medium bowl, mix the flax seed powder with 6 tbsp water and allow thickening for 5 to 10 minutes. Whisk in the almond milk, almond flour, maple syrup, salt, cinnamon powder, lemon zest, and pineapple juice. Soak the bread on both sides in the almond milk mixture and allow sitting on a plate for 2 to 3 minutes.

Heat a large skillet over medium heat and place the bread in the pan. Cook until golden brown on the bottom side. Flip the bread and cook further for until golden brown on the other side, 4 minutes in total. Transfer to a plate, drizzle some maple syrup on top and serve immediately.

Cashew Cheese Pimiento Biscuits

Ingredients for 4 servings

2 cups whole-wheat flour
2 tsp baking powder
1 tsp salt
½ tsp baking soda
½ tsp garlic powder
¼ tsp black pepper
¼ cup plant butter, cold and cubed
¾ cup coconut milk
1 cup shredded cashew cheese
1 (4 oz) jar chopped pimientos,
1 tbsp melted unsalted plant butter

Directions and Total Time: 30 minutes

Preheat the oven to 450 F and line a baking sheet with parchment paper. Set aside. In a medium bowl, mix the flour, baking powder, salt, baking soda, garlic powder, and black pepper.

Add the cold butter using a hand mixer until mixture is the size of small peas.

Pour in ¾ of the coconut milk and continue whisking. Continue adding the remaining coconut milk, a tablespoonful at a time, until dough forms.

Mix in the cashew cheese and pimientos. (If the dough is too wet to handle, mix in a little bit more of flour until it is manageable). Place the dough on a lightly floured surface and flatten the dough into ½-inch thickness.

Use a 2 ½-inch round cutter to cut out biscuits' pieces from the dough. Gather, re-roll the dough once and continue cutting out biscuits. Arrange the biscuits on the prepared pan and brush the tops with the melted butter. Bake for 12-14 minutes, or until the biscuits are golden brown. Cool and serve.

Vanilla Crepes with Berry Cream Compote Topping

Ingredients for 4 servings

For the berry cream:

1 knob plant butter
2 tbsp pure date sugar
1 tsp vanilla extract
½ cup fresh blueberries
½ cup fresh raspberries
½ cup whipped coconut cream

For the crepes:

2 tbsp flax seed powder
1 tsp vanilla extract
1 tsp pure date sugar
¼ tsp salt
2 cups almond flour
1 ½ cups almond milk
1 ½ cups water
3 tbsp plant butter for frying

Directions and Total Time: 35 minutes

Melt butter in a pot over low heat and mix in the date sugar, and vanilla. Cook until the sugar melts and then, toss in berries. Allow softening for 2-3 minutes. Set aside to cool.

In a medium bowl, mix the flax seed powder with 6 tbsp water and allow thickening for 5 minutes to make the flax egg. Whisk in vanilla, date sugar, and salt. Pour in a quarter cup of almond flour and whisk, then a quarter cup of almond milk, and mix until no lumps remain. Repeat the mixing process with the remaining almond flour and almond milk in the same quantities until exhausted.

Mix in 1 cup of water until the mixture is runny like that of pancakes and add the remaining water until the mixture is lighter. Brush a large non-stick skillet with some butter and place over medium heat to melt. Pour 1 tablespoon of the batter in the pan and swirl the skillet quickly and all around to coat the pan with the batter. Cook until the batter is dry and golden brown beneath, about 30 seconds.

Use a spatula to carefully flip the crepe and cook the other side until golden brown too. Fold the crepe onto a plate and set aside. Repeat making more crepes with the remaining batter until exhausted. Plate the crepes, top with the whipped coconut cream and the berry compote. Serve immediately.

Morning Naan Bread with Mango Jam

Ingredients for 4 servings

¾ cup almond flour
1 tsp salt + extra for sprinkling
1 tsp baking powder
1/3 cup olive oil
2 cups boiling water
2 tbsp plant butter for frying
4 cups heaped chopped mangoes
1 cup pure maple syrup
1 lemon, juiced
A pinch saffron powder
1 tsp cardamom powder

Directions and Total Time: 40 minutes

In a large bowl, mix the almond flour, salt, and baking powder. Mix in the olive oil and boiling water until smooth, thick batter forms. Allow the dough to rise for 5 minutes. Form balls out of the dough, place each on a baking paper and use your hands to flatten the dough.

Working in batches, melt the plant butter in a large skillet and fry the dough on both sides until set and golden brown on each side, 4 minutes per bread. Transfer to a plate and set aside for serving.

Add mangoes, maple syrup, lemon juice and 3 tbsp water in a pot and cook until boiling, 5 minutes. Mix in saffron and cardamom powders and cook further over low heat until the mangoes soften. Mash the mangoes with the back of the spoon until fairly smooth with little chunks of mangoes in a jam. Cool completely. Spoon the jam into sterilized jars and serve with the naan bread.

Sweet Orange Crepes

Ingredients for 4 servings

2 tbsp flax seed powder
1 tsp vanilla extract
1 tsp pure date sugar
¼ tsp salt
2 cups almond flour
1 ½ cups oat milk
½ cup melted plant butter
3 tbsp fresh orange juice
3 tbsp plant butter for frying

Directions and Total Time: 30 minutes

In a medium bowl, mix the flax seed powder with 6 tbsp water and allow thickening for 5 minutes to make the flax egg. Whisk in the vanilla, date sugar, and salt.

Pour in a quarter cup of almond flour and whisk, then a quarter cup of oat milk, and mix until no lumps remain. Repeat the mixing process with the remaining almond flour and almond milk in the same quantities until exhausted.

Mix in the plant butter, orange juice, and half of the water until the mixture is runny like that of pancakes. Add the remaining water until the mixture is lighter. Brush a large non-stick skillet with some butter and place over medium heat to melt.

Pour 1 tablespoon of the batter in the pan and swirl the skillet quickly and all around to coat the pan with the batter. Cook until the batter is dry and golden brown beneath, about 30 seconds.

Use a spatula to carefully flip the crepe and cook the other side until golden brown too. Fold the crepe onto a plate and set aside. Repeat making more crepes with the remaining batter until exhausted. Drizzle some maple syrup on the crepes and serve.

Cheddar Grits with Soy Chorizo

Ingredients for 6 servings

1 cup quick-cooking grits
½ cup grated plant-based cheddar
2 tbsp peanut butter
1 cup soy chorizo, chopped
1 cup corn kernels
2 cups vegetable broth

Directions and Total Time: 25 minutes

Preheat oven to 380 F.

Pour the broth in a pot and bring to a boil over medium heat. Stir in salt and grits. Lower the heat and cook until the grits are thickened, stirring often. Turn the heat off, put in the plant-based cheddar cheese, peanut butter, soy chorizo, and corn and stir well. Spread the mixture into a greased baking dish and bake for 45 minutes until slightly puffed and golden brown. Serve right away.

Pecan & Pumpkin Seed Oat Jars

Ingredients for 5 servings

2 ½ cups old-fashioned rolled oats
5 tbsp pumpkin seeds
5 tbsp chopped pecans
5 cups unsweetened soy milk
2 ½ tsp agave syrup
Salt to taste
1 tsp ground cardamom
1 tsp ground ginger

Directions and Total Time: 10 minutes + chilling time

In a bowl, put oats, pumpkin seeds, pecans, soy milk, agave syrup, salt, cardamom, and ginger and toss to combine. Divide the mixture between mason jars. Seal the lids and transfer to the fridge to soak for 10-12 hours.

Simple Apple Muffins

Ingredients for 4 servings

For the muffins:

1 flax seed powder + 3 tbsp water
1 ½ cups whole-wheat flour
¾ cup pure date sugar

2 tsp baking powder
¼ tsp salt
1 tsp cinnamon powder

1/3 cup melted plant butter
1/3 cup flax milk
2 apples, chopped

For topping:

1/3 cup whole-wheat flour
½ cup pure date sugar

½ cup cold plant butter, cubed
1 ½ tsp cinnamon powder

Directions and Total Time: 40 minutes

Preheat oven to 400 F and grease 6 muffin cups with cooking spray. In a bowl, mix the flax seed powder with water and allow thickening for 5 minutes to make the flax egg.

In a bowl, mix the flour, date sugar, baking powder, salt, and cinnamon powder. Whisk in the butter, flax egg, flax milk, and then fold in the apples. Fill the muffin cups two-thirds way up with the batter.

In a bowl, mix remaining flour, date sugar, cold butter, and cinnamon powder. Sprinkle the mixture on the muffin batter. Bake for 20 minutes. Remove the muffins onto a wire rack, allow cooling, and serve.

Orange-Glazed Raspberry Muffins

Ingredients for 4 servings

2 tbsp flax seed powder
2 cups whole-wheat flour
1½ tsp baking powder
A pinch salt

½ cup plant butter, softened
2 cups pure date sugar
½ cup oat milk
2 tsp vanilla extract

1 lemon, zested
1 cup dried raspberries
2 tbsp orange juice

Directions and Total Time: 40 minutes

Preheat oven to 400 F and grease 6 muffin cups with cooking spray. In a small bowl, mix the flax seed powder with 6 tbsp water and allow thickening for 5 minutes to make the flax egg. In a medium bowl, mix the flour, baking powder, and salt. In another bowl, cream the plant butter, half of the date sugar, and flax egg. Mix in the oat milk, vanilla, and lemon zest.

Combine both mixtures, fold in raspberries, and fill muffin cups two-thirds way up with the batter. Bake for 20-25 minutes. In a medium bowl, whisk orange juice and remaining date sugar until smooth. Remove the muffins when ready and transfer to a wire rack to cool. Drizzle the glaze on top to serve.

Almond Yogurt with Berries & Walnuts

Ingredients for 4 servings

4 cups almond milk
Dairy-Free yogurt, cold

2 tbsp pure malt syrup
2 cups mixed berries, chopped

¼ cup chopped toasted walnuts

Directions and Total Time: 10 minutes

In a medium bowl, mix the yogurt and malt syrup until well-combined. Divide the mixture into 4 breakfast bowls. Top with the berries and walnuts. Enjoy immediately.

Crispy Corn Cakes

Ingredients for 4 servings

1 tbsp flax seed powder
2 cups yellow cornmeal
1 tsp salt
2 tsp baking powder
4 tbsp olive oil
1 cup tofu mayonnaise for serving

Directions and Total Time: 35 minutes

In a medium bowl, mix the flax seed powder with 3 tbsp water and allow thickening for 5 minutes to form the flax egg. Mix in 1 cup of water and then whisk in the cornmeal, salt, and baking powder until soup texture forms but not watery.

Heat a quarter of the olive oil in a griddle pan and pour in a quarter of the batter. Cook until set and golden brown beneath, 3 minutes. Flip the cake and cook the other side until set and golden brown too. Plate the cake and make three more with the remaining oil and batter. Top the cakes with some tofu mayonnaise before serving.

Coconut Oat Bread

Ingredients for 4 servings

4 cups whole-wheat flour
¼ tsp salt
½ cup rolled oats
1 tsp baking soda
1 ¾ cups coconut milk, thick
2 tbsp pure maple syrup

Directions and Total Time: 50 minutes

Preheat the oven to 400 F.

In a bowl, mix flour, salt, oats, and baking soda. Add in coconut milk, maple syrup and whisk until dough forms. Dust your hands with some flour and knead the dough into a ball. Shape the dough into a circle and place on a baking sheet.

Cut a deep cross on the dough and bake in the oven for 15 minutes at 450 F. Then, reduce the temperature to 400 F and bake further for 20 to 25 minutes or until a hollow sound is made when the bottom of the bread is tapped. Slice and serve.

Banana French Toast with Strawberry Syrup

Ingredients for 8 servings

1 banana, mashed
1 cup coconut milk
1 tsp pure vanilla extract
¼ tsp ground nutmeg
½ tsp ground cinnamon
1 ½ tsp arrowroot powder
A pinch of salt
8 slices whole-grain bread
1 cup strawberries
2 tbsp water
2 tbsp maple syrup

Directions and Total Time: 40 minutes

Preheat oven to 350 F.

In a bowl, stir banana, coconut milk, vanilla, nutmeg, cinnamon, arrowroot, and salt. Dip each bread slice in the banana mixture and arrange on a baking tray. Spread the remaining banana mixture over the top. Bake for 30 minutes, until the tops are lightly browned. In a pot over medium heat, put the strawberries, water and maple syrup. Simmer for 15-10 minutes, until the berries breaking up and the liquid has reduced. Serve the banana toast topped with the strawberry syrup.

Spicy Quinoa Bowl with Black Beans

Ingredients for 4 servings

1 cup brown quinoa, rinsed
3 tbsp plant-based yogurt
½ lime, juiced
2 tbsp chopped fresh cilantro
1 (5 oz) can black beans, drained
3 tbsp tomato salsa
¼ avocado, sliced
2 radishes, shredded
1 tbsp pepitas (pumpkin seeds)

Directions and Total Time: 25 minutes

Cook the quinoa with 2 cups of slightly salted water in a medium pot over medium heat or until the liquid absorbs, 15 minutes. Spoon the quinoa into serving bowls and fluff with a fork.

In a small bowl, mix the yogurt, lime juice, cilantro, and salt. Divide this mixture on the quinoa and top with the beans, salsa, avocado, radishes, and pepitas. Serve immediately.

Orange Granola with Hazelnuts

Ingredients for 5 servings

2 cups rolled oats
¾ cup whole-wheat flour
1 tbsp ground cinnamon
1 tsp ground ginger
½ cup sunflower seeds
½ cup hazelnuts, chopped
½ cup pumpkin seeds
½ cup shredded coconut
1¼ cups orange juice
½ cup dried cherries
½ cup goji berries

Directions and Total Time: 50 minutes

Preheat oven to 350 F.

In a bowl, combine the oats, flour, cinnamon, ginger, sunflower seeds, hazelnuts, pumpkin seeds, and coconut. Pour in the orange juice, toss to combine well.

Transfer to a baking sheet and bake for 15 minutes. Turn the granola and continue baking until is crunchy, about 30 minutes. Stir in the cherries and goji berries and store in the fridge for up to 14 days.

Almond & Raisin Granola

Ingredients for 8 servings

5 ½ cups old-fashioned oats
1 ½ cups chopped walnuts
½ cup shelled sunflower seeds
1 cup golden raisins
1 cup shaved almonds
1 cup pure maple syrup
½ tsp ground cinnamon
¼ tsp ground allspice
A pinch of salt

Directions and Total Time: 20 minutes

Preheat oven to 325 F. In a baking dish, place the oats, walnuts and sunflower seeds. Bake for 10 minutes. Lower the heat from the oven to 300 F. Stir in the raisins, almonds, maple syrup, cinnamon, allspice, and salt. Bake for an additional 15 minutes. Allow to cool before serving.

Blueberry Muesli Breakfast

Ingredients for 5 servings

2 cups spelt flakes
2 cups puffed cereal
¼ cup sunflower seeds
¼ cup almonds
¼ cup raisins
¼ cup dried cranberries
¼ cup chopped dried figs
¼ cup shredded coconut
¼ cup non-dairy chocolate chips
3 tsp ground cinnamon
½ cup coconut milk
½ cup blueberries

Directions and Total Time: 10 minutes

In a bowl, combine the spelt flakes, puffed cereal, sunflower seeds, almonds, raisins, cranberries, figs, coconut, chocolate chips, and cinnamon. Toss to combine well. Pour in the coconut milk. Let sit for 1 hour and serve topped with blueberries.

Chocolate-Mango Quinoa Bowl

Ingredients for 2 servings

1 cup quinoa	1 large mango, chopped	1 tbsp hemp seeds
1 tsp ground cinnamon	3 tbsp unsweetened cocoa powder	1 tbsp walnuts
1 cup non-dairy milk	2 tbsp almond butter	¼ cup raspberries

Directions and Total Time: 35 minutes

In a pot combine the quinoa, cinnamon, milk, and 1 cup water over medium heat. Bring to a boil, low heat and simmer covered for 25-30 minutes. In a bowl mash the mango and mix cocoa powder, almond butter, and hemp seeds. In a serving bowl, place cooked quinoa and mango mixture. Top with walnuts and raspberries. Serve immediately.

Orange-Carrot Muffins with Cherries

Ingredients for 6 servings

1 tsp vegetable oil	2 tbsp ground flaxseed	¾ cup whole-wheat flour
2 tbsp almond butter	1 tsp apple cider vinegar	1 tsp baking powder
¼ cup non-dairy milk	1 tsp pure vanilla extract	½ tsp baking soda
1 orange, peeled	½ tsp ground cinnamon	½ cup rolled oats
1 carrot, coarsely chopped	½ tsp ground ginger	2 tbsp raisins
2 tbsp chopped dried cherries	¼ tsp ground nutmeg	2 tbsp sunflower seeds
3 tbsp molasses	¼ tsp allspice	

Directions and Total Time: 45 minutes

Preheat oven to 350 F. Grease 6 muffin cups with vegetable oil.

In a food processor, add the almond butter, milk, orange, carrot, cherries, molasses, flaxseed, vinegar, vanilla, cinnamon, ginger, nutmeg, and allspice, and blend until smooth.

In a bowl, combine the flour, baking powder and baking soda. Fold in the wet mixture and gently stir to combine. Mix in the oats, raisins and sunflower seeds. Divide the batter between muffin cups. Put in a baking tray and bake for 30 minutes.

Morning Pecan & Pear Farro

Ingredients for 4 servings

2 cups water	1 cup farro	2 pears, peeled, cored, and chopped
½ tsp salt	1 tbsp plant butter	¼ cup chopped pecans

Directions and Total Time: 20 minutes

Bring water to a boil in a pot over high heat. Stir in salt and farro. Lower the heat, cover and simmer for 15 minutes until the farro is tender and the liquid has absorbed. Turn the heat off and add in the butter, pears and pecans. Cover and rest for 12-15 minutes. Serve immediately.

Almond Oatmeal Porridge

Ingredients for 4 servings

2 ½ cups vegetable broth
2 ½ cups almond milk
½ cup steel-cut oats
1 tbsp pearl barley
½ cup slivered almonds
¼ cup nutritional yeast
2 cups old-fashioned rolled oats

Directions and Total Time: 25 minutes

Pour the broth and almond milk in a pot over medium heat and bring to a boil. Stir in oats, pearl barley, almond slivers, and nutritional yeast. Reduce the heat and simmer for 20 minutes. Add in the rolled oats, cook for an additional 5 minutes, until creamy. Allow to cool before serving.

Classic Walnut Waffles with Maple Syrup

Ingredients for 4 servings

1 ¾ cups whole-wheat flour
⅓ cup coarsely ground walnuts
1 tbsp baking powder
1 ½p cups soy milk
3 tbsp pure maple syrup
3 tbsp plant butter, melted

Directions and Total Time: 15 minutes

Preheat the waffle iron and grease with oil. Combine the flour, walnuts, baking powder, and salt in a bowl. Set aside. In another bowl, mix the milk, and butter. Pour into the walnut mixture and whisk until well combined. Spoon a ladleful of the batter onto the waffle iron. Cook for 3-5 minutes, until golden brown. Repeat the process until no batter is left. Top with maple syrup to serve.

Orange-Bran Cups with Dates

Ingredients for 12 servings

1 tsp vegetable oil
3 cups bran flakes cereal
1 ½ cups whole-wheat flour
½ cup dates, chopped
3 tsp baking powder
½ tsp ground cinnamon
½ tsp salt
⅓ cup brown sugar
¾ cup fresh orange juice

Directions and Total Time: 30 minutes

Preheat oven to 400 F. Grease a 12-cup muffin tin with oil.

Mix the bran flakes, flour, dates, baking powder, cinnamon, and salt in a bowl. In another bowl, combine the sugar and orange juice, until blended. Pour into the dry mixture and whisk. Divide the mixture between the cups of the muffin tin. Bake for 20 minutes or until golden brown and set. Cool for a few minutes before removing from the tin and serve warm or cooled.

Maple Banana Oats

Ingredients for 4 servings

3 cups water
1 cup steel-cut oats
2 bananas, mashed
¼ cup pumpkin seeds
2 tbsp maple syrup
A pinch of salt

Directions and Total Time: 35 minutes

Bring water to a boil in a pot, add in oats, and lower the heat. Cook for 20-30 minutes. Put in the mashed bananas, cook for 3-5 minutes more. Stir in maple syrup, pumpkin seeds and salt. Serve.

Mushroom Crepes

Ingredients for 4 servings

1 cup whole-wheat flour	1 cup pressed, crumbled tofu	½ cup finely chopped mushrooms
1 tsp onion powder	⅓ cup plant-based milk	½ cup finely chopped onion
½ tsp baking soda	¼ cup lemon juice	2 cups collard greens
¼ tsp salt	2 tbsp extra-virgin olive oil	

Directions and Total Time: 25 minutes

Combine the flour, onion powder, baking soda, and salt in a bowl. Blitz the tofu, milk, lemon juice, and oil in a food processor over high speed for 30 seconds. Pour over the flour mixture and mix to combine well. Add in the mushrooms, onion and collard greens.

Heat a skillet and grease with cooking spray. Lower the heat and spread a ladleful of the batter across the surface of the skillet. Cook for 4 minutes on both sides or until set.

Remove to a plate. Repeat the process until no batter is left, greasing with a little more oil, if needed. Serve.

Coconut Blueberry Muffins

Ingredients for 12 servings

1 tbsp coconut oil melted	¼ cup ground flaxseed	½ cup pure date sugar
1 cup quick-cooking oats	1 tsp almond extract	2 tsp baking soda
1 cup boiling water	1 tsp apple cider vinegar	A pinch of salt
½ cup almond milk	1 ½ cups whole-wheat flour	1 cup blueberries

Directions and Total Time: 30 minutes

Preheat oven to 400 F.

In a bowl, stir in the oats with boiling water until soften. Pour in the coconut oil, milk, flaxseed, almond extract, and vinegar. Add in the flour, sugar, baking soda, and salt. Gently stir in blueberries.

Divide the batter between a greased with coconut oil muffin tin. Bake for 20 minutes until lightly brown. Allow to cool for 10 minutes. Using a spatula run the sides of the muffins to take out. Serve.

Lemony Quinoa Muffins

Ingredients for 5 servings

2 tbsp coconut oil melted, plus more for coating the muffin tin	½ cup pure date sugar	2 tsp baking soda
	1 tsp apple cider vinegar	A pinch of salt
¼ cup ground flaxseed	2 ½ cups whole-wheat flour	½ cup raisins
2 cups unsweetened lemon curd	1 ½ cups cooked quinoa	

Directions and Total Time: 25 minutes

Preheat oven to 400 F.

In a bowl, combine the flaxseed and ½ cup water. Stir in the lemon curd, sugar, coconut oil, and vinegar. Add in flour, quinoa, baking soda, and salt. Put in the raisins, be careful to not fluffy.

Divide the batter between greased with coconut oil cups of the tin and bake for 20 minutes until golden and set. Allow to cool slightly before removing from the tin. Serve.

Blackberry Waffles

Ingredients for 4 servings

1 ½ cups whole-heat flour
½ cup old-fashioned oats
¼ cup date sugar
3 tsp baking powder
½ tsp salt
1 tsp ground cinnamon
2 cups soy milk
1 tbsp fresh lemon juice
1 tsp lemon zest
¼ cup plant butter, melted
½ cup fresh blackberries

Directions and Total Time: 15 minutes

Preheat the waffle iron.

In a bowl, mix flour, oats, sugar, baking powder, salt, and cinnamon. Set aside. In another bowl, combine milk, lemon juice, lemon zest, and butter. Pour into the wet ingredients and whisk to combine. Add the batter to the hot greased waffle iron, using approximately a ladleful for each waffle. Cook for 3-5 minutes, until golden brown. Repeat the process until no batter is left. Serve topped with blackberries.

Sweet Kiwi Oatmeal Bars

Ingredients for 12 servings

2 cups uncooked rolled oats
2 cups all-purpose flour
1 ½ cups pure date sugar
1 ½ tsp baking soda
½ tsp ground cinnamon
1 cup plant butter, melted
4 cups kiwi, chopped
¼ cup organic cane sugar
2 tbsp cornstarch

Directions and Total Time: 50 minutes

Preheat oven to 380 F. Grease a baking dish.

In a bowl, mix the oats, flour, date sugar, baking soda, salt, and cinnamon. Put in butter and whisk to combine. In another bowl, combine the kiwis, cane sugar and cornstarch until the kiwis are coated. Spread 3 cups of oatmeal mixture on a greased baking dish and top with kiwi mixture and finally put the remaining oatmeal mixture on top. Bake for 40 minutes. Allow to cool and slice into bars.

Scrambled Tofu with Swiss Chard

Ingredients for 5 servings

1 (14-oz) package tofu, crumbled
2 tsp olive oil
1 onion, chopped
3 cloves minced garlic
1 celery stalk, chopped
2 large carrots, chopped
1 tsp chili powder
½ tsp ground cumin
½ tsp ground turmeric
Salt and black pepper to taste
5 cups Swiss chard

Directions and Total Time: 35 minutes

Heat the oil in a skillet over medium heat. Add in the onion, garlic, celery, and carrots. Sauté for 5 minutes. Stir in tofu, chili powder, cumin, turmeric, salt, and pepper, cook for 7-8 minutes more. Mix in the Swiss chard and cook until wilted, about 3 minutes. Allow to cool and seal and serve.

Tangerine Banana Toast

Ingredients for 4 servings

3 bananas
1 cup almond milk
Zest and juice of 1 tangerine
1 tsp ground cinnamon
¼ tsp grated nutmeg
4 slices bread
1 tbsp olive oil

Directions and Total Time: 25 minutes

Blend the bananas, almond milk, tangerine juice, tangerine zest, cinnamon, and nutmeg until smooth in a food processor. Spread into a baking dish. Submerge the bread slices in the mixture for 3-4 minutes. Heat the oil in a skillet over medium heat. Fry the bread for 5 minutes until golden brown. Serve hot.

Spicy Apple Pancakes

Ingredients for 4 servings

2 cups almond milk	½ tsp baking soda	¼ tsp ground allspice
1 tsp apple cider vinegar	1 tsp sea salt	½ cup applesauce
2 ½ cups whole-wheat flour	½ tsp ground cinnamon	1 cup water
2 tbsp baking powder	¼ tsp grated nutmeg	1 tbsp coconut oil

Directions and Total Time: 30 minutes

Whisk the almond milk and apple cider vinegar in a bowl and set aside. In another bowl, combine the flour, baking powder, baking soda, salt, cinnamon, nutmeg, and allspice. Transfer the almond mixture to another bowl and beat with the applesauce and water.

Pour in the dry ingredients and stir. Melt some coconut oil in a skillet over medium heat. Pour a ladle of the batter and cook for 5 minutes, flipping once until golden. Repeat the process until the batter is exhausted. Serve warm.

Almond & Coconut Granola with Cherries

Ingredients for 6 servings

½ cup coconut oil, melted	4 cups rolled oats	½ cup slivered almonds
½ cup maple syrup	⅓ cup whole-wheat flour	½ cup shredded coconut
1 tsp vanilla extract	¼ cup ground flaxseed	½ cup dried cherries
3 tsp pumpkin pie spice	½ cup sunflower seeds	½ cup dried apricots, chopped

Directions and Total Time: 45 minutes

Preheat oven to 350 F.

In a bowl, combine the coconut oil, maple syrup and vanilla. Add in the pumpkin pie spice. Put oats, flour, flaxseed, sunflower seeds, almonds, and coconut in a baking sheet and toss to combine. Coat with the oil mixture. Spread the granola out evenly. Bake for 25 minutes. Once ready, break the granola into chunks and stir in the cherries and apricots. Bake another 5 minutes. Allow to cool and serve.

Cranberry Oat Cookies

Ingredients for 2 servings

½ cup rolled oats	2 tbsp pure date sugar	2 tbsp dried cranberries
1 tbsp whole-wheat flour	½ tsp ground cinnamon	
½ tsp baking powder	¼ cup applesauce	

Directions and Total Time: 20 minutes

Combine the oats, flour, baking powder, sugar, and cinnamon in a bowl. Add in applesauce and cranberries. Stir until well combined. Form 2 cookies out of the mixture and microwave for 1 ½ minutes. Allow to cool before serving.

Cinnamon Buckwheat with Almonds

Ingredients for 4 servings

1 cup almond milk
1 cup water
1 cup buckwheat groats, rinsed
1 tsp cinnamon
¼ cup chopped almonds
2 tbsp pure date syrup

Directions and Total Time: 20 minutes

Place almond milk, water and buckwheat in a pot over medium heat and bring to a boil. Lower the heat and simmer covered for 15 minutes. Allow to sit covered for 5 minutes. Mix in the cinnamon, almonds and date syrup. Serve warm.

Berry Quinoa Bowl

Ingredients for 4 servings

3 cups cooked quinoa
1 ⅓ cups unsweetened almond milk
2 bananas, sliced
1 cup raspberries
1 cup blueberries
½ cup chopped raw hazelnuts
¼ cup agave syrup

Directions and Total Time: 5 minutes

In a large bowl, combine the quinoa, milk, banana, raspberries, blueberries, and hazelnuts. Divide between serving bowls and top with agave syrup to serve.

Mango Rice Pudding

Ingredients for 4 servings

1 cup brown rice
1 ½ cups non-dairy milk
3 tbsp pure date sugar
2 tsp pumpkin pie spice
1 mango, chopped
2 tbsp chopped walnuts

Directions and Total Time: 55 minutes

In a pot over medium heat, add the rice, 2 cups water, milk, sugar, and pumpkin pie spice. Bring to a boil, then lower the heat and simmer for 50 minutes, until the rice is soft and the liquid is absorbed. Put in the mango and stir to combine. Top with walnuts to serve.

Strawberry & Pecan Breakfast

Ingredients for 2 servings

1 (14-oz) can coconut milk, refrigerated overnight
1 cup granola
½ cup pecans, chopped
1 cup sliced strawberries

Directions and Total Time: 15 minutes

Drain the coconut milk liquid. Layer the coconut milk solids, granola, and strawberries in small glasses. Top with chopped pecans and serve right away.

Simple Pear Oatmeal

Ingredients for 2 servings

1 ¼ cups apple cider
1 pear, peeled, cored, and chopped
⅔ cup rolled oats
1 tsp ground cinnamon
1 tbsp pure date syrup

Directions and Total Time: 20 minutes

Pour the apple cider in a pot over medium heat and bring to a boil. Add in the pear, oats and cinnamon. Lower the heat and simmer for 3-4 minutes, until the oatmeal thickens. Divide between bowls and drizzle with date syrup. Serve immediately.

Fresh Peach Smoothie

Ingredients for 2 servings

1 avocado
2 cups baby spinach
1 cup peach chunks
2 cups unsweetened almond milk
Juice of 1 lime
2 tbsp maple syrup

Directions and Total Time: 5 minutes

In a food processor, combine the avocado, spinach, pear, almond milk, lime, and maple syrup. Purée until smooth and serve right away.

Apple-Date Couscous with Macadamia Nuts

Ingredients for 4 servings

3 cups apple juice
1 ½ cups couscous
1 tsp ground cinnamon
¼ tsp ground cloves
½ cup dried dates
½ cup chopped macadamia nuts

Directions and Total Time: 20 minutes

Pour the apple juice in a pot over medium heat and bring to a boil. Stir in couscous, cinnamon and cloves. Turn the heat off and cover. Let sit for 5 minutes, until the liquid is absorbed. Using a fork fluff the couscous and add the dates and macadamia nuts, stir to combine. Serve warm.

Thyme Pumpkin Stir-Fry

Ingredients for 2 servings

1 cup pumpkin, shredded
1 tbsp olive oil
½ onion, chopped
1 carrot, peeled and chopped
2 garlic cloves, minced
½ tsp dried thyme
1 cup chopped kale
Salt and black pepper to taste

Directions and Total Time: 25 minutes

Heat the oil in a skillet over medium heat. Sauté onion and carrot for 5 minutes. Add in garlic and thyme, cook for 30 seconds until the garlic is fragrant. Place in pumpkin, cook for 10 minutes until tender. Stir in kale, cook for 4 minutes until the kale wilts. Season with salt and pepper. Serve hot.

Choco-Berry Smoothie

Ingredients for 2 servings

1 tbsp poppy seeds
2 cups unsweetened soy milk
2 cups blackberries
2 tbsp pure agave syrup
2 tbsp cocoa powder

Directions and Total Time: 10 minutes

Submerge poppy seeds in soy milk and let sit for 5 minutes. Transfer to a food processor and add in the soy milk, blackberries, agave syrup, and cocoa powder. Blitz until smooth. Serve right away in glasses.

Raspberry Almond Smoothie

Ingredients for 4 servings

1 ½ cups almond milk
½ cup raspberries
Juice from half lemon
½ tsp almond extract

Directions and Total Time: 5 minutes

In a blender or smoothie maker, pour the almond milk, raspberries, lemon juice, and almond extract. Puree the ingredients on high speed until the raspberries have blended almost entirely into the liquid. Pour the smoothie into serving glasses. Stick in some straws and serve immediately.

Banana-Strawberry Smoothie

Ingredients for 4 servings

4 bananas, sliced
4 cups strawberries
4 cups kale
4 cups plant-based milk

Directions and Total Time: 5 minutes

In a food processor, add in bananas, strawberries, kale, and milk and blitz until smooth. Divide between 4 glasses and serve.

Tropical Smoothie Bowl

Ingredients for 4 servings

4 bananas, sliced
1 cup papaya
1 cup baked granola, crushed
2 cups fresh raspberries
½ cup slivered almonds
4 cups plant-based milk

Directions and Total Time: 10 minutes

Put bananas, raspberries, and milk in a food processor and pulse until smooth. Transfer to a bowl and stir in granola. Top with almonds and serve.

Coconut Fruit Smoothie

Ingredients for 3 servings

1 cup strawberries
1 cup chopped watermelon
1 cup cranberries
1 tbsp chia seeds
½ cup coconut milk
1 cup water
1 tsp goji berries
2 tbsp fresh mint, chopped

Directions and Total Time: 5 minutes

In a food processor, put the strawberries, watermelon, cranberries, chia seeds, coconut milk, water, goji berries, and mint. Pulse until smooth, adding more water or milk if needed. Divide between 3 glasses and serve.

Amazing Yellow Smoothie

Ingredients for 4 servings

1 banana
1 cup chopped mango
1 cup chopped apricots
1 cup strawberries
1 carrot, peeled and chopped
1 cup water

Directions and Total Time: 5 minutes

Put the banana, mango, apricots, strawberries, carrot, and water in a food processor. Pulse until smooth, add more water if needed. Divide between glasses and serve.

Delicious Matcha Smoothie

Ingredients for 4 servings

1 cup chopped pineapple	1 cup chopped spinach	½ cup almond milk
1 cup chopped mango	½ avocado	1 tsp matcha green tea powder

Directions and Total Time: 5 minutes

Purée everything in a blender until smooth, adding 1 cup water if needed. In a food processor, place the pineapple, mango, spinach, avocado, almond milk, water, and matcha powder. Blitz until smooth, add more water or milk if necessary. Divide between 4 glasses and serve.

Hearty Smoothie

Ingredients for 3 servings

1 banana	1 cup broccoli sprouts	¼ tsp ground cinnamon
½ cup coconut milk	2 cherries, pitted	¼ tsp ground cardamom
1 cup water	1 tbsp hemp hearts	1 tbsp grated fresh ginger

Directions and Total Time: 5 minutes

In a food processor, place banana, coconut milk, water, broccoli, cherries, hemp hearts, cinnamon, cardamom, and ginger. Blitz until smooth. Divide between glasses and serve.

Apple Chocolate Smoothie

Ingredients for 4 servings

1 cup applesauce	1 tbsp peanut butter	1 cup water
2 tbsp plant protein powder	1 tbsp maple syrup	1 tsp matcha powder
1 tbsp flaxseed	1 cup spinach, chopped	1 tsp cocoa nibs
1 tbsp unsweetened cacao powder	½ cup non-dairy milk	

Directions and Total Time: 5 minutes

Put in a food processor the applesauce, protein powder, flaxseed, cacao powder, peanut butter, maple syrup, spinach, milk, water, matcha powder, and cocoa nibs. Pulse until smooth, add more water or milk if needed. Divide between glasses and serve.

Carrot-Strawberry Smoothie

Ingredients for 2 servings

1 cup peeled and diced carrots	1 apple, chopped	2 cups unsweetened almond milk
1 cup strawberries	2 tbsp maple syrup	

Directions and Total Time: 5 minutes

Place in a food processor the carrots, strawberries, apple, maple syrup and almond milk. Blitz until smooth. Pour in glasses and serve.

Power Green Smoothie

Ingredients for 2 servings

1 banana, sliced
2 cups kale

1 cup sliced kiwi
1 orange, cut into segments

1 cup unsweetened coconut milk

Directions and Total Time: 10 minutes

Put in a food processor the banana, kale, kiwi, orange, and coconut milk. Pulse until smooth. Serve right away in glasses.

Maple Blueberry Smoothie

Ingredients for 4 servings

4 cups chopped arugula
2 cups frozen blueberries

4 cups unsweetened almond milk
Juice of 2 limes

4 tbsp maple syrup

Directions and Total Time: 5 minutes

In a food processor, blitz the arugula, blueberries, almond milk, lime juice, and maple syrup, until smooth. Serve immediately.

Energy Chia-Peach Smoothie

Ingredients for 2 servings

1 banana, sliced
1 peach, chopped

1 cup almond milk
1 scoop plant-based protein powder

1 tbsp chia seeds
1 cucumber, chopped

Directions and Total Time: 5 minutes

Purée the banana, peach, almond milk, protein powder, chia seeds, and cucumber for 50 seconds until smooth in a food processor. Serve immediately in glasses.

Morning Green Smoothie

Ingredients for 2 servings

1 avocado
1 cup chopped cucumber
2 cups curly endive
2 apples, peeled and cored

2 tbsp lime juice
2 cups soy milk
½-inch piece peeled fresh ginger
2 tbsp chia seeds

1 cup unsweetened coconut yogurt
4 tbsp chopped fresh mint

Directions and Total Time: 5 minutes

Put in a food processor the avocado, cucumber, curly endive, apple, lime juice, soy milk, ginger, chia seeds, and coconut yogurt. Blend until smooth. Serve topped with mint.

SOUPS & STEWS

Spinach & Kale Soup with Fried Collards

Ingredients for 4 servings

4 tbsp plant butter
1 cup fresh spinach, chopped
1 cup fresh kale, chopped
1 large avocado

3 ½ cups coconut cream
4 cups vegetable broth
3 tbsp chopped fresh mint leaves
Salt and black pepper to taste

Juice from 1 lime
1 cup collard greens, chopped
2 garlic cloves, minced
1 pinch of green cardamom powder

Directions and Total Time: 16 minutes

Melt 2 tbsp of plant butter in a saucepan over medium heat and sauté spinach and kale for 5 minutes. Turn the heat off. Add the avocado, coconut cream, vegetable broth, salt, and pepper. Puree the ingredients with an immersion blender until smooth. Pour in the lime juice and set aside.

Melt the remaining plant butter in a pan and add the collard greens, garlic, and cardamom; sauté until the garlic is fragrant and has achieved a golden brown color, about 4 minutes. Fetch the soup into serving bowls and garnish with fried collards and mint. Serve warm.

Tofu Goulash Soup

Ingredients for 4 servings

1 ½ cups extra firm tofu, crumbled
3 tbsp plant butter
1 white onion
2 garlic cloves
8 oz chopped butternut squash

1 red bell pepper
1 tbsp paprika powder
¼ tsp red chili flakes
1 tbsp dried basil
½ tbsp crushed cardamom seeds

Salt and black pepper to taste
1 ½ cups crushed tomatoes
4 cups vegetable broth
1 ½ tsp red wine vinegar
Chopped cilantro to serve

Directions and Total Time: 25 minutes

Melt plant butter in a pot over medium heat and sauté onion and garlic for 3 minutes. Stir in tofu and cook for 3 minutes; add the butternut squash, bell pepper, paprika, red chili flakes, basil, cardamom seeds, salt, and pepper. Cook for 2 minutes. Pour in tomatoes and vegetable broth. Bring to a boil, reduce the heat and simmer for 10 minutes. Mix in red wine vinegar. Garnish with cilantro and serve.

Coconut Cream Pumpkin Soup

Ingredients for 4 servings

2 small red onions, cut into wedges
2 garlic cloves, pelled
10 oz pumpkin, cubed

10 oz butternut squash
2 tbsp olive oil
4 tbsp plant butter

Juice of 1 lime
¾ cup tofu mayonnaise
Toasted pumpkin seeds for garnis

Directions and Total Time: 55 minutes

Preheat oven to 400 F.

Place onions, garlic, and pumpkin in a baking sheet and drizzle with olive oil. Season with salt and pepper. Roast for 30 minutes or until the vegetables are golden brown and fragrant. Remove the vegetables from the oven and transfer to a pot. Add 2 cups of water, bring the ingredients to boil over medium heat for 15 minutes. Turn the heat off. Add in plant butter and puree until smooth. Stir in lime juice and tofu mayonnaise. Spoon into serving bowls and garnish with pumpkin seeds to serve.

Celery Dill Soup

Ingredients for 4 servings

2 tbsp coconut oil
½ lb celery root, trimmed
1 garlic clove
1 medium white onion

¼ cup fresh dill, roughly chopped
1 tsp cumin powder
¼ tsp nutmeg powder
1 head cauliflower, cut into florets

3 ½ cups seasoned vegetable stock
5 oz plant butter
Juice from 1 lemon
¼ cup coconut whipping cream

Directions and Total Time: 26 minutes

Set a pot over medium heat, add the coconut oil and allow heating until no longer shimmering.

Add the celery root, garlic clove, and onion; sauté the vegetables until fragrant and soft, about 5 minutes. Stir in the dill, cumin, and nutmeg, and fry further for 1 minute. Mix in the cauli florets and vegetable stock. Bring the soup to a boil for 12 to 15 minutes or until the cauliflower is soft. Turn the heat off. Add the plant butter and lemon juice. Puree the ingredients with an immersion blender until smooth. Mix in coconut whipping cream and season the soup with salt and black pepper. Serve warm.

Broccoli Fennel Soup

Ingredients for 4 servings

1 fennel bulb, chopped
10 oz broccoli, cut into florets
3 cups vegetable stock

Salt and black pepper to taste
1 garlic clove
1 cup cashew cream cheese

3 oz plant butter
½ cup chopped fresh oregano

Directions and Total Time: 25 minutes

Put the fennel and broccoli into a pot, and cover with the vegetable stock. Bring the ingredients to a boil over medium heat until the vegetables are soft, about 10 minutes. Season the liquid with salt and black pepper, and drop in the garlic. Simmer the soup for 5 to 7 minutes and turn the heat off.

Pour the cream cheese, plant butter, and oregano into the soup; puree the ingredients with an immersion blender until completely smooth. Adjust the taste with salt and black pepper. Spoon the soup into serving bowls and serve.

Medley of Mushroom Soup

Ingredients for 4 servings

4 oz unsalted plant butter
1 small onion, finely chopped
1 clove garlic, minced
5 oz button mushrooms, chopped

5 oz cremini mushrooms, chopped
5 oz shiitake mushrooms, chopped
½ lb celery root, chopped
½ tsp dried rosemary

1 vegetable stock cube, crushed
1 tbsp plain vinegar
1 cup coconut cream
4 – 6 leaves basil, chopped

Directions and Total Time: 40 minutes

Place a saucepan over medium-high heat, add the plant butter to melt, then sauté the onion, garlic, mushrooms, and celery root in the butter until golden brown and fragrant, about 6 minutes. Fetch out some mushrooms and reserve for garnishing. Add the rosemary, 3 cups of water, stock cube, and vinegar. Stir the mixture and bring to a boil for 6 minutes. After, reduce the heat and simmer the soup for 15 minutes or until the celery is soft.

Mix in the coconut cream and puree the ingredients using an immersion blender. Simmer for 2 minutes. Spoon the soup into serving bowls, garnish with the reserved mushrooms, and basil. Serve.

Asian-Style Bean Soup

Ingredients for 4 servings

- 1 cup canned cannellini beans
- 2 tsp curry powder
- 2 tsp olive oil
- 1 red onion, diced
- 1 tbsp minced fresh ginger
- 2 cubed sweet potatoes
- 1 cup sliced zucchini
- Salt and black pepper to taste
- 4 cups vegetable stock
- 1 bunch spinach, chopped
- Toasted sesame seeds

Directions and Total Time: 55 minutes

Mix the beans with 1 tsp of curry powder, until well combined. Warm the oil in a pot over medium heat. Place the onion and ginger and cook for 5 minutes until soft. Add in sweet potatoes and cook for 10 minutes. Put in zucchini and cook for 5 minutes. Season with the remaining curry, pepper and salt.

Pour in stock and bring to a boil. Lower the heat and simmer for 25 minutes. Stir in beans and spinach. Cook until the spinach wilts and remove from the heat. Garnish with sesame seeds to serve.

Carrot & Mushroom Broth

Ingredients for 6 servings

- 5 dried porcini mushrooms, soaked and liquid reserved
- 1 tbsp olive oil
- 1 onion, unpeeled and quartered
- 1 medium carrot, coarsely chopped
- 1 celery rib with leaves, chopped
- 8 oz Cremini mushrooms, chopped
- 1 onion, chopped
- ½ cup chopped fresh parsley
- Salt and black pepper to taste
- 5 cups water

Directions and Total Time: 1 hour 15 minutes

Warm the oil in a pot over medium heat. Place in onion, carrot, celery, and cremini mushrooms. Cook for 5 minutes until softened. Add in the dried mushrooms and reserved liquid, onion, salt, and water. Bring to a boil, then lower the heat and simmer uncovered for 1 hour.

Let cool for a few minutes, then pour over a strainer into a pot. Divide between glass mason jars and allow to cool completely. Seal and store in the fridge up to 5 days or 1 month in the freezer.

Mexican Tortilla Soup

Ingredients for 4 servings

- 1 (14.5-oz) can diced tomatoes
- 1 (4-oz) can chopped green chiles
- 2 tbsp olive oil
- 1 cup canned sweet corn
- 1 red onion, chopped
- 2 garlic cloves, minced
- 2 jalapeño peppers, sliced
- 4 cups vegetable broth
- 8 oz seitan, cut into ¼-inch strips
- Salt and black pepper to taste
- ¼ cup chopped fresh cilantro
- 3 tbsp fresh lime juice
- 4 corn tortillas, cut into strips
- 1 ripe avocado, chopped

Directions and Total Time: 40 minutes

Preheat oven to 350 F. Heat the oil in a pot over medium heat. Place sweet corn, garlic, jalapeño, and onion and cook for 5 minutes. Stir in broth, seitan, tomatoes, canned chiles, salt, and pepper. Bring to a boil, then lower the heat and simmer for 20 minutes. Put in the cilantro and lime juice, stir. Adjust the seasoning.

Meanwhile, arrange the tortilla strips on a baking sheet and bake for 8 minutes until crisp. Serve the soup into bowls and top with tortilla strips and avocado.

Spicy Bean Soup

Ingredients for 4 servings

2 tbsp olive oil
1 medium onion, chopped
2 large garlic cloves, minced
1 carrot, chopped
1 (15.5-oz) can cannellini beans, drained
5 cups vegetable broth
¼ tsp crushed red pepper
Salt and black pepper to taste
3 cups chopped baby spinach

Directions and Total Time: 40 minutes

Heat oil in a pot over medium heat. Place in carrot, onion, and garlic and cook for 3 minutes. Put in beans, broth, red pepper, salt, and black pepper and stir. Bring to a boil, then lower the heat and simmer for 25 minutes. Stir in baby spinach and cook for 5 minutes until the spinach wilts. Serve warm.

Celery & Potato Soup

Ingredients for 6 servings

2 tbsp olive oil
1 onion, chopped
1 carrot, chopped
1 celery stalk, chopped
2 garlic cloves, minced
1 golden beet, peeled and diced
1 yellow bell pepper, chopped
1 Yukon Gold potato, diced
6 cups vegetable broth
1 tsp dried thyme
Salt and black pepper to taste
1 tbsp lemon juice

Directions and Total Time: 55 minutes

Heat the oil in a pot over medium heat. Place the onion, carrot, celery, and garlic. Cook for 5 minutes until soften. Stir in beet, bell pepper and potato, cook uncovered for 1 minute. Pour in the broth and thyme. Season with salt and pepper. Cook for 45 minutes until the vegetables are tender. Serve sprinkled with lemon juice.

Cabbage & Red Bean Chili

Ingredients for 4 servings

2 tsp sesame oil
1 cup green onions, chopped
3 cloves garlic, minced
1 pound yellow squash, chopped
2 cups shredded napa cabbage
1 (14.5-oz) can red beans, drained
1 (14.5-oz) can diced tomatoes
2 cups vegetable broth
2 tbsp red miso paste
2 tbsp water
1 tbsp hot sauce
2 tsp tamari sauce

Directions and Total Time: 35 minutes

Heat the sesame oil in a pot over medium heat. Place in green onion, garlic and yellow squash and cook for 5 minutes. Stir in cabbage, beans, tomatoes, and broth. Bring to a boil, then lower the heat and simmer covered for 15 minutes.

Meanwhile, mix the miso paste with hot water. Set aside.

Remove the pot from heat and stir in the miso, tamari and hot sauces. Adjust the seasoning and serve.

Rice Wine Mushroom Soup

Ingredients for 4 servings

2 tbsp olive oil
4 green onions, chopped
1 carrot, chopped
8 oz shiitake mushrooms, sliced
3 tbsp rice wine
2 tbsp soy sauce
4 cups vegetable broth
Salt and black pepper to taste
2 tbsp parsley, chopped

Directions and Total Time: 25 minutes

Heat the oil in a pot over medium heat. Place the green onions and carrot and cook for 5 minutes. Stir in mushrooms, rice wine, soy sauce, broth, salt, and pepper. Bring to a boil, then lower the heat and simmer for 15 minutes. Top with parsley and serve warm.

Tangy Bean Tomato Soup

Ingredients for 5 servings

2 tsp olive oil	Sea salt to taste	1 (14-oz) can kidney beans, drained
1 onion, chopped	1 tbsp dried basil	5 cups water
2 garlic cloves, minced	½ tbsp dried oregano	2 cups chopped mustard greens
1 cup mushrooms, chopped	1 (19-oz) can diced tomatoes	

Directions and Total Time: 30 minutes

Heat the oil in a pot over medium heat. Place onion, garlic, mushrooms, salt and cook for 5 minutes. Stir in basil and oregano, tomatoes, and beans. Pour in water and stir. Simmer for 20 minutes and add in mustard greens; cook for 5 minutes until greens soften. Serve immediately.

Vegetable Chili

Ingredients for 4 servings

1 onion, chopped	1 carrot, chopped	1 (14-oz) can chickpeas
1 cup vegetable broth	2 tsp olive oil	1 tsp chili powder
2 garlic cloves, minced	1 (28-oz) can tomatoes	Salt and black pepper to taste
1 potato, cubed	1 tbsp tomato paste	¼ cup parsley leaves, chopped

Directions and Total Time: 30 minutes

Heat the oil in a pot over medium heat. Place the onion and garlic, sauté for 3 minutes until soften. Add in potato, carrot, tomatoes, vegetable broth, tomato paste, chickpeas, and chili powder. Season with salt and pepper. Simmer for 20 minutes. Serve garnished with parsley.

Turmeric Bean Soup

Ingredients for 6 servings

3 tbsp olive oil	2 garlic cloves, minced	1 tsp ground cayenne pepper
1 onion, chopped	4 tomatoes, chopped	1 (15.5-oz) can white beans, drained
2 carrots, chopped	6 cups vegetable broth	⅓ cup whole-wheat pasta
1 sweet potato, chopped	1 bay leaf	¼ tsp turmeric
1 yellow bell pepper, chopped	Salt to taste	

Directions and Total Time: 50 minutes

Heat the oil in a pot over medium heat. Place onion, carrots, sweet potato, bell pepper, and garlic. Cook for 5 minutes. Add in tomatoes, broth, bay leaf, salt, and cayenne pepper. Stir and bring to a boil. Lower the heat and simmer for 10 minutes. Put in white beans and simmer for 15 more minutes.

Cook the pasta in a pot with boiling salted water and turmeric for 8-10 minutes, until pasta is al dente. Strain and transfer to the soup. Discard the bay leaf. Spoon into bowl to serve.

Spinach & Potato Soup

Ingredients for 4 servings

2 tbsp olive oil
1 onion, chopped
2 garlic cloves, minced
4 cups vegetable broth
2 russet potatoes, cubed
½ tsp dried oregano
¼ tsp crushed red pepper
1 bay leaf
Salt to taste
4 cups chopped spinach
1 cup green lentils, rinsed

Directions and Total Time: 55 minutes

Warm the oil in a pot over medium heat. Place the onion and garlic, cook covered for 5 minutes. Stir in broth, potatoes, oregano, red pepper, bay leaf, lentils, and salt. Bring to a boil, then lower the heat and simmer uncovered for 30 minutes. Add in spinach and cook for another 5 minutes. Discard the bay leaf and serve immediately.

Arugula Coconut Soup

Ingredients for 4 servings

1 tsp coconut oil
1 onion, diced
2 cups green beans
4 cups water
1 cup arugula, chopped
1 tbsp fresh mint, chopped
Sea salt and black pepper to taste
¾ cup coconut milk

Directions and Total Time: 30 minutes

In a pot over medium heat, place coconut oil, onion and sauté for 5 minutes. Add in green beans and water. Bring to a boil, then lower the heat and stir in arugula, mint, salt, and pepper. Simmer for 10 minutes. Stir in coconut milk. Transfer to a food processor and blitz the soup until smooth. Serve.

Cayenne Pumpkin Soup

Ingredients for 6 servings

1 (2 pounds) pumpkin, sliced
3 tbsp olive oil
1 tsp salt
2 red bell peppers
1 onion, halved
1 head garlic
6 cups water
Zest and juice of 1 lime
¼ tsp cayenne pepper
½ tsp ground coriander
½ tsp ground cumin
Toasted pumpkin seeds

Directions and Total Time: 55 minutes

Preheat oven to 350 F.

Brush the pumpkin slices with oil and sprinkle with salt.

Arrange the slices skin side-down and on a greased baking dish and bake for 20 minutes. Brush the onion with oil. Cut the top of garlic head and brush with oil.

When the pumpkin is done, add in bell peppers, onion and garlic, and bake for another 10 minutes. Allow to cool.

Take out the flesh from the pumpkin skin and transfer to a food processor. Cut the pepper roughly, peel and cut the onion, and remove the cloves from the garlic head. Transfer to the food processor and pour in the water, lime zest and lime juice.

Blend the soup until smooth. If it's very thick, add a bit of water to reach your desired consistency. Sprinkle with salt, cayenne, coriander, and cumin. Serve.

Bell Pepper & Mushroom Soup

Ingredients for 6 servings

3 tbsp olive oil
1 onion, chopped
1 large carrot, chopped
1 lb mixed bell peppers, chopped
1 cup cremini mushrooms, quartered
1 cup white mushrooms, quartered
6 cups vegetable broth
¼ cup chopped fresh parsley
1 tsp minced fresh thyme
Salt and black pepper to taste

Directions and Total Time: 45 minutes

Heat the oil in a pot over medium heat. Place onion, carrot and celery and cook for 5 minutes. Add in bell peppers and broth and stir. Bring to a boil, lower the heat, and simmer for 20 minutes. Adjust the seasoning with salt and black pepper Serve in soup bowls topped with parsley and thyme.

Pumpkin & Garbanzo Chili with Kale

Ingredients for 6 servings

¾ cup dried garbanzo beans, soaked
1 (28-oz) can crushed tomatoes
2 cups chopped pumpkin
6 cups water
2 tbsp chili powder
1 tsp onion powder
½ tsp garlic powder
3 cups kale, chopped
½ tsp salt

Directions and Total Time: 60 minutes

In a saucepan over medium heat, place the garbanzo, tomatoes, pumpkin, 2 cups of water, chili powder, onion powder, salt, and garlic powder. Cover and bring to a boil. Reduce the heat and simmer for 50 minutes. Stir in kale and cook for 5 minutes until the kale wilts. Serve hot.

Cream Soup of Zucchini with Walnuts

Ingredients for 4 servings

3 zucchinis, chopped
2 tsp olive oil
Sea salt and black pepper to taste
1 onion, diced
4 cups vegetable stock
3 tsp ground sage
3 tbsp nutritional yeast
1 cup non-dairy milk
¼ cup toasted walnuts

Directions and Total Time: 45 minutes

Heat the oil in a skillet and place zucchini, onion, salt, and pepper; cook for 5 minutes. Pour in vegetable stock and bring to a boil. Lower the heat and simmer for 15 minutes. Stir in sage, nutritional yeast and milk. Purée the soup with a blender until smooth. Serve garnished with toasted walnuts and pepper.

Homemade Ramen Soup

Ingredients for 4 servings

7 oz Japanese buckwheat noodles
4 tbsp sesame paste
1 cup canned pinto beans, drained
2 tbsp fresh cilantro, chopped
2 scallions, thinly sliced

Directions and Total Time: 25 minutes

In a boiling salted water, add in the noodles and cook for 5 minutes over low heat. Remove a cup of the noodle water to a bowl and add in the sesame paste; stir until it has dissolved. Pour the sesame mix in the pot with the noodles, add in pinto beans, and stir until everything is hot. Serve topped with cilantro and scallions in individual bowls.

Vegetable & Rice Soup

Ingredients for 6 servings

3 tbsp olive oil
2 carrots, chopped
1 onion, chopped
1 celery stalk, chopped
2 garlic cloves, minced
2 cups chopped cabbage
½ red bell pepper, chopped
4 potatoes, unpeeled and quartered
6 cups vegetable broth
½ cup brown rice, rinsed
½ cup frozen green peas
2 tbsp chopped parsley

Directions and Total Time: 40 minutes

Heat the oil in a pot over medium heat. Place carrots, onion, celery, and garlic, cook for 5 minutes. Add in cabbage, bell pepper, potatoes, and broth. Bring to a boil, then lower the heat and add the brown rice, salt and pepper. Simmer uncovered for 25 minutes until vegetables are tender. Stir in peas and cook for 5 minutes. Top with parsley and serve warm.

Daikon & Sweet Potato Soup

Ingredients for 6 servings

6 cups water
2 tsp olive oil
1 chopped onion
3 garlic cloves, minced
1 tbsp thyme
2 tsp paprika
2 cups peeled and chopped daikon
2 cups chopped sweet potatoes
2 cups peeled and chopped parsnips
½ tsp sea salt
1 cup fresh mint, chopped
½ avocado
2 tbsp balsamic vinegar
2 tbsp pumpkin seeds

Directions and Total Time: 40 minutes

Heat the oil in a pot and place onion and garlic. Sauté for 3 minutes. Add in thyme, paprika, daikon, sweet potato, parsnips, water, and salt. Bring to a boil and cook for 30 minutes. Remove the soup to a food processor and add in balsamic vinegar; purée until smooth. Top with mint and pumpkin seeds to serve.

Pressure Cooker Green Onion & Potato Soup

Ingredients for 5 servings

3 green onions, chopped
4 garlic cloves, minced
1 tbsp olive oil
6 russet potatoes, chopped
½ (13.5-oz) can coconut milk
5 cups vegetable broth
Salt and black pepper to taste

Directions and Total Time: 25 minutes

Set your IP to Sauté. Place in green onions, garlic and olive oil. Cook for 3 minutes until soften. Add in potatoes, coconut milk, broth, and salt. Lock the lid in place, set time to 6 minutes on High. Once ready, perform a natural pressure release for 10 minutes. Unlock the lid and allow to cool for a few minutes. Using an immersion blender, blitz the soup until smooth. Serve.

Black-Eyed Pea Soup

Ingredients for 6 servings

2 carrots, chopped
1 onion, chopped
2 cups canned dried black-eyed peas
1 tbsp soy sauce
3 tsp dried thyme
1 tsp onion powder
½ tsp garlic powder
Salt and black pepper to taste
¼ cup chopped pitted black olives

Directions and Total Time: 45 minutes

Place carrots, onion, black-eyed peas, 3 cups water, soy sauce, thyme, onion powder, garlic powder, and pepper in a pot. Bring to a boil, then reduce the heat to low. Cook for 20 minutes. Allow to cool for a few minutes. Transfer to a food processor and blend until smooth. Stir in black olives. Serve.

Chickpea & Vegetable Soup

Ingredients for 5 servings

2 tbsp olive oil	1 (28-oz) can diced tomatoes	1 tsp za'atar spice
1 onion, chopped	2 tbsp tomato paste	¼ tsp ground cayenne pepper
1 carrot, chopped	1 (15.5-oz) can chickpeas, draine	6 cups vegetable broth
1 celery stalk, chopped	2 tsp smoked paprika	4 oz whole-wheat vermicelli
1 eggplant, chopped	1 tsp ground cumin	2 tbsp minced cilantro

Directions and Total Time: 35 minutes

Heat the oil in a pot over medium heat. Place onion, carrot and celery and cook for 5 minutes. Add in eggplant, tomatoes, tomato paste, chickpeas, paprika, cumin, za´atar spice, and cayenne pepper. Stir in broth and salt. Bring to a boil, then lower the heat and simmer for 15 minutes. Add in vermicelli and cook for another 5 minutes. Serve topped with cilantro.

Italian Bean Soups

Ingredients for 6 servings

3 tbsp olive oil	3 garlic cloves, minced	2 bay leaves
2 celery stalks, chopped	½ cup brown rice	Salt and black pepper to taste
2 carrots, chopped	6 cups vegetable broth	2 (15.5-oz) cans white beans
3 shallots, chopped	1 (14.5-oz) can diced tomatoes	¼ cup chopped basil

Directions and Total Time: 1 hour 25 minutes

Heat oil in a pot over medium heat. Place celery, carrots, shallots, and garlic and cook for 5 minutes. Add in brown rice, broth, tomatoes, bay leaves, salt, and pepper. Bring to a boil, then lower the heat and simmer uncovered for 20 minutes. Stir in beans and basil and cook for 5 minutes. Discard bay leaves and spoon into bowls. Sprinkle with basil and serve.

Brussels Sprouts & Tofu Soup

Ingredients for 4 servings

7 oz firm tofu, cubed	1 garlic clove, minced	2 tbsp soy sauce
2 tsp olive oil	½-inch piece fresh ginger, minced	1 tsp pure date sugar
1 cup sliced mushrooms	Salt to taste	¼ tsp red pepper flakes
1 cup shredded Brussels sprouts	2 tbsp apple cider vinegar	1 scallion, chopped

Directions and Total Time: 40 minutes

Heat the oil in a skillet over medium heat. Place mushrooms, Brussels sprouts, garlic, ginger, and salt. Sauté for 7-8 minutes until the veggies are soft.

Pour in 4 cups of water, vinegar, soy sauce, sugar, pepper flakes, and tofu. Bring to a boil, then lower the heat and simmer for 5-10 minutes. Top with scallions and serve.

Roasted Basil & Tomato Soup

Ingredients for 4 servings

2 pounds tomatoes, halved
2 tsp garlic powder
3 tbsp olive oil

1 tbsp balsamic vinegar
Salt and black pepper to taste
4 shallots, chopped

2 cups vegetable broth
½ cup basil leaves, chopped

Directions and Total Time: 60 minutes

Preheat oven to 450 F.

In a bowl, mix tomatoes, garlic, 2 tbsp of oil, vinegar, salt, and pepper. Arrange the tomatoes onto a baking dish. Sprinkle with some olive oil, garlic powder, balsamic vinegar, salt, and pepper. Bake for 30 minutes until the tomatoes get dark brown in colour. Take out from the oven; reserve.

Heat the remaining oil in a pot over medium heat. Place the shallots and cook for 3 minutes, stirring often. Add in roasted tomatoes and broth. Bring to a boil, then lower the heat and simmer for 10 minutes. Transfer to a food processor and blitz the soup until smooth. Serve topped with basil.

Pasta & Tomato Soup

Ingredients for 4 servings

4 cups cubed bread
¼ cup olive oil
2 garlic cloves, minced

8 oz whole-wheat pasta
1 (28-oz) can crushed tomatoes
4 cups vegetable broth

2 tbsp minced parsley
Salt and black pepper to taste
2 tbsp basil leaves, chopped

Directions and Total Time: 30 minutes

Preheat oven to 400 F. Arrange the bread cubes on a baking tray and toast for 10 minutes, shaking them once. Heat olive oil in a pot over medium heat. Place the garlic, cook for 1 minute. Add in pasta, tomatoes, broth, parsley, salt, and pepper. Bring to a boil, then lower the heat and simmer for 10 minutes. Share the toasted bread into soup bowls and spoon in the soup all over. Sprinkle with basil.

Rosemary White Bean Soup

Ingredients for 4 servings

2 tsp olive oil
1 carrot, chopped
1 onion, chopped

2 garlic cloves, minced
1 tbsp rosemary, chopped
2 tbsp apple cider vinegar

1 cup dried white beans
¼ tsp salt
2 tbsp nutritional yeast

Directions and Total Time: 30 minutes

Heat the oil in a pot over medium heat. Place carrots, onion and garlic, cook for 5 minutes.

Pour in vinegar to deglaze the bottom of the pot. Stir in 5 cups water and beans and bring to a boil. Lower the heat and simmer for 45 minutes until the beans are soft. Add in salt and nutritional yeast and stir. Serve topped with chopped rosemary.

Mushroom & Tofu Soup

Ingredients for 4 servings

4 cups water
2 tbsp soy sauce

4 white mushrooms, sliced
¼ cup chopped green onions

3 tbsp tahini
6 oz extra-firm tofu, diced

Directions and Total Time: 20 minutes

Pour the water and soy sauce in a pot and bring to a boil. Add in mushrooms and green onions. Lower the heat and simmer for 10 minutes. In a bowl, combine ½ cup of hot soup with tahini. Pour the mixture into the pot and simmer 2 minutes more, but not boil. Stir in tofu. Serve warm.

Rice Noodle Soup with Beans

Ingredients for 6 servings

2 carrots, chopped
2 celery stalks, chopped
6 cups vegetable broth
8 oz brown rice noodles
1 (15-oz) can pinto beans
1 tsp dried herbs

Directions and Total Time: 10 minutes

Place a pot over medium heat and add in the carrots, celery and vegetable broth. Bring to a boil. Add in noodles, beans, dried herbs, salt, and pepper. Reduce the heat and simmer for 5 minutes. Serve.

Brown Rice & Bean Chili

Ingredients for 6 servings

30 oz canned roasted tomatoes and peppers
3 tbsp olive oil
1 onion, chopped
4 garlic cloves, minced
1 (15-oz) can kidney beans, drained
½ cup brown rice
2 cups vegetable stock
3 tbsp chili powder
1 tsp sea salt

Directions and Total Time: 30 minutes

Heat the oil in a pot over medium heat. Place onion and garlic and cook for 3 minutes until fragrant. Stir in beans, rice, tomatoes and peppers, stock, chili powder, and salt. Cook for 20 minutes. Serve.

Butternut Squash Coconut Cream Soup

Ingredients for 5 servings

1 (2-lb) butternut squash, cubed
1 red bell pepper, chopped
1 large onion, chopped
3 garlic cloves, minced
4 cups vegetable broth
1 cup coconut cream

Directions and Total Time: 30 minutes

Place the squash, bell pepper, onion, garlic, and broth in a pot. Bring to a boil. Lower the heat and simmer for 20 minutes. Stir in coconut cream, salt and pepper. Transfer to a food processor purée the soup until smooth. Serve warm.

Cauliflower Soup with Leeks

Ingredients for 4 servings

2 tbsp olive oil
3 leeks, thinly sliced
1 head cauliflower, cut into florets
4 cups vegetable stock
Salt and black pepper to taste
3 tbsp chopped fresh chives

Directions and Total Time: 25 minutes

Heat the oil in a pot over medium heat. Place the leeks and sauté for 5 minutes. Add in broccoli, vegetable stock, salt, and pepper and cook for 10 minutes. Blend the soup until purée in a food processor. Top with chives and serve.

Lime Lentil Soup

Ingredients for 2 servings

1 tsp olive oil
1 onion, chopped
6 garlic cloves, minced
1 tsp chili powder
½ tsp ground cinnamon
Salt to taste
1 cup yellow lentils
1 cup canned crushed tomatoes
2 cups water
1 celery stalk, chopped
2 cups chopped collard greens

Directions and Total Time: 35 minutes

Heat oil in a pot over medium heat. Place onion and garlic and cook for 5 minutes. Stir in chili powder, celery, cinnamon and salt. Pour in lentils, tomatoes and juices, and water. Bring to a boil, then lower the heat and simmer for 15 minutes. Stir in collard greens. Cook for an additional 5 minutes. Serve.

Spinach, Rice & Bean Soup

Ingredients for 6 servings

6 cups baby spinach
2 tbsp olive oil
1 onion, chopped
2 garlic cloves, minced
1 (15.5-oz) can black-eyed peas
6 cups vegetable broth
Salt and black pepper to taste
½ cup brown rice
Tabasco sauce, for serving

Directions and Total Time: 45 minutes

Heat oil in a pot over medium heat. Place the onion and garlic and sauté for 3 minutes. Poor in broth and season with salt, and pepper. Bring to a boil, then lower the heat and stir in rice. Simmer for 15 minutes. Stir in peas and spinach and cook for another 5 minutes. Serve topped with Tabasco sauce.

Ginger Broccoli Soup

Ingredients for 4 servings

1 onion, chopped
1 tbsp minced peeled fresh ginger
2 tsp olive oil
2 carrots, chopped
1 head broccoli, chopped into florets
1 cup coconut milk
3 cups vegetable broth
½ tsp turmeric
Salt and black pepper to taste

Directions and Total Time: 50 minutes

In a pot over medium heat, place the onion, ginger and olive oil, cook for 4 minutes. Add in carrots, broccoli, broth, turmeric, pepper, and salt. Bring to a boil and cook for 15 minutes. Transfer the soup to a food processor and blend until smooth. Stir in coconut milk and serve warm.

Coconut Mushroom Soup

Ingredients for 2 servings

2 tsp olive oil
1 onion, chopped
2 garlic cloves, minced
2 cups chopped mushrooms
Salt and black pepper to taste
2 tbsp whole-wheat flour
1 tsp dried rosemary
4 cups vegetable broth
1 cup coconut cream

Directions and Total Time: 20 minutes

In a pot over medium heat, warm the oil. Place the onion, garlic, mushrooms, and salt and cook for 5 minutes. Stir in the flour and cook for another 1-2 minutes. Add in rosemary, vegetable broth, coconut cream, and pepper. Lower the heat and simmer for 10 minutes. Serve.

Mustard Green & Potato Soup

Ingredients for 6 servings

2 tbsp olive oil
1 red onion, chopped
1 leek, white part only, chopped
2 garlic cloves, minced
6 cups vegetable broth
1 pound red potatoes, chopped
1 lb sweet potatoes, diced
¼ tsp crushed red pepper
1 bunch mustard greens, chopped

Directions and Total Time: 30 minutes

Heat the oil in a pot over medium heat. Place onion, leek and garlic and sauté for 5 minutes. Pour in broth, potatoes and red pepper. Bring to a boil, then lower the heat and season with salt and pepper. Simmer for 15 minutes. Add in mustard greens, cook for 5 minutes until the greens are tender. Serve.

Sunday Soup

Ingredients for 5 servings

2 tbsp vegetable oil
1 onion, chopped
1 carrot, chopped
2 garlic cloves, minced
3 small new potatoes, sliced
1 zucchini, sliced
1 yellow summer squash, sliced
2 ripe tomatoes, diced
Salt and black pepper to taste
5 cups vegetable broth
2 cups chopped kale
¼ cup fresh basil leaves, chopped

Directions and Total Time: 45 minutes

Heat oil in a pot over medium heat. Place onion, carrot, and garlic and cook covered for 5 minutes. Add in potatoes, zucchini, yellow squash, tomatoes, salt, and pepper. Cook for 5 minutes. Stir in broth and bring to a boil. Lower the heat and simmer for 30 minutes. Stir in kale and basil. Serve in bowls.

Pumpkin Soup with Apples

Ingredients for 4 servings

1 tsp olive oil
1 onion, chopped
1-inch piece fresh ginger, diced
1 apple, cored and chopped
1 tsp curry powder
½ tsp pumpkin pie spice
½ tsp smoked paprika
¼ tsp red pepper flakes
3 cups canned pumpkin purée
Salt and black pepper to taste
½ cup almond milk
4 tbsp nutritional yeast

Directions and Total Time: 25 minutes

Warm oil in a pot and place in onion, ginger and apple and cook for 5 minutes. Add in curry powder, pumpkin pie spice, paprika, and pepper flakes. Stir in 4 cups water, pumpkin, salt, and pepper. Cook for 10 minutes. Puree with an immersion blender until smooth. Pour in milk and nutritional yeast.

Pomodoro Cream Soup

Ingredients for 5 servings

1 (28-oz) can tomatoes
2 tbsp olive oil
1 tsp smoked paprika
2 cups vegetable broth
2 tsp dried herbs
1 red onion, chopped
1 cup unsweetened non-dairy milk
Salt and black pepper to taste

Directions and Total Time: 15 minutes

Place the tomatoes, olive oil, paprika, broth, dried herbs, onion, milk, salt, and pepper in a pot. Bring to a boil and cook for 10 minutes. Transfer to a food processor and blend the soup until smooth.

Potato Soup with Kale

Ingredients for 4 servings

2 tbsp olive oil
1 onion, chopped
1 ½ pounds potatoes, chopped
4 cups vegetable broth
⅓ cup plant butter
¼ tsp ground cayenne pepper
⅛ tsp ground nutmeg
Salt and black pepper to taste
4 cups kale

Directions and Total Time: 45 minutes

Heat the oil in a pot over medium heat. Place in the onion and sauté for 5 minutes. Pour in potatoes and broth and cook for 20 minutes. Stir in butter, cayenne pepper, nutmeg, salt, and pepper. Add in kale and cook 5 minutes until wilted. Serve warm.

Mediterranean Soup

Ingredients for 4 servings

2 tsp olive oil
1 leek, chopped
4 garlic cloves, minced
2 carrots, peeled and chopped
1 tbsp dried herbs
4 cups vegetable broth
2 (15-oz) cans white beans
2 tbsp lemon juice
2 cups green beans

Directions and Total Time: 20 minutes

Heat the oil in a pot over medium heat. Place in leek, garlic, carrots, pepper, and salt. Cook for 5 minutes until fragrant. Season with dried herbs. Stir in broth, green beans, and white beans, reduce the heat and simmer for 10 minutes. Stir in lemon juice and serve.

Hot Bean & Corn Soup

Ingredients for 4 servings

3 tbsp olive oil
1 onion, chopped
3 garlic cloves, chopped
1 cup sweet corn
1 (14.5-oz) can crushed tomatoes
1 (15.5-oz) can black beans
1 (4-oz) can chopped hot chilies
1 tsp ground cumin
½ tsp dried oregano
4 cups vegetable broth
Salt and black pepper to taste
¼ cup chopped cilantro

Directions and Total Time: 30 minutes

Warm oil in a pot over medium heat. Place in the onion and garlic and sauté for 3 minutes. Add in sweet corn, tomatoes, beans, chilies, cumin, oregano, broth, salt, and pepper. Reduce the heat and simmer for 15 minutes. Divide between bowls and garnish with cilantro to serve.

Vegetable Soup with Vermicelli

Ingredients for 6 servings

1 tbsp olive oil 1 onion, chopped
4 garlic cloves, minced
1 (14.5-oz) can diced tomatoes
6 cups vegetable broth
8 oz vermicelli
1 (5-oz) package baby spinach

Directions and Total Time: 20 minutes

Preparing the Ingredients

Warm the oil in a pot over medium heat. Place in onion and garlic and cook for 3 minutes. Stir in tomatoes, broth, salt, and pepper. Bring to a boil, then lower the heat and simmer for 5 minutes. Pour in vermicelli and spinach and cook for another 5 minutes. Serve warm.

Mushroom Curry Soup

Ingredients for 4 servings

1 tbsp coconut oil
1 red onion, sliced
1 carrot, chopped
½ cup sliced shiitake mushrooms

2 garlic cloves, minced
1 (13.5-oz) can coconut milk
4 cups vegetable stock
1 (8-oz) can tomato sauce

2 tbsp cilantro, chopped
Juice from 1 lime
Salt to taste
2 tbsp red curry paste

Directions and Total Time: 15 minutes

Melt the coconut oil in a pot over medium heat. Place in onion, garlic, carrot and mushrooms and sauté for 5 minutes. Pour in coconut milk, vegetable stock, tomato sauce, cilantro, lime juice, salt and curry paste. Cook until heated through. Serve warm.

Garlicky Broccoli Soup

Ingredients for 6 servings

2 tbsp olive oil
3 spring onions, chopped
6 cups vegetable broth

3 potatoes, chopped
2 cups broccoli florets, chopped
2 garlic cloves, minced

1 cup plain unsweetened soy milk
Salt and black pepper to taste
1 tbsp minced chives

Directions and Total Time: 35 minutes

Heat the oil in a pot over medium heat. Place in spring onions and garlic and sauté for 5 minutes until translucent. Add in broth, potatoes, and broccoli. Bring to a boil, then lower the heat and simmer for 20 minutes. Mix in soy milk, salt and pepper. Cook for 5 more minutes. Serve topped with chives.

Spanish Gazpacho

Ingredients for 4 servings

3 tbsp olive oil
2 garlic cloves, crushed
Salt and black pepper to taste

2 cucumbers
2 tsp lemon juice
2 lb ripe plum tomatoes, chopped

1 (14.5-oz) can crushed tomatoes
1 cup tomato juice
2 tbsp chopped dill

Directions and Total Time: 15 minutes

In a food processor, put the garlic, olive oil, and salt and pulse until a paste-like consistency forms. Add in 1 cucumber and lemon juice. Blitz until smooth. Put in tomatoes, tomato juice, salt and pepper. Blend until smooth. Transfer to a bowl, close the lid and let chill in the fridge before serving.

Celery Butternut Squash Soup

Ingredients for 6 servings

2 tbsp olive oil
1 onion, chopped
1 celery stalk, chopped

½ tsp ground allspice
1 potato, peeled and chopped
1 pound butternut squash, chopped

6 cups vegetable broth
Salt to taste
2 tbsp fresh orange juice

Directions and Total Time: 30 minutes

Heat the oil in a pot over medium heat. Place in onion and celery and sauté for 5 minutes until tender. Add in allspice, potato, squash, broth, and salt. Cook for 20 minutes. Stir in orange juice. Using an immersion blender, blitz the soup until purée. Return to the pot and heat. Serve immediately.

Vegetable & Black Bean Soup

Ingredients for 4 servings

- 2 tbsp olive oil
- 1 onion, chopped
- 1 celery stalk, chopped
- 2 medium carrots, chopped
- 1 small green bell pepper, chopped
- 2 garlic cloves, minced
- 2 tomatoes, chopped
- 4 cups vegetable broth
- 1 (15.5-oz) can black beans
- 1 tsp dried thyme
- ¼ tsp cayenne pepper
- 1 tbsp minced cilantro

Directions and Total Time: 50 minutes

Heat the oil in a pot over medium heat. Place in onion, celery, carrots, bell pepper, garlic, and tomatoes. Sauté for 5 minutes, stirring often. Stir in broth, beans, thyme, salt, and cayenne. Bring to a boil, then lower the heat and simmer for 15 minutes. Transfer the soup to a food processor and pulse until smooth. Serve in soup bowls garnished with cilantro.

Basil Coconut Soup

Ingredients for 4 servings

- 2 tbsp coconut oil
- 1½ cups vegetable broth
- 2 garlic cloves, minced
- 1 onion, chopped
- 1 tbsp minced fresh ginger
- 1 cup green bell peppers, sliced
- 1 (13.5-oz) can coconut milk
- Juice of ½ lime
- 2 tbsp chopped basil
- 1 tbsp chopped cilantro
- 4 Lime wedges

Directions and Total Time: 15 minutes

Warm the coconut oil in a pot over medium heat. Place in onion, garlic, and ginger and sauté for 3 minutes. Add in bell peppers and broth. Bring to a boil, then lower the heat and simmer. Stir in coconut milk, lime juice, and chopped cilantro. Simmer for 5 minutes. Serve garnished with basil and lime.

Habanero Bean Soup with Brown Rice

Ingredients for 6 servings

- 2 tbsp olive oil
- 3 garlic cloves, minced
- 1 tbsp chili powder
- 1 tsp dried oregano
- 3 (15.5-oz) cans kidney beans
- 1 habanero pepper, chopped
- ¼ cup sun-dried tomatoes, chopped
- 6 cups vegetable broth
- Salt and black pepper to taste
- ½ cup brown rice
- 1 tbsp chopped cilantro

Directions and Total Time: 40 minutes

Heat the oil in a pot over medium heat. Place in garlic and sauté for 1 minute. Add in chili powder, oregano, beans, habanero, tomatoes, broth, rice, salt, and pepper. Cook for 30 minutes.

Meanwhile, put the rice in a pot with boiling salted water and cook for 5 minutes. Spoon the soup in individual bowls and garnish with cilantro to serve.

Classic Minestrone Soup

Ingredients for 4 servings

- 2 tbsp olive oil
- 1 onion, chopped
- 1 carrot, chopped
- 1 stalk celery, chopped
- 2 garlic cloves, minced
- 4 cups vegetable stock
- 1 cup green peas
- ½ cup orzo
- 1 (15-oz) can chopped tomatoes
- 2 tsp Italian seasoning
- Sea salt and black pepper to taste

Directions and Total Time: 20 minutes

Heat the oil in a pot over medium heat. Place in onion, garlic, carrot and celery and sauté for 5 minutes until tender. Stir in vegetable stock, green peas, orzo, tomatoes, salt, pepper, and Italian seasoning. Cook for 10 minutes. Serve right away.

Turnip & Rutabaga Soup

Ingredients for 5 servings

2 tbsp olive oil
1 onion, diced
3 garlic cloves, minced
1 carrot, chopped
1 rutabaga, chopped
1 turnip chopped
1 red potato, chopped
5 cups vegetable stock
2 tsp dried thyme

Directions and Total Time: 30 minutes

Heat the oil in a pot over medium heat. Place the onion and garlic and sauté for 3 minutes until translucent. Stir in carrot, rutabaga, turnip, potato, vegetable stock, salt, pepper, and thyme. Simmer for 10 minutes. In a food processor, put the soup and blend until purée. Serve warm.

Green Onion Corn & Bean Soup

Ingredients for 4 servings

2 tbsp olive oil
1 red onion, chopped
1 red bell pepper, chopped
1 carrot, chopped
2 garlic cloves, minced
1 tsp ground cumin
1 tsp dried oregano
1 (14.5-oz) can diced tomatoes
1 (15.5-oz) can pinto beans
4 cups vegetable broth
2 cups corn kernels
1 tsp fresh lemon juice
Salt and black pepper to taste
2 stalks green onions, chopped
Tabasco sauce for garnish

Directions and Total Time: 55 minutes

Heat the oil in a pot over medium heat. Place in onion, bell pepper, carrot, and garlic. Sauté for 5 minutes. Add in cumin, oregano, tomatoes, beans, salt, pepper, and broth. Bring to a boil, then lower the heat and simmer for 15 minutes.

In a food processor, transfer ⅓ of the soup and blend until smooth. Return to the pot and stir in the corn. Cook for 10 minutes. Drizzle with lemon juice before serving and garnish with green onions and hot sauce to serve.

Mushroom, Chickpea & Eggplant Stew

Ingredients for 4 servings

2 tbsp olive oil
1 onion, chopped
1 eggplant, chopped
2 medium carrots, sliced
1 red potato, chopped
1 cup mushrooms, sliced
2 garlic cloves, minced
1 (15.5-oz) cans chickpeas, drained
1 (28-oz) can diced tomatoes
1 tbsp minced parsley
½ tsp dried oregano
½ tsp dried basil
1 tbsp soy sauce
½ cup vegetable broth
Salt and black pepper to taste

Directions and Total Time: 30 minutes

Heat the oil in a pot over medium heat. Place in onion, garlic, eggplant and carrots and sauté for 5 minutes. Lower the heat and stir in potato, mushrooms, chickpeas, tomatoes, oregano, basil, soy sauce, salt, pepper, and broth. Simmer for 15 minutes. Serve sprinkled with parsley.

Sweet African Soup

Ingredients for 4 servings

1 tbsp canola oil
1 onion, chopped
1 carrot, chopped
1 garlic clove, minced
3 Granny Smith apples, chopped
2 tbsp curry powder
2 tsp tomato paste
3 cups vegetable broth
Salt to taste
1 cup soy milk
4 tsp sugar-free apricot preserves

Directions and Total Time: 45 minutes

Heat the oil in a pot over medium heat. Place onion, carrot, and garlic and sauté for 5 minutes. Stir in apples and cook for 5 minutes, until the apples soften. Add in tomato paste, broth, and salt. Cook for 10 minutes. Blend the soup in a food processor until smooth. Transfer to a bowl and mix with soy milk. Close the lid and let chill in the fridge for 3 hours. Serve topped with apricot preserves.

Cold Vegetable Soup

Ingredients for 4 servings

2 pounds tomatoes, chopped
1 cucumber, peeled, chopped
1 green bell pepper, chopped
1 cup cold water
1 slice whole-wheat bread
4 green onions, white part only
2 garlic cloves, minced
2 tbsp olive oil
2 tbsp white wine vinegar
Salt to taste
2 tbsp minced fresh parsley

Directions and Total Time: 15 minutes

In a food processor, place half of tomatoes, cucumber, bell pepper, water, bread, green onions, and garlic. Blitz until smooth. Pour in oil, salt, and vinegar and pulse until combined. Transfer to a bowl and combine with remaining tomatoes. Close the lid and let chill in the fridge for 1-2 hours. Serve garnished with parsley.

Lime Pumpkin Soup

Ingredients for 4 servings

2 tsp olive oil
3 cups pumpkin, chopped
1 onion, chopped
1 garlic clove, minced
2 cups water
1 (15-oz) can black-eyed peas
2 tbsp lime juice
1 tbsp pure date sugar
1 tsp paprika
1 tbsp red pepper flakes
3 cups shredded cabbage
1 cup mushrooms, chopped

Directions and Total Time: 30 minutes

Warm the oil in a pot over medium heat. Place in pumpkin, onion, garlic, and salt. Cook for 5 minutes. Stir in water, peas, lime juice, sugar, paprika, and pepper flakes. Bring to a boil and cook for 15 minutes. Add in cabbage and mushrooms and cook for 5 minutes. Allow to cool before serving.

Easy Garbanzo Soup

Ingredients for 4 servings

2 tbsp olive oil
1 onion, chopped
1 green bell pepper, diced
1 carrot, peeled and diced
4 garlic cloves, minced
1 (15-oz) can garbanzo beans
1 cup spinach, chopped
4 cups vegetable stock
¼ tsp ground cumin
Sea salt to taste
¼ cup chopped cilantro

Directions and Total Time: 25 minutes

Heat the oil in a pot over medium heat. Place in onion, garlic, bell pepper and carrot and sauté for 5 minutes until tender. Stir in garbanzo beans, spinach, vegetable stock, cumin, and salt. Cook for 10 minutes. Mash the garbanzo using a potato masher, leaving some chunks. Top with cilantro and serve.

Garlic Veggie Bisque

Ingredients for 6 servings

1 red onion, chopped
2 carrots, chopped
1 potato, peeled and chopped
1 zucchini, sliced
1 ripe tomato, quartered
2 garlic cloves, crushed
3 tbsp olive oil
½ tsp dried rosemary
Salt and black pepper to taste
6 cups vegetable broth
1 tbsp minced fresh parsley

Directions and Total Time: 25 minutes

Preheat oven to 400 F.

Arrange the onion, carrots, potato, zucchini, tomato, and garlic on a greased baking dish. Sprinkle with oil, rosemary, salt, and pepper. Cover with foil and roast for 30 minutes. Uncover and turn them. Roast for another 10 minutes.

Transfer the veggies into a pot and pour in the broth. Bring to a boil, then lower the heat and simmer for 5 minutes. Transfer to a food processor and blend the soup until smooth. Return to the pot and cook until hot. Serve topped with parsley.

Coconut Artichoke Soup with Almonds

Ingredients for 4 servings

1 tbsp olive oil
2 medium shallots, chopped
2 (10-oz) packages artichoke hearts
3 cups vegetable broth
1 tsp fresh lemon juice
Salt to taste
⅓ cup plant butter
⅛ tsp ground cayenne pepper
1 cup plain coconut cream
1 tbsp snipped fresh chives
2 tbsp sliced toasted almonds

Directions and Total Time: 30 minutes

Heat the oil in a pot over medium heat. Place in shallots and sauté until softened, about 3 minutes. Add in artichokes, broth, lemon juice, and salt. Bring to a boil, lower the heat, and simmer for 10 minutes. Stir in butter and cayenne pepper. Transfer to a food processor and blend until purée. Return to the pot. Mix in the coconut cream and simmer for 5 minutes. Serve topped with chives and almonds.

Noodle Soup

Ingredients for 6 servings

2 tbsp olive oil
1 onion, chopped
1 carrot, sliced
2 garlic cloves, minced
1 (28-oz) can crushed tomatoes
1 cup Chana dal, rinsed, and drained
1 tsp dried thyme
6 cups vegetable broth
4 oz soba noodles, broken into thirds

Directions and Total Time: 30 minutes

Warm the oil in a pot over medium heat. Place in onion, carrot and garlic and sauté for 5 minutes. Add in tomatoes, chana dal, thyme, and broth. Bring to a boil, then lower the heat and season with salt and pepper. Simmer for 15 minutes. Stir in soba noodles, cook 5 minutes more. Serve immediately.

Coconut & Tofu Soup

Ingredients for 4 servings

- 1 tbsp canola oil
- 1 onion, chopped
- 2 tbsp minced fresh ginger
- 2 tbsp soy sauce
- 1 cup shiitake mushrooms, sliced
- 1 tbsp pure date sugar
- 1 tsp chili paste
- 2 cups light vegetable broth
- 8 oz extra-firm tofu, chopped
- 2 (13.5-oz) cans coconut milk
- 1 tbsp fresh lime juice
- 3 tbsp chopped fresh cilantro

Directions and Total Time: 30 minutes

Heat the oil in a pot over medium heat. Place in onion and ginger and sauté for 3 minutes until softened. Add in soy sauce, mushrooms, sugar, and chili paste. Stir in broth. Bring to a boil, then lower the heat and simmer for 15 minutes. Stain the liquid and discard solids. Return the broth to the pot. Stir in tofu, coconut milk and lime juice. Cook for 5 minutes. Garnish with cilantro and serve.

Hot Lentil Soup with Zucchini

Ingredients for 4 servings

- 2 tbsp olive oil
- 1 onion, chopped
- 1 zucchini, chopped
- 1 garlic clove, minced
- 1 tbsp hot paprika
- 1 (14.5-oz) can crushed tomatoes
- 1 cup red lentils, rinsed
- 4 cups vegetable broth
- 3 cups chopped Swiss chard

Directions and Total Time: 30 minutes

Heat the oil in a pot over medium heat. Place in onion, zucchini, and garlic and sauté for 5 minutes until tender. Add in paprika, tomatoes, lentils, broth, salt, and pepper. Bring to a boil, then lower the heat and simmer for 15 minutes, stirring often. Add in the Swiss chard and cook for another 3-5 minutes. Serve immediately.

Shallot Lentil Soup with Walnuts

Ingredients for 4 servings

- 2 tbsp olive oil
- 3 shallots, chopped
- 3 cups vegetable broth
- 1 cup apple juice
- 4 cups fresh spinach
- ½ cup lentils
- 1 tsp minced fresh sage
- ¼ tsp ground allspice
- Salt and black pepper to taste
- 1 cup soy milk
- ¼ cup toasted walnuts, chopped

Directions and Total Time: 30 minutes

Heat the oil in a pot over medium heat. Place in the shallots and sauté for 3 minutes until translucent. Add in vegetable, apple juice, spinach, sage, allspice, salt, and pepper. Bring to a boil, lower the heat and simmer for 10 minutes. With an immersion blender, pulse the soup until purée. Mix in soy milk and heat until hot. Top with walnuts to serve.

Fennel & Corn Chowder

Ingredients for 4 servings

- 2 tbsp olive oil
- 1 onion, chopped
- 1 cup chopped fennel bulb
- 2 carrots, chopped
- 1 cup mushrooms, chopped
- ¼ cup whole-wheat flour
- 4 cups vegetable stock
- 2 cups canned corn
- 2 cups cubed red potatoes
- 1 cup almond milk
- ½ tsp chili paste
- Sea salt and black pepper to taste

Directions and Total Time: 30 minutes

Heat the oil in a pot over medium heat. Place in onion, fennel, carrots, and mushrooms. Sauté for 5 minutes until tender. Stir in flour. Pour in vegetable stock. Lower the heat. Add in corn, potatoes, almond milk, and chili paste. Simmer for 20 minutes. Sprinkle with salt and pepper. Serve immediately.

Ginger Squash Soup

Ingredients for 4 servings

- 1/3 cup toasted pumpkin seeds
- 1 tbsp chopped ginger paste
- 1 tbsp canola oil
- 1 onion, chopped
- 1 celery stalk, chopped
- 4 cups vegetable broth
- 1 acorn squash, peeled, chopped
- 1 tbsp soy sauce
- ¼ tsp ground allspice
- Salt and black pepper to taste
- 1 cup plain unsweetened soy milk

Directions and Total Time: 30 minutes

Heat the oil in a pot over medium heat. Place in onion and celery and sauté for 5 minutes until tender. Add in broth and squash, bring to a boil. Lower the heat and simmer for 20 minutes. Stir in soy sauce, ginger paste, allspice, salt, and pepper. Transfer to a food processor and blend the soup until smooth. Return to the pot. Mix in soy milk and cook until hot. Serve garnished with pumpkin seeds.

Fennel & Parsnip Bisque

Ingredients for 6 servings

- 1 tbsp olive oil
- 2 green onions, chopped
- ½ fennel bulb, sliced
- 2 large carrots, shredded
- 2 parsnips, shredded
- 1 potato, chopped
- 2 garlic cloves, minced
- ½ tsp dried thyme
- ¼ tsp dried marjoram
- 6 cups vegetable broth
- 1 cup plain unsweetened soy milk
- 1 tbsp minced fresh parsley

Directions and Total Time: 30 minutes

Heat the oil in a pot over medium heat. Place in green onions, fennel, carrots, parsnips, potato, and garlic. Sauté for 5 minutes until softened. Add in thyme, marjoram and broth. Bring to a boil, then lower the heat and simmer for 20 minutes. Transfer to a blender and pulse the soup until smooth. Return to the pot and mix in soy milk. Top with parsley to serve.

Spicy Potato Soup

Ingredients for 6 servings

- 3 tbsp olive oil
- 1 onion, chopped
- 1 garlic clove, minced
- 1 tbsp hot powder
- 1 pound carrots, chopped
- 2 potatoes, chopped
- 6 cups vegetable broth
- Salt to taste
- 1 (13.5-oz) can coconut milk
- 1 tbsp minced fresh parsley
- Chopped roasted cashews

Directions and Total Time: 25 minutes

Heat the oil in a pot over medium heat. Place in onion and garlic, cook for 3 minutes. Add in hot powder, cook for 30 seconds. Stir in carrots, potatoes, broth, and salt. Bring to a boil, lower the heat and simmer for 15 minutes.

With an immersion blender, blitz the soup until smooth. Sprinkle with salt and pepper. Mix in coconut milk and cook until hot. Garnish with parsley and chopped cashews to serve.

Spinach Soup with Gnocchi

Ingredients for 4 servings

1 tsp olive oil
1 cup green bell peppers
Salt and black pepper to taste
2 garlic cloves, minced
2 carrots, chopped
3 cups vegetable broth
1 cup gnocchi
¾ cup unsweetened non-dairy milk
¼ cup nutritional yeast
2 cups chopped fresh spinach
¼ cup pitted black olives, chopped
Croutons, for topping

Directions and Total Time: 25 minutes

Heat the oil in a pot over medium heat. Place in bell peppers, garlic, carrots, and salt and cook for 5 minutes. Stir in broth. Bring to a boil. Put in gnocchi, cook for 10 minutes. Add in spinach and cook for another 5 minutes. Stir in milk, nutritional yeast, and olives. Serve topped with croutons.

Mushroom Rice Soup

Ingredients for 6 servings

3 tbsp olive oil
1 onion, chopped
1 carrot, chopped
1 celery stalk, chopped
1 cup wild mushrooms, sliced
½ cup brown rice
7 cups vegetable broth
1 tsp dried dill weed
Salt and black pepper to taste

Directions and Total Time: 30 minutes

Heat the oil in a pot over medium heat. Place in onion, carrot and celery and sauté for 5 minutes. Add in mushrooms, rice, broth, dill weed, salt, and pepper. Bring to a boil, then lower the heat and simmer uncovered for 20 minutes. Serve immediately.

Chili Gazpacho

Ingredients for 4 servings

2 tbsp olive oil
2 cups water
1 red onion, chopped
6 tomatoes, chopped
1 red bell pepper, diced
2 garlic cloves, minced
juice of 1 lemon
2 tbsp chopped fresh basil
½ tsp chili pepper

Directions and Total Time: 15 minutes

In a food processor, place the olive oil, half of the onion, half of the tomato, half of bell pepper, garlic, lemon juice, basil, and chili pepper. Season with salt and pepper. Blitz until smooth. Transfer to a bowl and add in the reserved onion, tomatoes and bell pepper. Let chill in the fridge before serving.

Butternut Squash Soup

Ingredients for 4 servings

2 tbsp olive oil
1 onion, chopped
½ pound butternut squash, chopped
1 red bell pepper, chopped
4 cups vegetable broth
Salt and black pepper to taste
½ cup plant butter
¼ cup toasted pumpkin seeds

Directions and Total Time: 30 minutes

Heat oil in a pot over medium heat. Place in onion, squash, and bell pepper and sauté for 5 minutes until soft. Stir in broth, salt and pepper. Bring to a boil, then lower the heat and simmer for 20 minutes. Stir in butter and blend the soup using an immersion blender. Top with toasted seeds and serve.

Green Bean & Rice Soup

Ingredients for 4 servings

2 tbsp olive oil	2 garlic cloves minced	1 cup green beans, chopped
1 medium onion, minced	1 cup brown rice	¼ cup chopped parsley

Directions and Total Time: 50 minutes

Heat oil in a pot over medium heat. Place in onion and garlic and sauté for 3 minutes until translucent. Add in rice, 4 cups water, salt, and pepper. Bring to a boil, then lower the heat and simmer covered for 15 minutes. Stir in green beans and cook for 10 minutes. Top with parsley and serve.

Celery & Potato Rice Soup

Ingredients for 6 servings

3 tbsp olive oil	1 pound potatoes, chopped	2 bay leaves
1 onion, chopped	½ cup long-grain brown rice	½ tsp ground cumin
1 medium carrot, chopped	1 (14.5-oz) can crushed tomatoes	Salt and black pepper to taste
1 celery stalk, chopped	2 cups tomato juice	1 tbsp minced fresh parsley

Directions and Total Time: 40 minutes

Heat oil in a pot and sauté onion, carrot, and celery for 10 minutes. Add in potatoes, rice, tomatoes, tomato juices, bay leaves, cumin, 6 cups water, salt, and pepper. Bring to a boil, then lower the heat and simmer uncovered for 20 minutes. Discard the bay leaves. Scatter with parsley. Serve immediately.

Rotini & Tomato Soup

Ingredients for 4 servings

1 tbsp olive oil	1 (28-oz) can crushed tomatoes	2 bay leaves
1 medium onion, chopped	3 cups chopped fresh ripe tomatoes	1 cup plain unsweetened soy milk
1 celery rib, minced	2 tbsp tomato paste	½ cup whole-wheat rotini pasta
3 garlic cloves, minced	3 cups vegetable broth	2 tbsp chopped fresh basil

Directions and Total Time: 35 minutes

Heat oil in a pot and sauté onion, celery, and garlic for 5 minutes. Add in tomatoes, tomato paste, broth, sugar, and bay leaves. Sprinkle with salt and pepper. Bring to a boil, lower the heat, and simmer for 10 minutes. Add in pasta and cook for 10 minutes. Discard bay leaves. Garnish with basil to serve.

Green Bean & Zucchini Velouté

Ingredients for 6 servings

3 tbsp olive oil	2 cups green beans	½ tsp dried marjoram
1 onion, chopped	4 cups vegetable broth	½ cup plain almond milk
1 garlic clove, minced	3 medium zucchini, sliced	2 tbsp minced jarred pimiento

Directions and Total Time: 30 minutes

Heat oil in a pot and sauté onion and garlic for 5 minutes. Add in green beans and broth. Cook for 10 minutes. Stir in zucchini and cook for 10 minutes. Transfer to a food processor and pulse until smooth. Return to the pot and mix in almond milk; cook until hot. Serve topped with pimiento.

Kale & Potato Stew

Ingredients for 4 servings

- 2 onions, diced
- 2 tbsp olive oil or coconut oil
- 2 potatoes, peeled and chopped
- ⅓ cup chunky almond butter
- 1 tsp paprika
- ¼ tsp red pepper flakes
- Salt and black pepper to taste
- 2 cups kale, chopped

Directions and Total Time: 30 minutes

In a saucepan over medium heat, warm olive oil and cook onions for 3 minutes. Add in potatoes, almond butter, paprika, pepper flakes, 2 cups of water, and salt; stir. Bring to a boil and reduce the heat. Simmer 20 for minutes. Add in the kale and cook for another 5 minutes until wilted. Serve warm.

Caribbean Lentil Stew

Ingredients for 4 servings

- 2 tbsp olive oil
- 1 onion, chopped
- 1 carrot, sliced
- 2 garlic cloves, minced
- 1 sweet potato, chopped
- ¼ tsp crushed red pepper
- 1 cup red lentils, rinsed
- 1 (14.5-oz) can diced tomatoes
- 1 tsp hot curry powder
- 1 tsp chopped thyme
- ¼ tsp ground allspice
- Salt and black pepper to taste
- 1 cup water
- 1 (13.5-oz) can coconut milk

Directions and Total Time: 50 minutes

Warm oil in a pot and sauté onion and carrot for 5 minutes, stirring occasionally until softened. Add in garlic, sweet potato, and crushed red pepper. Put in red lentils, tomatoes, curry powder, allspice, salt, and black pepper, stir to combine. Pour in water and simmer for 30 minutes until the vegetables are tender. Stir in coconut milk and simmer for 10 minutes. Serve hot topped with thyme.

Moroccan Bean Stew

Ingredients for 4 servings

- 3 cups cooked red kidney beans
- 2 tbsp olive oil
- 1 yellow onion, chopped
- 2 carrots, sliced
- 3 garlic cloves, minced
- 1 tsp grated fresh ginger
- ½ tsp ground cumin
- 1 tsp ras el hanout
- 2 russet potatoes, chopped
- 1 (14.5-oz) can crushed tomatoes
- 1 (4-oz) can diced green chiles, drained
- 1 ½ cups vegetable broth
- Salt and black pepper to taste
- 3 cups eggplants, chopped
- ⅓ cup chopped roasted peanuts

Directions and Total Time: 40 minutes

Heat the oil in a pot over medium heat. Place the onion, garlic, ginger, and carrots and sauté for 5 minutes until tender. Stir in cumin, ras el hanout, potatoes, beans, tomatoes, chiles, and broth. Season with salt and pepper. Bring to a boil, then lower the heat and simmer for 20 minutes. Add in eggplants and cook for 10 minutes. Serve garnished with peanuts.

Pearl Barley & Vegetable Stew

Ingredients for 6 servings

- 3 tbsp olive oil
- 1 onion, chopped
- 2 garlic cloves, minced
- 2 turnips, chopped
- 4 potatoes, chopped
- 1 cup pearl barley
- 1 (28-oz) can diced tomatoes
- 3 tsp dried mixed herbs
- Salt and black pepper to taste

Directions and Total Time: 30 minutes

Warm oil in a pot over medium heat. Add in onion and garlic and sauté for 3 minutes until fragrant. Stir in the turnips, potatoes, barley, tomatoes, 3 cups water, and herbs. Cook for 20 minutes. Serve.

Chicago-Style Vegetable Stew

Ingredients for 4 servings

- 2 tbsp olive oils
- 3 shallots, chopped
- 1 carrot, sliced
- ½ cup dry white wine
- 3 new potatoes, cubed
- 1 red bell pepper, chopped
- 1½ cups vegetable broth
- 2 zucchini, sliced
- 1 yellow summer squash, sliced
- 1 pound plum tomatoes, chopped
- 2 Salt and black pepper to taste
- 3 cups fresh corn kernels
- 1 cup green beans
- ¼ cup fresh basil
- ¼ cup chopped fresh parsley

Directions and Total Time: 35 minutes

Heat oil in a pot over medium heat. Place shallots and carrot and cook for 5 minutes. Pour in white wine, potatoes, bell pepper and broth. Bring to a boil, lower the heat, and simmer for 5 minutes. Stir in zucchini, yellow squash and tomatoes. Sprinkle with salt and pepper. Simmer for 20 more minutes. Put in corn, green peas, basil, and parsley. Simmer an additional 5 minutes. Serve hot.

Mushroom & Bean Stew

Ingredients for 4 servings

- 2 tbsp olive oil
- 1 onion, chopped
- 1 carrot, chopped
- 2 garlic cloves, minced
- 1 red bell pepper, chopped
- ½ cup capers
- 1 medium zucchini, chopped
- 1 (14.5-oz) can diced tomatoes
- 1 cup vegetable broth
- Salt and black pepper to taste
- 8 oz porcini mushrooms, sliced
- 3 cups fresh baby spinach
- 1 (15.5-oz) can cannellini beans,
- ½ tsp dried basil
- 2 tbsp minced fresh parsley

Directions and Total Time: 35 minutes

Heat oil in a pot and sauté onion, carrot, garlic, mushrooms, and bell pepper for 5 minutes. Stir in capers, zucchini, tomatoes, broth, salt, and pepper. Bring to a boil, then lower the heat and simmer for 20 minutes. Add in beans, and basil. Simmer an additional 2-3 minutes. Serve topped with parsley.

Asian Veggie Stew

Ingredients for 5 servings

- 2 tbsp canola oil
- 1 onion, chopped
- 2 garlic cloves, minced
- 2 fresh hot chilies, minced
- 1 tbsp grated fresh ginger
- 1 russet potato, chopped
- 1 medium eggplant, chopped
- 8 oz green peas
- 2 cups cauliflower florets
- 2 cups vegetable broth
- 1 (14.5-oz) can crushed tomatoes
- 2 tbsp soy sauce
- ½ tsp ground turmeric
- 1 (13.5-oz) can coconut milk
- 1 tbsp tamarind paste
- 2 tbsp fresh lime juice
- 3 tbsp minced fresh cilantro
- 2 tbsp minced scallions

Directions and Total Time: 40 minutes

Warm the oil in a pot over medium heat. Place onion, garlic, chilies, and ginger and cook for 5 minutes. Stir in potato, eggplant, green peas, cauliflower, broth, tomatoes, soy sauce, and turmeric. Cook for 20 minutes. Lower the heat and pour in coconut milk, tamarind paste, salt, and pepper. Simmer for 5 minutes. Mix in lime juice. Garnish with cilantro and scallions to serve.

Mediterranean Vegetable Stew

Ingredients for 4 servings

2 tbsp olive oil
1 onions, chopped
2 carrots, chopped
½ tsp ground cumin
½ tsp ground ginger
½ tsp paprika
½ tsp saffron
1 (14.5-oz) can diced tomatoes
½ head broccoli, cut into florets
2 cups winter squash, chopped
1 russet potato, cubed
1 ½ cups vegetable broth
1 (15.5-oz) can chickpeas, drained
1 tsp lemon zest
Salt and black pepper to taste
½ cup pitted green olives
1 tbsp minced cilantro for garnish
½ cup toasted slivered almonds

Directions and Total Time: 30 minutes

Heat the oil in a pot over medium heat. Place onions and carrots and sauté for 5 minutes. Add in cumin, ginger, paprika, salt, pepper, and saffron and cook for 30 seconds. Stir in tomatoes, broccoli, squash, potato, chickpeas, and broth. Bring to a boil, then lower the heat and simmer for 20 minutes. Add in olives and lemon zest and simmer for 2-3 minutes. Garnish with cilantro and almonds to serve.

Tomato Lentil Stew

Ingredients for 4 servings

2 tsp olive oil
4 carrots, chopped
1 onion, chopped
½ green bell pepper, chopped
1 tbsp paprika
2 garlic cloves, sliced
4 cups vegetable broth
1 (28-oz) can crushed tomatoes
2 (15-oz) cans lentils, drained

Directions and Total Time: 25 minutes

Heat the oil in a pot over medium heat. Place in carrots, onion, bell pepper, paprika, and garlic. Sauté for 5 minutes until tender. Stir in broth, tomatoes and lentils. Bring to a boil, then lower the heat and simmer for 15 minutes. Sprinkle with salt and pepper. Serve warm.

Sudanese Veggie Stew

Ingredients for 6 servings

3 potatoes, cubed
3 tbsp olive oil
2 carrots, sliced
4 shallots, chopped
2 garlic cloves, minced
1 tbsp ground turmeric
1 tsp ground ginger
1 ½ cups vegetable broth
4 cups shredded spinach

Directions and Total Time: 30 minutes

Cook the potatoes in salted water over medium heat, about 15 minutes. Drain and reserve. Heat the oil in a saucepan over medium heat. Place in carrots and shallots and cook for 5 minutes. Stir in garlic, turmeric, ginger, and salt. Cook for 1 minute more. Add in cooked potatoes and broth. Bring to a boil, then lower the heat. Stir in the spinach and cook for another 3 minutes until wilted.

Fall Medley Stew

Ingredients for 4 servings

2 tbsp olive oil
8 oz seitan, cubed
1 leek, chopped
2 garlic cloves, minced
1 russet potato, chopped
1 carrot, chopped
1 parsnip, chopped
1 cup butternut squash, cubed
1 head savoy cabbage, chopped
1 (14.5-oz) can diced tomatoes
1 (15.5-oz) can white beans
2 cups vegetable broth
½ cup dry white wine
½ tsp dried thyme
½ cup crumbled angel hair pasta

Directions and Total Time: 65 minutes

Heat oil in a pot over medium heat. Place in seitan and cook for 3 minutes. Sprinkle with salt and pepper. Add in leek and garlic and cook for another 3 minutes. Stir in potato, carrot, parsnip, and squash, cook for 10 minutes. Add in cabbage, tomatoes, white beans, broth, wine, thyme, salt, and pepper. Bring to a boil, lower the heat and simmer for 15 minutes. Put in pasta and cook for 5 minutes.

Homemade Succotash Stew

Ingredients for 4 servings

- 1 cup canned chickpeas
- 2 tbsp olive oil
- 1 onion, chopped
- 2 russet potatoes, chopped
- 2 carrots, sliced
- 1 (14.5-oz) can diced tomatoes
- 1 (16-oz) package frozen succotash
- 2 cups vegetable broth
- 2 tbsp soy sauce
- 1 tsp dry mustard
- ½ tsp dried thyme
- ½ tsp ground allspice
- ¼ tsp ground cayenne pepper
- Salt and black pepper to taste

Directions and Total Time: 30 minutes

Heat oil in a saucepan. Place in onion and sauté for 3 minutes. Stir in chickpeas, potatoes, carrots, tomatoes, succotash, broth, soy sauce, mustard, sugar, thyme, allspice, and cayenne pepper. Sprinkle with salt and pepper. Bring to a boil, then lower the heat and simmer for 20 minutes. Serve hot.

Balsamic Veggie & Rice Stew

Ingredients for 6 servings

- 2 tsp olive oil
- 1 cups bell peppers
- Salt and black pepper to taste
- 1 onion, chopped
- 2 garlic cloves, minced
- 1 tbsp dried herbs
- 1 cup brown rice
- 2 cups vegetable broth
- 4 tbsp balsamic vinegar
- 1 cup frozen peas, thawed
- 1 cup unsweetened non-dairy milk
- 2 cups chopped kale, or chard

Directions and Total Time: 30 minutes

Heat the oil in a pot over medium heat. Place in bell peppers, onion, garlic, and salt and cook for 5 minutes until tender. Put in dried herbs, brown rice, broth, vinegar, and pepper. Bring to a boil, then lower the heat and simmer for 20 minutes. Stir in peas, milk and kale until the kale wilts. Serve.

Chili Cannellini Bean Stew

Ingredients for 4 servings

- 2 tbsp olive oil
- 1 onion, chopped
- 2 potatoes, chopped
- 2 (15.5-oz) cans cannellini beans
- 1 (28-oz) can crushed tomatoes
- 1 (4-oz) can mild chopped green chilies
- 2 tbsp tamarind paste
- ¼ cup pure agave syrup
- 1 cup vegetable broth
- 2 tbsp chili powder
- 1 tsp ground coriander
- ½ tsp ground cumin
- Salt and black pepper to taste
- 1 cup frozen peas, thawed

Directions and Total Time: 40 minutes

Heat the oil in a pot over medium heat. Place in the onion and sauté for 3 minutes until translucent. Stir in potatoes, beans, tomatoes, and chilies. Cook for 5 minutes more. In a bowl, whisk the tamarind paste with agave syrup and broth. Pour the mixture into the pot. Stir in chili powder, coriander, cumin, salt, and pepper. Bring to a boil, then lower the heat and simmer for 20 minutes until the potatoes are tender. Add in peas and cook for another 5 minutes. Serve warm.

SALADS & ENTRÉES

Greek Salad

Ingredients for 2 servings

½ yellow bell pepper, cut into pieces
3 tomatoes cut into bite-size pieces
½ cucumber, cut into bite-size pieces
½ red onion, peeled and sliced
½ cup tofu cheese, cut into squares
10 Kalamata olives, pitted
½ tbsp red wine vinegar
4 tbsp olive oil
2 tsp dried oregano

Directions and Total Time: 10 minutes

Pour the bell pepper, tomatoes, cucumber, red onion, tofu cheese, and olives into a salad bowl. Drizzle the red wine vinegar and olive oil over the vegetables. Season with salt, black pepper, and oregano, and toss the salad with two spoons. Share the salad into two bowls and serve immediately.

Squash Salad

Ingredients for 4 servings

2 lb green squash, cubed
2 tbsp plant butter
Salt and black pepper to taste
3 oz fennel, sliced
2 oz chopped green onions
1 cup tofu mayonnaise
2 tbsp fresh chives, finely chopped
A pinch of mustard powder
Chopped dill to garnish

Directions and Total Time: 20 minutes

Put a pan over medium heat and melt plant butter. Fry in squash cubes until slightly softened but not browned, about 7 minutes. Allow the squash to cool. In a salad bowl, mix the cooled squash, fennel slices, green onions, tofu mayonnaise, chives, and mustard powder. Garnish with dill and serve.

Beet Tofu Salad

Ingredients for 4 servings

8 oz red beets
2 oz tofu, chopped into little bits
2 tbsp plant butter
½ red onion
1 cup tofu mayonnaise
1 small romaine lettuce, torn
Freshly chopped chives
Salt and black pepper to taste

Directions and Total Time: 50 minutes

Put beets in a pot, cover with water and bring to a boil for 40 minutes. Melt plant butter in a non-stick pan over medium heat and fry tofu until browned. Set aside to cool. When the bits are ready, drain through a colander and allow cooling. Slip the skin off after and slice them. In a salad bowl, combine the beets, tofu, red onions, lettuce, salt, pepper, and tofu mayonnaise and mix until the vegetables are adequately coated with the mayonnaise. Garnish the salad with chives and serve immediately.

African Zucchini Salad

Ingredients for 2 servings

1 lemon, half zested and juiced, half cut into wedges
1 tsp olive oil 1 zucchini, chopped
½ tsp ground cumin
½ tsp ground ginger
¼ tsp turmeric
¼ tsp ground nutmeg
A pinch of salt
2 tbsp capers
1 tbsp chopped green olives
1 garlic clove, pressed
2 tbsp fresh mint, finely chopped
2 cups spinach, chopped

Directions and Total Time: 20 minutes

Warm olive oil in a skillet over medium heat. Place the zucchini and sauté for 10 minutes. Stir in cumin, ginger, turmeric, nutmeg, and salt. Pour in lemon zest, lemon juice, capers, garlic, and mint, cook for 2 minutes more. Divide the spinach between serving plates and top with the zucchini mixture. Garnish with lemon wedges and olives.

Tangy Nutty Brussel Sprout Salad

Ingredients for 4 servings

1 lb Brussels sprouts, grated
1 lemon, juice and zest
½ cup olive oil

1 tbsp plant butter
1 tsp chili paste
2 oz pecans

1 oz pumpkin seeds
1 oz sunflower seeds
½ tsp cumin powder

Directions and Total Time: 20 minutes

Put Brussels sprouts in a salad bowl. In a small bowl, mix lemon juice, zest, olive oil, salt, and pepper, and drizzle the dressing over the Brussels sprouts. Toss and allow the vegetable to marinate for 10 minutes. Melt plant butter in a pan. Stir in chili paste and toss the pecans, pumpkin seeds, sunflower seeds, cumin powder, and salt in the chili butter. Sauté on low heat for 3-4 minutes just to heat the nuts but. Allow cooling. Pour the nuts and seeds mix in the salad bowl, toss, and serve.

Roasted Mushrooms and Green Beans Salad

Ingredients for 4 servings

1 lb cremini mushrooms, sliced
½ cup green beans

3 tbsp melted plant butter
Salt and black pepper to taste

Juice of 1 lemon
4 tbsp toasted hazelnuts

Directions and Total Time: 25 minutes

Preheat oven to 450 F.

Arrange the mushrooms and green beans in a baking dish, drizzle the plant butter over, and sprinkle with salt and black pepper. Use your hands to rub the vegetables with the seasoning and roast in the oven for 20 minutes or until the vegetables are soft. Transfer the vegetables into a salad bowl, drizzle with the lemon juice, and toss the salad with the hazelnuts. Serve the salad immediately.

Seitan & Spinach Salad a la Puttanesca

Ingredients for 4 servings

4 tbsp olive oil
8 oz seitan, cut into strips
2 garlic cloves, minced
½ cup kalamata olives, halved

½ cup green olives, halved
2 tbsp capers
3 cups baby spinach, cut into strips
1 ½ cups cherry tomatoes, halved

2 tbsp balsamic vinegar
2 tbsp torn fresh basil leaves
2 tbsp minced fresh parsley
1 cup pomegranate seeds

Directions and Total Time: 11 minutes

Heat half of the olive oil in a skillet over medium heat. Place the seitan and brown for 5 minutes on all sides. Add in garlic and cook for 30 seconds. Remove to a bowl and let cool. Stir in olives, capers, spinach, and tomatoes. Set aside.

In another bowl, whisk the remaining oil, vinegar, salt, and pepper until well mixed. Pour this dressing over the seitan salad and toss to coat. Top with basil, parsley and pomegranate seeds. Serve.

Bean & Farro Salad

Ingredients for 4 servings

1 (14-oz) can black beans
1 cup corn kernels
¼ cup fresh cilantro, chopped
Zest and juice of 1 lime
3 tsp chili powder
Sea salt and black pepper to taste
1 ½ cups cherry tomatoes, halved
1 red bell pepper, chopped
2 scallions, chopped
4 large whole-grain tortillas
2 tsp olive oil
1 tbsp oregano
1 tsp cayenne pepper
4 cups watercress and arugula mix
¾ cup cooked faro
¼ cup chopped avocado
¼ cup mango salsa

Directions and Total Time: 20 minutes

Combine black beans, corn, cilantro, lime juice, lime zest, chili powder, salt, pepper, cherry tomatoes, bell peppers, and scallions in a bowl. Set aside. Brush the tortillas with olive oil and season with salt, pepper, oregano, and cayenne pepper. Slice into 8 pieces. Line with parchment paper a baking sheet. Arrange tortilla pieces and bake for 3-5 minutes until browned. On a serving platter, put the watercress and arugula mix, top with faro, bean mixture, avocado, and sprinkle with mango salsa all over to serve.

Warm Collard Salad

Ingredients for 2 servings

¾ cup coconut whipping cream
2 tbsp tofu mayonnaise
A pinch of mustard powder
2 tbsp coconut oil
1 garlic clove, minced
Salt and black pepper to taste
2 oz plant butter
1 cup collards, rinsed
4 oz tofu cheese

Directions and Total Time: 10 minutes

In a small bowl, whisk the coconut whipping cream, tofu mayonnaise, mustard powder, coconut oil, garlic, salt, and black pepper until well mixed; set aside. Melt the plant butter in a large skillet over medium heat and sauté the collards until wilted and brownish. Season with salt and black pepper to taste. Transfer the collards to a salad bowl and pour the creamy dressing over. Mix the salad well and crumble the tofu cheese over. Serve.

Fried Broccoli Salad with Tempeh & Cranberries

Ingredients for 4 servings

3 oz plant butter
¾ lb tempeh slices, cubed
1 lb broccoli florets
Salt and black pepper to taste
2 oz almonds
½ cup frozen cranberries

Directions and Total Time: 15 minutes

In a skillet, melt the plant butter over medium heat until no longer foaming, and fry the tempeh cubes until brown on all sides. Add the broccoli and stir-fry for 6 minutes. Season with salt and pepper. Turn the heat off. Stir in the almonds and cranberries to warm through. Share salad into bowls and serve.

Savory Pasta Salad with Cannellini Beans

Ingredients for 4 servings

2 ½ cups whole-wheat bow tie pasta
1 tbsp olive oil
1 medium zucchini, sliced
2 garlic cloves, minced
2 large tomatoes, chopped
1 (15 oz) can cannellini beans
1 (2 ¼ oz) can green olives, sliced
½ cup crumbled tofu cheese

Directions and Total Time: 35 minutes

Cook the pasta until al dente, 10 minutes. Drain and set aside. Heat olive oil in a skillet and sauté zucchini and garlic for 4 minutes. Stir in tomatoes, beans, and olives. Cook until the tomatoes soften, 10 minutes. Mix in pasta. Allow warming for 1 minute. Stir in tofu cheese and serve warm.

Bean & Couscous Salad

Ingredients for 4 servings

¼ cup olive oil	1 cup couscous	¼ cup golden raisins
1 medium shallot, minced	2 cups vegetable broth	¼ cup chopped roasted cashews
½ tsp ground coriander	1 yellow bell pepper, chopped	1 (15.5-oz) can white beans
½ tsp turmeric	1 carrot, shredded	2 tbsp minced fresh cilantro leaves
¼ tsp ground cayenne	½ cup chopped dried apricots	2 tbsp fresh lemon juice

Directions and Total Time: 15 minutes

Heat 1 tbsp of oil in a pot over medium heat. Place in shallot, coriander, turmeric, cayenne pepper, and couscous. Cook for 2 minutes, stirring often. Add in broth and salt. Bring to a boil. Turn the heat off and let sit covered for 5 minutes. Remove to a bowl and stir in bell pepper, carrot, apricots, raisins, cashews, beans, and cilantro. Set aside. In another bowl, whisk the remaining oil with lemon juice until blended. Pour over the salad and toss to combine. Serve immediately.

Tomato & Avocado Lettuce Salad

Ingredients for 4 servings

1 garlic clove, chopped	¼ tsp pure date sugar	12 ripe grape tomatoes, halved
1 red onion, sliced	3 tbsp white wine vinegar	½ cup frozen peas, thawed
½ tsp dried basil	1/3 cup olive oil	8 black olives, pitted
Salt and black pepper to taste	1 head Iceberg lettuce, shredded	1 avocado, sliced

Directions and Total Time: 15 minutes

In a food processor, place the garlic, onion, oil, basil, salt, pepper, sugar, and vinegar. Blend until smooth. Set aside. Place the lettuce, tomatoes, peas, and olives in a nice serving plate. Top with avocado slices and drizzle the previously prepared dressing all over. Serve.

Balsamic Lentil Salad

Ingredients for 4 servings

2 tsp olive oil	1 cup lentils	2 cups water
1 red onion, diced	1 tbsp dried basil	Sea salt to taste
1 garlic clove, minced	1 tbsp dried oregano	2 cups chopped Swiss chard
1 carrot, diced	1 tbsp balsamic vinegar	2 cups torn curly endive

Directions and Total Time: 40 minutes

In a bowl mix the balsamic vinegar, olive oil and salt. Set aside. Warm 1 tsp of oil in a pot over medium heat. Place the onion and carrot and cook for 5 minutes. Mix in lentils, basil, oregano, balsamic vinegar and water and bring to a boil. Lower the heat and simmer for 20 minutes.

Mix in two-thirds of the dressing. Add in the Swiss chard and cook for 5 minutes on low. Let cool. Coat the endive with the remaining dressing. Transfer to a plate and top with lentil mixture to serve.

Warm Green Bean & Potato Salad

Ingredients for 4 servings

Salt and black pepper to taste
1 cup green beans, chopped
4 potatoes, quartered
2 carrots, sliced
1 tbsp extra-virgin olive oil
1 tbsp lime juice
2 tsp dried dill
1 cup cashew cream

Directions and Total Time: 25 minutes

Pour salted water in a pot over medium heat. Add in potatoes, bring to a boil and cook for 8 minutes. Put in carrots and green beans and cook for 8 minutes. Drain and put in a bowl. Mix in olive oil, lime juice, dill, cashew cream, salt, and pepper. Toss to coat. Allow to cool before serving.

Mango Rice Salad with Lime Dressing

Ingredients for 4 servings

3 ½ cups cooked brown rice
½ cup chopped roasted peanuts
½ cup sliced mango
4 green onions, chopped
3 tbsp fresh lime juice
2 tsp agave nectar
1 tsp grated fresh ginger
1/3 cup grapeseed oil
Salt and black pepper to taste

Directions and Total Time: 15 minutes

In a bowl, mix the rice, peanuts, mango, and green onions. Set aside. In another bowl, whisk the lime juice, agave nectar and ginger. Add in oil, salt and pepper, stir to combine. Pour over the rice bowl and toss to coat. Serve immediately.

Orange & Kale Salad

Ingredients for 4 servings

2 tbsp Dijon mustard
2 tbsp olive oil
¼ cup fresh orange juice
1 tsp agave nectar
2 tbsp minced fresh parsley
1 tbsp minced green onions
4 cups fresh kale, chopped
1 orange, peeled and segmented
½ red onion, sliced paper-thin

Directions and Total Time: 10 minutes

In a food processor, place the mustard, oil, orange juice, agave nectar, salt, pepper, parsley, and green onions. Blend until smooth. Set aside. In a bowl, combine the kale, orange and onion. Pour over the dressing and toss to coat. Serve immediately.

Millet Salad with Olives & Cherries

Ingredients for 4 servings

1 cup millet
1 (15.5-oz) can navy beans
1 celery stalk, finely chopped
1 carrot, shredded
3 green onions, minced
½ cup chopped kalamata olives
½ cup dried cherries
½ cup toasted pecans, chopped
½ cup minced fresh parsley
1 garlic clove, pressed
3 tbsp sherry vinegar
¼ cup grapeseed oil

Directions and Total Time: 40 minutes

Cook the millet in salted water for 30 minutes. Remove to a bowl. Mix in beans, celery, carrot, green onions, olives, cherries, pecans, and parsley. Set aside. In another bowl, whisk the garlic, vinegar, salt, and pepper until well mixed. Pour over the millet mixture and toss to coat. Serve immediately.

Daikon Salad with Caramelized Onion

Ingredients for 4 servings

- 1 pound daikon, peeled
- 2 cups sliced sweet onions
- 2 tsp olive oil
- Salt to taste
- 1 tbsp rice vinegar

Directions and Total Time: 50 minutes

Place the daikon in a pot with salted water and cook 25 minutes, until tender. Drain and let cool. In a skillet over low heat, warm olive oil and add the onion. Sauté for 10-15 minutes until caramelized. Sprinkle with salt. Remove to a bowl. Chop the daikon into wedges and add to the onion bowl. Stir in the vinegar. Serve.

Cucumber, Lettuce & Tomato Salad

Ingredients for 4 servings

- ¾ cup olive oil
- ¼ cup white wine vinegar
- 2 tsp Dijon mustard
- 1 garlic clove
- 1 tbsp minced green onions
- ½ head romaine lettuce, chopped
- ½ head iceberg lettuce, chopped
- 1 (15.5-oz) can lentils, drained
- 2 ripe tomatoes, chopped
- 1 cucumber, peeled and chopped
- 1 carrot, chopped
- ½ cup halved pitted kalamata olives
- 3 small red radishes, chopped
- 2 tbsp chopped fresh parsley
- 1 ripe avocado, chopped

Directions and Total Time: 15 minutes

Put the oil, vinegar, mustard, garlic, green onions, salt, and pepper in a food processor. Pulse until blended. Set aside. In a bowl, place the lettuces, lentils, tomatoes, cucumber, carrot, olives, radishes, parsley, and avocado. Pour enough dressing over the salad and toss to coat. Serve immediately.

Quick Fresh Salad

Ingredients for 4 servings

- 1 pound carrots, shredded
- 2 oranges, chopped
- ½ cup roasted walnuts
- ¼ cup chopped fresh parsley
- 2 tbsp fresh orange juice
- 2 tbsp fresh lime juice
- 2 tsp pure date sugar
- Salt and black pepper to taste
- ¼ cup olive oil

Directions and Total Time: 15 minutes

In a bowl, mix the carrots, oranges, walnuts, and parsley. Set aside. In another bowl, whisk the orange juice, lime juice, sugar, salt, pepper, and oil. Mix until blended. Pour over the carrots mixture and toss to coat. Adjust the seasoning. Serve immediately.

Radish & Tomato Salad

Ingredients for 4 servings

- 2 tomatoes, sliced
- 6 small red radishes, sliced
- 2 ½ tbsp white wine vinegar
- ½ tsp chopped chervil
- Salt and black pepper to taste
- ¼ cup olive oil

Directions and Total Time: 15 minutes

Mix the tomatoes and radishes in a bowl. Set aside.

In another bowl, whisk the vinegar, chervil, salt, and pepper until mixed. Pour over the salad and toss to coat. Serve immediately.

Carrot & Cabbage Salad with Avocado & Capers

Ingredients for 4 servings

1 carrot, shredded
1 cup finely shredded red cabbage
1 cup cherry tomatoes, halved
1 yellow bell pepper, cut into sticks
1 (15.5-oz) can chickpeas
¼ cup capers
1 avocado, sliced
¼ cup olive oil
1 ½ tbsp fresh lemon juice

Directions and Total Time: 15 minutes

Combine the carrot, cabbage, tomatoes, bell pepper, chickpeas, capers, and avocado in a bowl. Set aside. In another bowl, mix the oil, lemon juice, salt, and pepper until thoroughly combined. Pour over the cabbage mixture and toss to coat. Serve immediately.

Chickpea & Celery Salad

Ingredients for 4 servings

1 (15.5-oz) can chickpeas
1 head fennel bulb, sliced
½ cup sliced red onion
½ cup celery leaves, chopped
¼ cup vegan mayonnaise
Salt and black pepper to taste

Directions and Total Time: 5 minutes

In a bowl, mash the chickpeas until chunky. Stir in fennel bulb, onion, celery, vegan mayonnaise, salt, and pepper. Serve.

Tropical Salad

Ingredients for 4 servings

½ tsp minced garlic
½ tsp grated fresh ginger
¼ cup olive oil
¼ tsp crushed red pepper
3 tbsp rice vinegar
3 tbsp water
1 tbsp soy sauce
2 cups snow peas, sliced and blanched
3 papaya, chopped
1 large carrot, shredded
1 cucumber, peeled and sliced
3 cups shredded romaine lettuce
½ cup chopped roasted almonds
Salt to taste

Directions and Total Time: 15 minutes

Combine the garlic, ginger, olive oil, red pepper, vinegar, water, salt, and soy sauce in a bowl. Set aside. In another bowl, add in papaya, snow peas, cucumber slices, and carrot. Drizzle with the dressing and toss to coat. Place a bed of lettuce on a plate and top with the salad. Serve topped with almonds.

Traditional Lebanese Salad

Ingredients for 4 servings

1 cup cooked bulgur
1 cup boiling water
Zest and juice of 1 lemon
1 garlic clove, pressed
Sea salt to taste
1 tbsp olive oil
½ cucumber, sliced
1 tomato, sliced
1 cup fresh parsley, chopped
¼ cup fresh mint, chopped
2 scallions, chopped
4 tbsp sunflower seeds

Directions and Total Time: 25 minutes

In a bowl, mix the lemon juice, lemon zest, garlic, salt, and olive oil. Stir in cucumber, tomato, parsley, mint, and scallions. Toss to coat. Using a fork, fluff the bulgur and put into the cucumber mix. Stir to combine. Top with sunflower seeds and serve.

Mediterranean Pasta Salad

Ingredients for 4 servings

8 oz whole-wheat pasta
1 (15.5-oz) can chickpeas
½ cup pitted black olives
½ cup minced sun-dried tomatoes
1 (6-oz) jar dill pickles, sliced
2 roasted red peppers, chopped
½ cup frozen peas, thawed
1 tbsp capers
3 tsp dried chives
½ cup olive oil
¼ cup white wine vinegar
½ tsp dried basil
1 garlic clove, minced
Salt and black pepper to taste

Directions and Total Time: 15 minutes

Cook the pasta in salted water for 8-10 minutes until al dente. Drain and remove to a bowl. Stir in chickpeas, olives, tomatoes, dill pickles, roasted peppers, peas, capers, and chives. In another bowl, whisk oil, vinegar, basil, garlic, sugar, salt, and pepper. Pour over the pasta and toss to coat. Serve.

Mexican Bean Salad

Ingredients for 4 servings

¼ cup vegan salad dressing
1 tsp chili powder
2 (14.5-oz) cans kidney beans
2 cups frozen corn, thawed
1 cup cooked pearl barley
1 head chopped Iceberg lettuce

Directions and Total Time: 15 minutes

Mix the salad dressing and chili powder in a bowl. Add in kidney beans, corn, barley and lettuce. Serve.

Zucchini & Bell Pepper Salad with Beans

Ingredients for 2 servings

1 tbsp olive oil
2 tbsp balsamic vinegar
1 tsp minced fresh chives
1 garlic clove, minced
1 tbsp fresh rosemary, chopped
1 tbsp fresh oregano, chopped
A pinch of salt
1 (14-oz) can cannellini beans
1 green bell pepper, sliced
1 zucchini, diced
2 carrots, diced
2 tbsp fresh basil, chopped

Directions and Total Time: 40 minutes

In a bowl, mix the olive oil, balsamic vinegar, chives, garlic, rosemary, oregano, and salt. Stir in the beans, bell pepper, zucchini, carrots, and basil. Serve.

Cashew & Raisin Salad with & Haricots Verts

Ingredients for 4 servings

3 cups haricots verts, chopped
2 carrots, sliced
3 cups shredded cabbage
1/3 cup golden raisins
¼ cup roasted cashew
1 garlic clove, minced
1 medium shallot, chopped
1 ½ tsp grated fresh ginger
⅓ cup creamy peanut butter
2 tbsp soy sauce
2 tbsp fresh lemon juice
Salt to taste
⅛ tsp ground cayenne
¾ cup coconut milk

Directions and Total Time: 15 minutes

Place the haricots verts, carrots and cabbage in a pot with water and steam for 5 minutes. Drain and transfer to a bowl. Add in raisins and cashew. Let cool. In a food processor, put the garlic, shallot and ginger. Pulse until puréed. Add in peanut butter, soy sauce, lemon juice, salt, cayenne pepper. Blitz until smooth. Stir in coconut milk. Sprinkle the salad with the dressing and toss to coat.

Lettuce & Tomato Salad with Quinoa

Ingredients for 4 servings

1 ½ cups dry quinoa, drained
2 ¼ cups water
⅓ cup white wine vinegar

2 tbsp extra-virgin olive oil
1 tbsp chopped fresh dill
Salt and black pepper to taste

2 cups sliced sweet onions
2 tomatoes, sliced
4 cups shredded lettuce

Directions and Total Time: 25 minutes

Place the quinoa in a pot with salted water. Bring to a boil. Lower the heat and simmer covered for 15 minutes. Turn the heat off and let sit for 5 minutes. Using a fork fluff the quinoa and set aside. In a small bowl, whisk the vinegar, olive oil, dill, salt, and pepper; set aside. In a serving plate, combine onions, tomatoes, quinoa, and lettuce. Pour in the dressing and toss to coat. Serve.

Minty Eggplant Salad

Ingredients for 2 servings

1 lemon, half zested and juiced, half cut into wedges
1 tsp olive oil
1 eggplant, chopped
½ tsp ground cumin

½ tsp ground ginger
¼ tsp turmeric
¼ tsp ground nutmeg
Sea salt to taste
2 tbsp capers

1 tbsp chopped green olives
1 garlic clove, pressed
2 tbsp fresh mint, finely chopped
2 cups watercress, chopped

Directions and Total Time: 45 minutes

In a skillet over medium heat, warm the oil. Place the eggplant and cook for 5 minutes. Add in cumin, ginger, turmeric, nutmeg, and salt. Cook for another 10 minutes. Stir in lemon zest, lemon juice, capers, olives, garlic, and mint. Cook for 1-2 minutes more. Place some watercress on each plate and top with the eggplant mixture. Serve immediately.

Artichoke & Potato Salad

Ingredients for 4 servings-6

1 (10-oz) package frozen artichoke hearts, cooked
1 ½ pounds potatoes, chopped
2 cups halved cherry tomatoes

½ cup sweet corn
3 green onions, minced
1 tbsp minced fresh parsley
⅓ cup olive oil

2 tbsp fresh lemon juice
1 garlic clove, minced
Salt and black pepper to taste

Directions and Total Time: 30 minutes

Place the potatoes in a pot with salted water and boil for 15 minutes. Drain and remove to a bowl.

Cut the artichokes by quarts and mix into the potato bowl. Stir in tomatoes, corn, green onions, and parsley. Set aside. Whisk the oil, lemon juice, garlic, salt, and pepper in a bowl. Pour over the potatoes and toss to coat. Let sit for 20 minutes. Serve.

Lemon Potato Salad with Kalamata Olives

Ingredients for 4 servings

4 potatoes, chopped
Salt and black pepper to taste
¼ cup olive oil

2 tbsp apple cider vinegar
2 tbsp lemon juice
1 tsp dried dill

½ cucumber, chopped
¼ red onion, diced
¼ cup chopped kalamata olives

Directions and Total Time: 30 minutes

In a pot with salted water, place the potatoes. Bring to a boil and cook for 20 minutes. Drain and let cool. Mix the olive oil, vinegar, lemon juice, and dill in a bowl. Add in cucumber, red onion and olives, toss to coat. Stir in the potatoes. Season with salt and pepper. Serve.

Italian Vegetable Relish

Ingredients for 6 servings

- ¼ cup sliced pimiento-stuffed green olives
- 1 carrot, sliced
- 1 medium red bell pepper, sliced
- 1 cup cauliflower florets
- 2 celery stalks, chopped
- ½ cup chopped red onion
- 1 garlic clove, minced
- 1 jalapeño pepper, chopped
- 3 tbsp white wine vinegar
- ⅓ cup olive oil

Directions and Total Time: 15 minutes

Combine the carrot, bell pepper, cauliflower, celery, and onion in a bowl. Add in salt and cold water. Cover and transfer to the fridge for 4-6 hours. Strain and wash the veggies. Remove to a bowl and mix in olives. Set aside. In another bowl, mix the garlic, jalapeño pepper, vinegar, and oil. Pour over the veggies and toss to coat. Let chill cover in the fridge overnight and serve.

Bulgur & Kale Salad

Ingredients for 4 servings

- 1 avocado, peeled and pitted
- 1 tbsp fresh lemon juice
- 1 tbsp fresh dill
- 1 small garlic clove, pressed
- 1 scallion, chopped
- Sea salt to taste
- 8 large kale leaves, chopped
- ½ cup chopped green beans, steamed
- 1 cup cherry tomatoes, halved
- 1 bell pepper, chopped
- 2 scallions, chopped
- 2 cups cooked bulgur

Directions and Total Time: 30 minutes

In a food processor, place the avocado, lemon juice, dill, garlic, scallion, salt, and ¼ cup water. Blend until smooth. Set aside the dressing.

Put kale, green beans, cherry tomatoes, bell pepper, scallions, and bulgur in a serving bowl. Add in the dressing and toss to coat. Serve.

Potato & Green Bean Salad

Ingredients for 4 servings-6

- 1 ½ lb small potatoes, unpeeled
- 1 cup frozen green beans, thawed
- ½ cup shredded carrots
- 4 green onions, chopped
- 1 tbsp grapeseed oil
- 1 garlic clove, minced
- 1/3 cup peanut butter
- ½ tsp Asian chili paste
- 2 tbsp soy sauce
- 1 tbsp rice vinegar
- ¾ cup coconut milk
- 3 tbsp chopped roasted peanuts

Directions and Total Time: 30 minutes

Place the potatoes in a pot with boiling salted water and cook for 20 minutes. Drain and let cool. Chop into chunks and place in a bowl. Stir in green beans, carrots and green onions. Set aside.

Heat the oil in a pot over medium heat. Place in garlic and cook for 30 seconds. Add in peanut butter, chili paste, soy sauce, vinegar, coconut milk and cook for 5 minutes, stirring often. Pour over the potatoes and toss to coat. Serve garnished with peanuts.

Beet & Cucumber Salad with Balsamic Dressing

Ingredients for 2 servings

3 beets, peeled and sliced
1 tsp olive oil
1 cucumber, sliced
2 cups mixed greens
4 tbsp balsamic dressing
2 tbsp chopped almonds

Directions and Total Time: 40 minutes

Preheat oven to 390 F.

In a bowl, stir the beets, oil, and salt. Toss to coat. Transfer to a baking dish and roast for 20 minutes, until golden brown. Once the beets are ready, divide between 2 plates and place a cucumber slice on each beet. Top with mixed greens. Pour over the dressing and garnish with almonds to serve.

Colorful Quinoa Salad

Ingredients for 6 servings

1 cup canned mandarin oranges in juice, drained
3 tbsp olive oil
Juice of 1 ½ lemons
1 tsp garlic powder
½ tsp dried oregano
1 bunch baby spinach
2 cups cooked tricolor quinoa
1 cup diced yellow summer squash
1 red bell pepper, diced
½ red onion, sliced
½ cup dried cranberries
½ cup slivered almonds

Directions and Total Time: 15 minutes

Mix the oil, lemon juice, garlic powder, and oregano in a bowl. In another bowl, place the spinach and pour over the dressing, toss to coat. Stir in quinoa, oranges, squash, bell pepper, and red onion. Share into bowls and garnish with cranberries and almonds to serve.

Chinese-Style Cabbage Salad

Ingredients for 6 servings

4 cups shredded red cabbage
2 cups thinly sliced napa cabbage
1 cup red radishes, sliced
¼ cup fresh orange juice
2 tbsp Chinese black vinegar
1 tbsp soy sauce
2 tbsp toasted sesame oil
1 tsp grated fresh ginger
1 tbsp black sesame seeds

Directions and Total Time: 15 minutes

Mix the red cabbage, napa cabbage and radishes in a bowl. In another bowl, whisk the orange juice, vinegar, soy sauce, sesame oil, and ginger. Pour over the slaw and toss to coat. Marinate covered in the fridge for 2 hours. Serve topped with sesame seeds.

Radicchio & Cabbage Coleslaw

Ingredients for 2 servings

½ head white cabbage, shredded
¼ head radicchio, shredded
1 large carrot, shredded
¾ cup vegan mayonnaise
¼ cup soy milk
1 tbsp cider vinegar
½ tsp dry mustard
¼ tsp celery seeds
Salt and black pepper to taste

Directions and Total Time: 10 minutes

Combine cabbage, radicchio and carrot in a bowl. In another bowl, whisk mayonnaise, soy milk, mustard, vinegar, celery seeds, salt, and pepper. Pour over the slaw and toss to coat. Serve immediately.

Avocado Salad with Sesame Seeds

Ingredients for 4 servings-6

- 2 medium avocados, sliced
- 3 tbsp sesame oil
- 2 tbsp soy sauce
- 1 tbsp mirin
- 2 tsp rice vinegar
- 2 tbsp toasted sesame seeds

Directions and Total Time: 15 minutes

Place the avocado in a bowl. Set aside. In another bowl, mix the oil, soy sauce, mirin, and vinegar. Pour over the avocado and toss to coat. Let sit for 10 minutes. Serve in bowls topped with sesame seeds.

Cilantro Chickpea & Corn Salad

Ingredients for 4 servings

- 1 cup corn kernels
- 1 (15.5-oz) can chickpeas
- 1 celery stalk, sliced
- 2 green onions, minced
- 2 tbsp chopped fresh cilantro
- ¼ cup olive oil
- 2 tbsp white wine vinegar
- ½ tsp ground cumin
- Salt and black pepper to taste

Directions and Total Time: 10 minutes

Combine the corn, chickpeas, celery, green onions, and cilantro in a bowl. Set aside. In another bowl, mix the oil, vinegar, cumin, salt, and pepper. Pour over the salad and toss to coat. Serve immediately.

Radish & Cabbage Ginger Salad

Ingredients for 4 servings

- 8 oz napa cabbage, cut crosswise into strips
- 1 cup grated carrots
- 1 cup sliced radishes
- 2 green onions, minced
- 2 tbsp chopped fresh parsley
- 2 tbsp rice vinegar
- 2 tsp toasted sesame oil
- 1 tbsp soy sauce
- 1 tsp grated fresh ginger
- ½ tsp dry mustard
- Salt and black pepper to taste
- 2 tbsp chopped roasted hazelnuts

Directions and Total Time: 15 minutes

Place the napa cabbage, carrot, radishes, green onions, and parsley in a bowl, stir to combine. In another bowl, mix vinegar, sesame oil, soy sauce, ginger, mustard, salt, and pepper. Pour over the slaw and toss to coat. Marinate covered in the fridge for 2 hours. Serve topped with hazelnuts.

Coleslaw & Spinach Salad with Grapefruit

Ingredients for 4 servings

- 1 large grapefruit
- 2 cups coleslaw mix
- 2 cups green leaf lettuce, torn
- 2 cups baby spinach
- 1 bunch watercress
- 6 radishes, sliced
- Juice of 1 lemon
- 2 tsp date syrup
- 1 tsp white wine vinegar
- Sea salt and black pepper
- ¼ cup extra-virgin olive oil

Directions and Total Time: 10 minutes

Slice the grapefruit by cutting the ends, peeling all the white pith and making an incise in the membrane to take out on each segment. Transfer to a bowl. Stir in coleslaw, lettuce, spinach, watercress, and radishes. In a bowl, mix the lemon juice, date syrup, vinegar, salt, and pepper. Gently beat the olive oil until emulsified. Pour over the salad and toss to coat. Serve right away.

Easy Pineapple & Jicama Salad

Ingredients for 6 servings

1 jicama, peeled and grated
1 pineapple, peeled and sliced
¼ cup non-dairy milk
2 tbsp fresh basil, chopped
1 large scallion, chopped
Sea salt to taste
1 ½ tbsp tahini
Arugula for serving
Chopped cashews

Directions and Total Time: 15 minutes

Place jicama in a bowl. In a food processor, put the pineapple and enough milk. Blitz until puréed. Add in basil, scallions, tahini, and salt. Pour over the jicama and cover. Transfer to the fridge and marinate for 1 hour. Place a bed of arugula on a plate and top with the salad. Serve garnished with cashews.

Broccoli & Mango Rice Salad

Ingredients for 4 servings

½ cup brown rice, rinsed
3 cups broccoli florets, blanched
1 mango, chopped
1 small red bell pepper, chopped
1 jalapeño, seeded and minced
1 tsp grated fresh ginger
2 tbsp fresh lemon juice
3 tbsp grapeseed oil
1/3 cup roasted almonds, chopped

Directions and Total Time: 25 minutes

Place the rice in a bowl with salted water and cook for 18-20 minutes. Remove to a bowl. Stir in broccoli, mango, bell pepper, and chili. In another bowl, mix the ginger, lemon juice and oil. Pour over the rice and toss to combine. Top with almonds to serve.

Mom´s Caesar Salad

Ingredients for 4 servings

½ cup cashews
½ cup water
3 tbsp olive oil
Juice of ½ lime
1 tbsp white miso paste
1 tsp soy sauce
1 tsp Dijon mustard
1 tsp garlic powder
Sea salt and black pepper to taste
2 heads romaine lettuce, chopped
2 tsp capers
1 cup cherry tomatoes, halved
Plant-based Parmesan cheese
Whole-what bread croutons

Directions and Total Time: 10 minutes

In a blender, put cashews, water, olive oil, lime juice, miso paste, soy sauce, mustard, garlic powder, salt, and pepper. Blend until smooth. Mix the lettuce with half of dressing in a bowl. Divide in individual bowls and add in capers, tomatoes and plant-based Parmesan cheese. Serve topped with croutons.

Fantastic Green Salad

Ingredients for 4 servings

1 head Iceberg lettuce
8 asparagus spears, chopped
2 mini seedless cucumbers, sliced
1 small zucchini, cut into ribbons
1 carrot, cut into ribbons
1 avocado, sliced
½ cup vegan green goddess dressing
2 scallions, thinly sliced

Directions and Total Time: 10 minutes

Share the lettuce into 4 bowls, Add in some asparagus, cucumber, zucchini, carrot, and avocado. Sprinkle each bowl with 2 tbsp of dressing. Serve garnished with scallions.

Carrot Salad with Cherries & Pecans

Ingredients for 4 servings

1 pound carrots, shredded
1 cup sweetened dried cherries
2 ½ cup toasted pecans
3 tbsp fresh lemon juice
3 tbsp avocado oil
Black pepper to taste

Directions and Total Time: 15 minutes

Combine the carrots, cherries and pecans in a bowl. In another bowl, mix the lemon juice, avocado oil and pepper. Pour over the salad and toss to coat. Serve immediately.

Apple & Spinach Salad with Walnut Crunch

Ingredients for 4 servings

¼ cup tahini
2 tbsp Dijon mustard
3 tbsp maple syrup
1 tbsp lemon juice
½ cup finely chopped walnuts
2 tsp soy sauce
1 pound baby spinach
1 green apple, cored and sliced

Directions and Total Time: 20 minutes

Preheat oven to 360 F. Line with parchment paper a baking sheet.

In a bowl, mix the tahini, mustard, 2 tbsp maple syrup, lemon juice, and salt. Set aside the dressing.

In a bowl, combine the walnuts, soy sauce and the remaining maple syrup. Spread evenly on the baking sheet and bake for 5 minutes, shaking once until crunchy. Allow to cool for 3 minutes.

Combine the spinach and apples in a bowl. Pour over the dressing and toss to coat. Serve garnished with the walnut crunch.

Apple & Kale Salad with Raspberry Vinaigrette

Ingredients for 2 servings

1 cup kale
½ apple, cored and chopped
¼ red onion, thinly sliced
2 tbsp sunflower seeds
2 tbsp raisins
2 tbsp raspberry vinaigrette

Directions and Total Time: 5 minutes

Place the kale on a plate. Add in apple, red onion, sunflower seeds, and raisins. Sprinkle with the vinaigrette and serve.

Dijon Potato Salad

Ingredients for 4 servings-6

1 ½ lb small potatoes, unpeeled
2 celery stalks, sliced
¼ cup sweet pickle relish
3 tbsp minced green onions
¾ cup vegan mayonnaise
1 tbsp soy milk
1 tbsp white wine vinegar
1 tsp Dijon mustard
10 black olives, pitted and sliced

Directions and Total Time: 25 minutes

Place the potatoes in a pot with boiling salted water and cook for 20 minutes. Drain and let cool. Once the potatoes are cooled, peel them and cut into small cubes. Remove to a bowl. Stir in celery, pickle relish and green onions. In another bowl, mix the mayonnaise, soy milk, vinegar, mustard, salt, and pepper. Pour over the salad and toss to coat. Serve immediately.

Baked Potato & Black-Eyed Pea Salad

Ingredients for 4 servings

1 ½ pounds potatoes, chopped
1 red onion, sliced
¼ cup olive oil
Salt and black pepper to taste
3 tbsp white wine vinegar
1 (15.5-oz) can black-eyed peas
⅓ cup chopped sun-dried tomatoes
¼ cup green olives, halved
¼ cup chopped fresh parsley

Directions and Total Time: 25 minutes

Preheat oven to 420 F.

In a bowl, mix the potatoes, onion and 1 tbsp of oil. Sprinkle with salt and pepper. Spread on a baking sheet and roast for 20 minutes. Remove to a bowl and let cool. In another bowl, combine the remaining oil, vinegar and pepper. Stir the peas, tomatoes, olives, and parsley into the potato bowl. Pour over the dressing and toss to coat. Adjust seasonings if needed. Serve hot or chilled.

Bean & Roasted Parsnip Salad

Ingredients for 3 servings

4 parsnips, sliced
2 tsp olive oil
½ tsp ground cinnamon
Salt to taste
1 (15-oz) can cannellini beans
3 cups chopped spinach
⅓ cup pomegranate seeds
⅓ cup sunflower seeds
¼ cup raspberry vinaigrette

Directions and Total Time: 40 minutes

Preheat oven to 390 F.

In a bowl, combine the parsnips, olive oil, cinnamon, and salt. Spread on a baking tray and roast for 15 minutes. Flip the parsnips and add the beans. Roast for another 15 minutes. Allow to cool. Divide the spinach among plates and place the pomegranate seeds, sunflower seeds and roasted parsnips and beans. Sprinkle with raspberry vinaigrette and serve.

Beet Slaw with Apples

Ingredients for 4 servings

2 tbsp olive oil
Juice of 1 lemon
½ beet, shredded
Sea salt to taste
2 apples, peeled and julienned
4 cups shredded red cabbage

Directions and Total Time: 10 minutes

Mix the olive oil, lemon juice, beet, and salt in a bowl. In another bowl, combine the apples and cabbage. Pour over the vinaigrette and toss to coat. Serve right away.

Spinach Salad with Blackberries & Pecans

Ingredients for 4 servings

10 oz baby spinach
1 cup raisins
1 cup fresh blackberries
¼ red onion, thinly sliced
½ cup chopped pecans
¼ cup balsamic vinegar
¾ cup olive oil
Sea salt and black pepper to taste

Directions and Total Time: 10 minutes

Combine the spinach, raisins, blackberries, red onion, and pecans in a bowl. In another bowl, mix the vinegar, olive oil, salt, and pepper. Pour over the salad and toss to coat. Serve immediately.

Festive Nicoise Salad Potato Salad

Ingredients for 4 servings

1½ lb small potatoes, unpeeled
1 cup firm tofu, drained and cubed
2 tbsp minced fresh parsley
1 tbsp minced fresh chives
1 tsp minced fresh tarragon
⅓ cup olive oil
2 tbsp white wine vinegar
Black pepper to taste

Directions and Total Time: 25 minutes

Place the potatoes in a pot with boiling salted water and cook for 20 minutes. Drain, cool, and slice. Remove to a bowl. Stir in tofu, parsley, chives, and tarragon. In another bowl, mix the oil, vinegar and pepper. Pour over the salad and toss to coat. Let chill and serve.

Cowboy Salad

Ingredients for 4 servings

2 heads romaine lettuce, chopped
2 cups cherry tomatoes, halved
1 avocado, peeled, pitted, and diced
1 cup corn kernels
1 large cucumber, peeled and diced
4 oz soy chorizo
4 scallions, thinly sliced
Vegan ranch dressing

Directions and Total Time: 15 minutes

Place a bed of romaine lettuce in a serving bowl. Layer tomatoes, avocado, corn, cucumber, and soy chorizo. Serve topped with scallions and vegan ranch dressing.

Christmas Potato Salad

Ingredients for 4 servings

1 ½ pounds potatoes, chopped
½ cup olive oil
4 portobello mushrooms, chopped
1 bunch green onions, chopped
1 tbsp whole-wheat flour
2 tbsp pure date sugar
⅓ cup white wine vinegar
¼ cup water
Salt and black pepper to taste

Directions and Total Time: 15 minutes

Place the potatoes in a pot with boiling salted water and cook for 20 minutes. Drain and remove to a bowl. Heat oil in a skillet over medium heat. Place the mushrooms and sauté for 5 minutes. Add the mushrooms to the potatoes. To the skillet, add in green onions and cook for 1 minute. Mix in flour, sugar, vinegar, water, salt, and pepper. Bring to a boil and cook until creamy. Pour the resulting sauce over the potatoes and mushrooms and toss to coat. Serve immediately.

Dijon Potato & Carrot Salad

Ingredients for 4 servings

6 potatoes, chopped
2 carrots, chopped
Salt to taste
½ cup tahini dressing
1 tsp dried dill
1 tsp Dijon mustard
4 celery stalks, chopped
2 scallions, chopped

Directions and Total Time: 25 minutes

Place the potatoes and carrots in a pot with salted water. Bring to a boil and cook for 20 minutes. Drain and let cool. In a bowl, mix the dressing, dill and mustard. Add in celery and scallions, toss to coat. Stir in carrots and potatoes. Serve.

Chickpea & Quinoa Salad with Capers

Ingredients for 4 servings

1 cup quinoa, rinsed
1 (15.5-oz) can chickpeas
1 cup cherry tomatoes, halved
2 green onions, minced
½ cucumber, peeled and chopped
¼ cup capers
2 tbsp toasted pine nuts
1 medium shallot, sliced
1 garlic clove, chopped
1 tsp Dijon mustard
2 tbsp white wine vinegar
¼ cup olive oil

Directions and Total Time: 25 minutes

Boil salted water in a pot over medium heat. Add in quinoa, lower the heat and simmer for 15 minutes. Remove to a bowl. Stir in chickpeas, tomatoes, green onions, cucumber, capers, and pine nuts. Set aside. In a food processor, put the shallot, garlic, mustard, vinegar, oil, salt, and pepper. Pulse until blend. Pour over the salad and toss to coat. Serve immediately.

Cucumber & Pear Rice Salad

Ingredients for 4 servings

1 cup brown rice
¼ cup olive oil
¼ cup orange juice
1 pear, cored and diced
½ cucumber, diced
¼ cup raisins

Directions and Total Time: 15 minutes

Place the rice in a pot with 2 cups of salted water. Bring to a boil, then lower the heat and simmer for 15 minutes. In a bowl, whisk together the olive oil, orange juice, salt, and pepper. Stir in the pear, cucumber, raisins, and cooked rice. Serve.

Apple & Arugula Salad with Walnuts

Ingredients for 4 servings

¼ cup chopped walnuts
10 oz arugula
1 apple, thinly sliced
1 tbsp finely minced shallot
2 tbsp champagne vinegar
2 tbsp olive oil
Sea salt and black pepper to taste
¼ tsp English mustard

Directions and Total Time: 20 minutes

Preheat oven to 360 F.

In a baking sheet, spread the walnuts and toast for 6 minutes. Let cool. In a bowl, combine the walnuts, arugula and apple. In another bowl, mix the shallot, vinegar, olive oil, salt, pepper, and mustard. Pour over the salad and toss to coat. Serve right away.

Lemony Ditalini Salad with Chickpeas

Ingredients for 4 servings

¼ cup olive oil
2 tbsp freshly squeezed lemon juice
A pinch of salt
1 ½ cups canned chickpeas
2 cups cooked ditalini pasta
2 cups raw spinach, finely chopped
1 cup chopped cucumber
¼ red onion, finely diced

Directions and Total Time: 25 minutes

Mix the olive oil, lemon juice and salt in a bowl. Stir in chickpeas and ditalini pasta. Add in spinach, cucumber and red onion, stir to combine. Serve.

Tomato Bean & Bulgur Salad

Ingredients for 4 servings

3 cups water
1 ½ cups bulgur, rinsed
Salt and black pepper to taste
1 (15.5-oz) can black beans
4 ripe plum tomatoes, sliced
1 red onion, sliced
¼ cup chopped fresh parsley
¼ cup olive oil
2 tbsp sherry vinegar

Directions and Total Time: 25 minutes

Place the bulgur in a pot with boiling salted water. Lower the heat and simmer for 20 minutes. Remove to a bowl. Stir in black beans, tomatoes, onion, and parsley. In another bowl, mix the olive oil, vinegar, salt, and pepper. Pour over the bulgur mixture and toss to coat. Let sit covered for 20 minutes. Serve.

Bell Pepper & Quinoa Salad

Ingredients for 4 servings

2 cups cooked quinoa
½ red onion, diced
1 red bell pepper, diced
1 orange bell pepper, diced
1 carrot, diced
¼ cup olive oil
2 tbsp rice vinegar
1 tbsp soy sauce
1 garlic clove, minced
1 tbsp grated fresh ginger
Sea salt and black pepper to taste

Directions and Total Time: 15 minutes

Combine the quinoa, onion, bell peppers, and carrots in a bowl. In another bowl, mix the olive oil, rice vinegar, soy sauce, garlic, ginger, salt, and pepper. Pour over the quinoa and toss to coat. Serve.

Apple & Spinach Salad with Nuts & Cranberries

Ingredients for 4 servings

Juice of 1 lemon
2 tbsp olive oil
1 tbsp maple syrup
1 (5-oz) package baby spinach
1 cup corn kernels
½ red onion, thinly sliced
2 apples, cored and sliced
½ cup pine nuts
¼ cup dried cranberries

Directions and Total Time: 10 minutes

Mix the lemon juice, oil, maple syrup, and salt in a bowl. Combine the spinach, corn, red onion, and apples in another bowl. Pour over the lemon dressing and toss to coat. Separate into 4 plates and serve topped with pine nuts and cranberries.

Chickpea & Faro Entrée

Ingredients for 4 servings

2 tbsp olive oil
½ cup chopped green onions
2 tsp minced fresh ginger
1 cup faro
½ cup dried apricots, quartered
¼ cup golden raisins
¼ tsp ground cumin
¼ tsp ground cayenne
1 tsp turmeric
1/3 cup pomegranate molasses
1 (15.5-oz) can chickpeas, drained
¼ cup minced fresh cilantro

Directions and Total Time: 30 minutes

Heat oil in a pot and sauté green onions, ginger, apricots, raisins, cumin, cayenne, turmeric, salt, and pepper for 2 minutes. Add in pomegranate molasses, faro, and 2 cups water. Bring to a boil, lower the heat, and simmer for 10 minutes. Stir in chickpeas and cilantro and cook for 10 minutes. Serve warm.

LUNCH

Tofu Cabbage Stir-Fry

Ingredients for 4 servings

2 ½ cups baby bok choy, quartered
5 oz plant butter
2 cups tofu, cubed
1 tsp garlic powder

1 tsp onion powder
1 tbsp plain vinegar
2 garlic cloves, minced
1 tsp chili flakes

1 tbsp fresh ginger, grated
3 green onions, sliced
1 tbsp sesame oil
1 cup tofu mayonnaise

Directions and Total Time: 45 minutes

Melt half of the butter in a wok over medium heat, add the bok choy, and stir-fry until softened. Season with salt, black pepper, garlic powder, onion powder, and plain vinegar. Sauté for 2 minutes; set aside. Melt the remaining butter in the wok, add and sauté garlic, chili flakes, and ginger until fragrant. Put the tofu in the wok and cook until browned on all sides. Add the green onions and bok choy, heat for 2 minutes and add the sesame oil. Stir in tofu mayonnaise, cook for 1 minute, and serve.

Smoked Tempeh with Broccoli Fritters

Ingredients for 4 servings

4 tbsp flax seed powder
1 tbsp soy sauce
3 tbsp olive oil
1 tbsp grated ginger
3 tbsp fresh lime juice

Cayenne pepper to taste
10 oz tempeh slices
1 head broccoli, grated
8 oz tofu, grated
3 tbsp almond flour

½ tsp onion powder
4 ¼ oz plant butter
½ cup mixed salad greens
1 cup tofu mayonnaise
Juice of ½ a lemon

Directions and Total Time: 40 minutes

In a bowl, mix the flax seed powder with 12 tbsp water and set aside to soak for 5 minutes. In another bowl, combine soy sauce, olive oil, grated ginger, lime juice, salt, and cayenne pepper. Brush the tempeh slices with the mixture. Heat a grill pan over medium and grill the tempeh on both sides until golden brown and nicely smoked. Remove the slices into a plate and set aside.

In a bowl, mix the tofu with broccoli. Add in flax egg, almond flour, onion powder, salt, and black pepper. Mix and form 12 patties out of the mixture. Melt the plant butter in a skillet and fry the patties on both sides until golden brown. Remove to a plate. Add the grilled tempeh with the broccoli fritters, and salad greens. Mix the tofu mayonnaise with the lemon juice and drizzle over the salad.

Cheesy Cauliflower Casserole

Ingredients for 4 servings

2 oz plant butter
1 white onion, finely chopped
½ cup celery stalks, finely chopped

1 green bell pepper, chopped
Salt and black pepper to taste
1 small head cauliflower, chopped

1 cup tofu mayonnaise
4 oz grated plant-based Parmesan
1 tsp red chili flakes

Directions and Total Time: 35 minutes

Preheat oven to 400 F. Season onion, celery, and bell pepper with salt and black pepper. In a bowl, mix cauliflower, tofu mayonnaise, Parmesan cheese, and red chili flakes. Pour the mixture into a greased baking dish and add the vegetables; mix to distribute. Bake for 20 minutes. Remove and serve warm.

Spicy Veggie Steaks with Green Salad

Ingredients for 2 servings

1 eggplant, sliced
1 zucchini, sliced
¼ cup coconut oil
Juice of ½ a lemon

5 oz plant-based cheddar, cubed
10 Kalamata olives
2 tbsp pecans
1 oz mixed salad greens

½ cup tofu mayonnaise
Salt to taste
½ tsp Cayenne pepper to taste

Directions and Total Time: 35 minutes

Set oven to broil and line a baking sheet with parchment paper. Arrange eggplant and zucchini on the baking sheet. Brush with coconut oil and sprinkle with cayenne pepper. Broil for 15-20 minutes.

Remove to a serving platter and drizzle with the lemon juice. Arrange the plant-based cheddar cheese, Kalamata olives, pecans, and mixed greens by the grilled veggies. Top with tofu mayonnaise and serve.

Mushroom Curry Pie

Ingredients for 8 servings

Piecrust

1 tbsp flax seed powder + 3 tbsp water
¾ cup coconut flour
4 tbsp chia seeds

4 tbsp almond flour
1 tbsp psyllium husk powder
1 tsp baking powder

1 pinch of salt
3 tbsp olive oil
4 tbsp water

Filling

1 cup chopped shiitake mushrooms
1 cup tofu mayonnaise
3 tbsp flax seed powder + 9 tbsp water

½ red bell pepper, finely chopped
1 tsp turmeric
½ tsp paprika

½ tsp garlic powder
½ cup cashew cream cheese
1 ¼ cups grated plant-based Parmesan

Directions and Total Time: 70 minutes

In two separate bowls, mix the different portions of flax seed powder with the respective quantity of water and set aside to absorb for 5 minutes.

Preheat oven to 350 F. When the flax egg is ready, pour the smaller quantity into a food processor, add in the pie crust ingredients and blend until a ball forms out of the dough. Line a springform pan with parchment paper and grease with cooking spray. Spread the dough in the bottom of the pan and bake for 15 minutes. In a bowl, add the remaining flax egg and all the filling ingredients, combine the mixture evenly, and fill the piecrust. Bake further for 40 minutes. Remove, slice, and serve the pie.

Vegan Mushroom Pizza

Ingredients for 4 servings

2 tsp plant butter
1 cup chopped button mushrooms
½ cup sliced mixed bell peppers

Salt and black pepper to taste
1 pizza crust
1 cup tomato sauce

1 cup plant-based Parmesan cheese
5-6 basil leaves

Directions and Total Time: 35 minutes

Melt plant butter in a skillet and sauté mushrooms and bell peppers for 10 minutes until soften. Season with salt and black pepper. Put the pizza crust on a pizza pan, spread the tomato sauce all over and scatter vegetables evenly on top. Sprinkle with plant-based Parmesan cheese. Bake for 20 minutes until the cheese has melted. Garnish with basil, slice and serve.

Avocado Coconut Pie

Ingredients for 4 servings

Piecrust

1 tbsp flax seed powder + 3 tbsp water
1 cup coconut flour
4 tbsp chia seeds
1 tbsp psyllium husk powder
1 tsp baking soda
1 pinch salt
3 tbsp coconut oil
4 tbsp water

Filling

2 ripe avocados, chopped
1 cup tofu mayonnaise
3 tbsp flax seed powder + 9 tbsp water
2 tbsp fresh parsley, chopped
1 jalapeno, finely chopped
½ tsp onion powder
¼ tsp salt
½ cup cream cheese
1 ¼ cups grated plant-based Parmesan

Directions and Total Time: 80 minutes

In 2 separate bowls, mix the different portions of flax seed powder with the respective quantity of water. Allow absorbing for 5 minutes.

Preheat oven to 350 F. In a food processor, add the piecrust ingredients and the smaller portion of the flax egg. Blend until the resulting dough forms into a ball. Line a springform pan with parchment paper and spread the dough in the pan. Bake for 10-15 minutes.

Put avocado in a bowl and add the tofu mayonnaise, remaining flax egg, parsley, jalapeno, onion powder, salt, cream cheese, and plant-based Parmesan cheese. Combine well. Remove the piecrust when ready and fill with the creamy mixture. Bake for 35 minutes. Cool before slicing and serving.

Tofu & Spinach Lasagna with Red Sauce

Ingredients for 4 servings

2 tbsp plant butter
1 white onion, chopped
1 garlic clove, minced
2 ½ cups crumbled tofu
3 tbsp tomato paste
½ tbsp dried oregano
Salt and black pepper to taste
1 cup baby spinach
8 tbsp flax seed powder
1 ½ cup cashew cream cheese
5 tbsp psyllium husk powder
2 cups coconut cream
5 oz grated plant-based mozzarella
2 oz grated plant-based Parmesan
½ cup fresh parsley, finely chopped

Directions and Total Time: 65 minutes

Melt plant butter in a medium pot and sauté onion and garlic until fragrant and soft, about 3 minutes. Stir in tofu and cook until brown. Mix in tomato paste, oregano, salt, and black pepper. Pour ½ cup of water into the pot, stir, and simmer the ingredients until most of the liquid has evaporated.

Preheat oven to 300 F. Mix flax seed powder with 1 ½ cups water in a bowl to make flax egg. Allow sitting to thicken for 5 minutes. Combine flax egg with cashew cream cheese and salt. Add psyllium husk powder a bit at a time while whisking and allow the mixture to sit for a few minutes. Line a baking sheet with parchment paper and spread the mixture in. Cover with another parchment paper and flatten the dough into the sheet. Bake for 10-12 minutes. Slice the pasta into sheets.

In a bowl, combine coconut cream and two-thirds of the plant-based mozzarella cheese. Fetch out 2 tablespoons of the mixture and reserve. Mix in plant-based Parmesan cheese, salt, pepper, and parsley. Set aside. Grease a baking dish with cooking spray, layer a single line of pasta, spread with some tomato sauce, 1/3 of the spinach, and ¼ of the coconut cream mixture. Repeat layering the ingredients twice in the same manner making sure to top the final layer with the coconut cream mixture and the reserved cream cheese. Bake for 30 minutes at 400 F. Slice and serve with salad.

Curried Tofu with Buttery Cabbage

Ingredients for 4 servings

2 cups tofu, cubed
1 tbsp + 3 ½ tbsp coconut oil
½ cup grated coconut

1 tsp yellow curry powder
½ tsp onion powder
2 cups Napa cabbage, grated

4 oz plant butter
Salt and black pepper to taste
Lemon wedges for serving

Directions and Total Time: 55 minutes

Drizzle 1 tablespoon of coconut oil on the tofu. In a bowl, mix the shredded coconut, yellow curry powder, salt, and onion powder. Toss the tofu cubes in the spice mixture. Heat the remaining coconut oil in a non-stick skillet and fry the coated tofu until golden brown on all sides. Transfer to a plate.

In another skillet, melt half of the plant butter, add, and sauté the cabbage until slightly caramelized. Then, season with salt and black pepper. Dish the cabbage into serving plates with the tofu and lemon wedges. Melt the remaining plant butter in the skillet and drizzle over the cabbage and tofu. Serve.

Green Avocado Carbonara

Ingredients for 4 servings

8 tbsp flax seed powder
1 ½ cups cashew cream cheese
5 ½ tbsp psyllium husk powder
1 avocado, chopped

1 ¾ cups coconut cream
Juice of ½ lemon
1 teaspoon onion powder
½ teaspoon garlic powder

¼ cup olive oil
Salt and black pepper to taste
½ cup grated plant-based Parmesan
4 tbsp toasted pecans

Directions and Total Time: 30 minutes

Preheat oven to 300 F.

In a medium bowl, mix the flax seed powder with 1 ½ cups water and allow sitting to thicken for 5 minutes. Add the cashew cream cheese, salt, and psyllium husk powder. Whisk until smooth batter forms. Line a baking sheet with parchment paper, pour in the batter and cover with another parchment paper. Use a rolling pin to flatten the dough into the sheet. Bake for 10-12 minutes. Remove, take off the parchment papers and use a sharp knife to slice the pasta into thin strips lengthwise. Cut each piece into halves, pour into a bowl, and set aside.

In a blender, combine avocado, coconut cream, lemon juice, onion powder, and garlic powder; puree until smooth. Pour the olive oil over the pasta and stir to coat properly. Pour the avocado sauce on top and mix. Season with salt and black pepper. Divide the pasta into serving plates, garnish with Parmesan cheese and pecans, and serve immediately.

Mushroom Lettuce Wraps

Ingredients for 4 servings

2 tbsp plant butter
4 oz baby bella mushrooms, sliced

1 ½ lb tofu, crumbled
1 iceberg lettuce, leaves extracted

1 cup grated plant-based cheddar
1 large tomato, sliced

Directions and Total Time: 25 minutes

Melt the plant butter in a skillet, add in mushrooms and sauté until browned and tender, about 6 minutes. Transfer to a plate. Add the tofu to the skillet and cook until brown, about 10 minutes. Spoon the tofu and mushrooms into the lettuce leaves, sprinkle with the plant-based cheddar cheese, and share the tomato slices on top. Serve the burger immediately.

Kale & Mushroom Pierogis

Ingredients for 4 servings

Stuffing

2 tbsp plant butter
2 garlic cloves, finely chopped
1 small red onion, finely chopped

3 oz baby bella mushrooms, sliced
2 oz fresh kale
½ tsp salt

¼ tsp freshly ground black pepper
½ cup dairy free cream cheese
2 oz plant-based Parmesan, grated

Pierogi

1 tbsp flax seed powder
½ cup almond flour
4 tbsp coconut flour

½ tsp salt
1 tsp baking powder
1½ cups grated plant-based Parmesan

5 tbsp plant butter
Olive oil for brushing

Directions and Total Time: 45 minutes

Put the plant butter in a skillet and melt over medium heat, then add and sauté the garlic, red onion, mushrooms, and kale until the mushrooms brown. Season the mixture with salt and black pepper and reduce the heat to low. Stir in the cream cheese and plant-based Parmesan cheese and simmer for 1 minute. Turn the heat off and set the filling aside to cool.

Make the pierogis: In a small bowl, mix the flax seed powder with 3 tbsp water and allow sitting for 5 minutes. In a bowl, combine almond flour, coconut flour, salt, and baking powder. Put a small pan over low heat, add, and melt the plant-based Parmesan cheese and plant butter while stirring continuously until smooth batter forms. Turn the heat off.

Pour the flax egg into the cream mixture, continue stirring, while adding the flour mixture until a firm dough forms. Mold the dough into four balls, place on a chopping board, and use a rolling pin to flatten each into ½ inch thin round pieces. Spread a generous amount of stuffing on one-half of each dough, then fold over the filling, and seal the dough with your fingers. Brush with olive oil, place on a baking sheet, and bake for 20 minutes at 380 F. Serve the pierogis with salad.

Cashew Buttered Quesadillas with Leafy Greens

Ingredients for 4 servings

3 tbsp flax seed powder
½ cup cashew cream cheese
1½ tsp psyllium husk powder

1 tbsp coconut flour
½ tsp salt
1 tbsp cashew butter

5 oz grated plant-based cheddar
1 oz leafy greens

Directions and Total Time: 30 minutes

Preheat oven to 400 F.

In a bowl, mix the flax seed powder with ½ cup water and allow sitting to thicken for 5 minutes. Whisk cashew cream cheese into the flax egg until the batter is smooth. In another bowl, combine psyllium husk powder, coconut flour, and salt. Add the flour mixture to the flax egg batter and fold in until fully incorporated. Allow sitting for a few minutes. Line a baking sheet with parchment paper and pour in the mixture. Spread into the baking sheet and bake for 5-7 minutes. Slice into 8 pieces. Set aside.

For the filling, spoon a little cashew butter into a skillet and place a tortilla in the pan. Sprinkle with some plant-based cheddar cheese, leafy greens, and cover with another tortilla. Brown each side of the quesadilla for 1 minute or until the cheese melts. Transfer to a plate. Repeat assembling the quesadillas using the remaining cashew butter. Serve immediately with avocado salad.

Grilled Zucchini with Spinach Avocado Pesto

Ingredients for 4 servings

3 oz spinach, chopped
1 ripe avocado, chopped
Juice of 1 lemon
1 garlic clove, minced

2 oz pecans
Salt and black pepper to taste
¾ cup olive oil
2 zucchini, sliced

1 tbsp fresh lemon juice
2 tbsp melted plant butter
1 ½ lb tempeh slices

Directions and Total Time: 20 minutes

Place the spinach in a food processor along with the avocado, lemon juice, garlic, and pecans. Blend until smooth and then, season with salt and black pepper. Add the olive oil and process a little more. After, pour the pesto into a bowl and set aside.

Place zucchini in a bowl. Season with the remaining lemon juice, salt, black pepper, and the plant butter. Also, season the tempeh with salt and black pepper, and brush with olive oil. Preheat a grill pan and cook both the tempeh and zucchini slices until browned on both sides. Plate the tempeh and zucchini, spoon some pesto to the side, and serve immediately.

Baked Cheesy Spaghetti Squash

Ingredients for 4 servings

2 lb spaghetti squash
1 tbsp coconut oil
Salt and black pepper to taste
2 tbsp melted plant butter

½ tbsp garlic powder
1/5 tsp chili powder
1 cup coconut cream
2 oz cashew cream cheese

1 cup plant-based mozzarella
2 oz grated plant-based Parmesan
2 tbsp fresh cilantro, chopped
Olive oil for drizzling

Directions and Total Time: 40 minutes

Preheat oven to 350 F.

Cut the squash in halves lengthwise and spoon out the seeds and fiber. Place on a baking dish, brush with coconut oil, and season with salt and pepper. Bake for 30 minutes. Remove and use two forks to shred the flesh into strands. Empty the spaghetti strands into a bowl and mix with plant butter, garlic powder, chili powder, coconut cream, cream cheese, half of the plant-based mozzarella, and plant-based Parmesan. Spoon the mixture into the squash cups and sprinkle with the remaining mozzarella cheese. Bake further for 5 minutes. Sprinkle with cilantro and drizzle with some olive oil. Serve warm.

Baked Tofu with Roasted Pepper

Ingredients for 4 servings

3 oz cashew cream cheese
¾ cup tofu mayonnaise
2 oz cucumber, diced

1 large tomato, chopped
2 tsp dried parsley
4 medium orange bell peppers

2 ½ cups cubed tofu
1 tbsp melted plant butter
1 tsp dried basil

Directions and Total Time: 20 minutes

Preheat oven's broiler to 450 F and line a baking sheet with parchment paper. In a salad bowl, combine cashew cream cheese, tofu mayonnaise, cucumber, tomato, salt, pepper, and parsley. Refrigerate.

Arrange the bell peppers and tofu on the baking sheet, drizzle with melted plant butter, and season with basil, salt, and pepper. Bake for 10-15 minutes or until the peppers have charred lightly and the tofu browned. Remove from the oven and serve with the salad.

Zoodle Bolognese

Ingredients for 4 servings

3 oz olive oil
1 white onion, chopped
1 garlic clove, minced
3 oz carrots, chopped

3 cups crumbled tofu
2 tbsp tomato paste
1 ½ cups crushed tomatoes
Salt and black pepper to taste

1 tbsp dried basil
1 tbsp vegan Worcestershire sauce
2 lb zucchini, spiralized
2 tbsp plant butter

Directions and Total Time: 45 minutes

Pour olive oil into a saucepan and heat over medium heat. Add in onion, garlic, and carrots and sauté for 3 minutes or until the onions are soft and the carrots caramelized. Pour in tofu, tomato paste, tomatoes, salt, pepper, basil, and Worcestershire sauce. Stir and cook for 15 minutes. Mix in some water if the mixture is too thick and simmer further for 20 minutes. Melt plant butter in a skillet and toss in the zoodles quickly, about 1 minute. Season with salt and black pepper. Divide into serving plates and spoon the Bolognese on top. Serve immediately.

Tofu Skewers with Salsa Verde & Squash Mash

Ingredients for 4 servings

7 tbsp fresh cilantro, finely chopped
4 tbsp fresh basil, finely chopped
2 garlic cloves
Juice of ½ a lemon

4 tbsp capers
2/3 cup olive oil
1 lb extra firm tofu, cubed
½ tbsp sugar-free BBQ sauce

1 tbsp melted plant butter
3 cups butternut squash, cubed
½ cup cold plant butter
2 oz grated plant-based Parmesan

Directions and Total Time: 20 minutes

In a blender, add cilantro, basil, garlic, lemon juice, capers, olive oil, salt, and pepper. Process until smooth; set aside. Thread the tofu cubes on wooden skewers. Season with salt and brush with BBQ sauce. Melt plant butter in a grill pan and fry the tofu until browned. Remove to a plate. Pour the squash into a pot, add some lightly salted water, and bring the vegetable to a boil until soft, about 6 minutes. Drain and pour into a bowl. Add the cold plant butter, plant-based Parmesan cheese, salt, and black pepper. Mash the vegetable with an immersion blender until the consistency of mashed potatoes is achieved. Serve the tofu skewers with the mashed cauliflower, and salsa verde.

Zucchini Boats with Vegan Cheese

Ingredients for 2 servings

1 medium-sized zucchini
4 tbsp plant butter
2 garlic cloves, minced

1 ½ oz baby kale
Salt and black pepper to taste
2 tbsp unsweetened tomato sauce

1 cup grated plant-based mozzarella
Olive oil for drizzling

Directions and Total Time: 40 minutes

Preheat oven to 375 F.

Use a knife to slice the zucchini in halves and scoop out the pulp with a spoon into a plate. Keep the flesh. Grease a baking sheet with cooking spray and place the zucchini boats on top. Put the plant butter in a skillet and melt over medium heat. Sauté the garlic for 1 minute. Add in kale and zucchini pulp. Cook until the kale wilts; season with salt and black pepper. Spoon tomato sauce into the boats and spread to coat the bottom evenly. Then, spoon the kale mixture into the zucchinis and sprinkle with the plant-based mozzarella cheese. Bake for 20-25 minutes. Serve immediately.

Asparagus with Creamy Puree

Ingredients for 4 servings

4 tbsp flax seed powder
2 oz plant butter, melted
3 oz cashew cream cheese
½ cup coconut cream
Powdered chili pepper to taste
1 tbsp olive oil
½ lb asparagus, hard stalks removed
3 oz plant butter
Juice of ½ a lemon

Directions and Total Time: 15 minutes

In a safe microwave bowl, mix the flax seed powder with ½ cup water and set aside to thicken for 5 minutes. Warm the flax egg in the microwave for 1-2 minutes, then, pour into a blender. Add in plant butter, cashew cream cheese, coconut cream, salt, and chili pepper. Puree until smooth.

Heat olive oil in a saucepan and roast the asparagus until lightly charred. Season with salt and black pepper and set aside. Melt plant butter in a frying pan until nutty and golden brown. Stir in lemon juice and pour the mixture into a sauce cup. Spoon the creamy blend into the center of four serving plates and use the back of the spoon to spread out lightly. Top with the asparagus and drizzle the lemon butter on top. Serve immediately.

Roasted Butternut Squash with Chimichurri

Ingredients for 4 servings

Zest and juice of 1 lemon
½ medium red bell pepper, chopped
1 jalapeno pepper, chopped
1 cup olive oil
½ cup chopped fresh parsley
2 garlic cloves, minced
1 lb butternut squash
1 tbsp plant butter, melted
3 tbsp toasted pine nuts

Directions and Total Time: 15 minutes

In a bowl, add the lemon zest and juice, red bell pepper, jalapeno, olive oil, parsley, garlic, salt, and black pepper. Use an immersion blender to grind the ingredients until your desired consistency is achieved; set aside the chimichurri.

Slice the butternut squash into rounds and remove the seeds. Drizzle with the plant butter and season with salt and black pepper. Preheat a grill pan over medium heat and cook the squash for 2 minutes on each side or until browned. Remove the squash to serving plates, scatter the pine nuts on top, and serve with the chimichurri and red cabbage salad.

Sweet and Spicy Brussel Sprout Stir-Fry

Ingredients for 4 servings

4 oz plant butter + more to taste
4 shallots, chopped
1 tbsp apple cider vinegar
Salt and black pepper to taste
1 lb Brussels sprouts
Hot chili sauce

Directions and Total Time: 15 minutes

Put the plant butter in a saucepan and melt over medium heat. Pour in the shallots and sauté for 2 minutes, to caramelize and slightly soften.

Add the apple cider vinegar, salt, and black pepper. Stir and reduce the heat to cook the shallots further with continuous stirring, about 5 minutes. Transfer to a plate after.

Trim the Brussel sprouts and cut in halves. Leave the small ones as wholes. Pour the Brussel sprouts into the saucepan and stir-fry with more plant butter until softened but al dente. Season with salt and black pepper, stir in the onions and hot chili sauce, and heat for a few seconds. Serve immediately.

Spicy Cheese with Tofu Balls

Ingredients for 4 servings

1/3 cup tofu mayonnaise	1 tbsp mustard powder	1 tbsp flax seed powder
¼ cup pickled jalapenos	1 pinch cayenne pepper	2 ½ cup crumbled tofu
1 tsp paprika powder	4 oz grated plant-based cheddar	2 tbsp plant butter

Directions and Total Time: 40 minutes

In a bowl, mix tofu mayonnaise, jalapenos, paprika, mustard powder, cayenne powder, and plant-based cheddar cheese; set aside. In another bowl, combine flax seed powder with 3 tbsp water and allow absorbing for 5 minutes. Add the flax egg to the cheese mixture, crumbled tofu, salt, and pepper and combine well. Form large meatballs out of the mix. Melt plant butter in a skillet and fry the tofu balls until cooked and browned. Serve the tofu balls with roasted cauliflower mash and tofu mayonnaise.

Seitan Cakes with Broccoli Mash

Ingredients for 4 servings

1 tbsp flax seed powder	2 oz olive oil	2 oz grated plant-based Parmesan
1½ lb crumbled seitan	1 lb broccoli	4 oz plant butter, room temperature
½ white onion	5 oz cold plant butter	2 tbsp lemon juice

Directions and Total Time: 30 minutes

Preheat oven to 220 F. In a bowl, mix the flax seed powder with 3 tbsp water and allow sitting to thicken for 5 minutes. When the flax egg is ready, add in crumbled seitan, white onion, salt, and pepper. Mix and mold out 6-8 cakes out of the mixture. Melt plant butter in a skillet and fry the patties on both sides until golden brown. Remove onto a wire rack to cool slightly.

Pour salted water into a pot, bring to a boil, and add in broccoli. Cook until the broccoli is tender but not too soft. Drain and transfer to a bowl. Add in cold plant butter, plant-based Parmesan, salt, and pepper. Puree the ingredients until smooth and creamy. Set aside. Mix the soft plant butter with lemon juice, salt, and pepper in a bowl. Serve the seitan cakes with the broccoli mash and lemon butter.

White Pizza with Mixed Mushrooms

Ingredients for 4 servings

2 tbsp flax egg	1 tsp baking powder	Salt and black pepper to taste
½ cup tofu mayonnaise	2 oz mixed mushrooms, sliced	½ cup coconut cream
¾ cup almond flour	1 tbsp plant-based basil pesto	¾ cup grated plant-based Parmesan
1 tbsp psyllium husk powder	2 tbsp olive oil	

Directions and Total Time: 35 minutes

Preheat oven to 350 F.

Combine flax seed powder with 6 tbsp water and allow sitting to thicken for 5 minutes. Whisk in tofu mayonnaise, almond flour, psyllium husk powder, baking powder, and salt. Allow sitting for 5 minutes. Pour the batter into a baking sheet and spread out with a spatula. Bake for 10 minutes.

In a bowl, mix mushrooms with the pesto, olive oil, salt, and black pepper. Remove the crust from the oven and spread the coconut cream on top. Add the mushroom mixture and plant-based Parmesan cheese. Bake the pizza further until the cheese has melted, 5-10 minutes. Slice and serve with salad.

Eggplant Fries with Chili Aioli & Beet Salad

Ingredients for 4 servings

Eggplant Fries

2 tbsp flax seed powder
2 eggplants, sliced

2 cups almond flour
Salt and black pepper to taste

2 tbsp olive oil

Beet salad

3½ oz beets, peeled and thinly cut
3½ oz red cabbage, grated

2 tbsp fresh cilantro
2 tbsp olive oil

1 tbsp freshly squeezed lime juice
Salt and black pepper to taste

Spicy Aioli

1 tbsp flax seed powder
2 garlic cloves, minced

¾ cup light olive oil
½ tsp red chili flakes

1 tbsp freshly squeezed lemon juice
3 tbsp dairy-free yogurt

Directions and Total Time: 35 minutes

Preheat oven to 400 F. In a bowl, combine the flax seed powder with 6 tbsp water and allow sitting to thicken for 5 minutes. In a deep plate, mix almond flour, salt, and black pepper. Dip the eggplant slices into the flax egg, then in the almond flour, and then in the flax egg, and finally in the flour mixture. Place the eggplants on a greased baking sheet and drizzle with olive oil. Bake until the fries are crispy and brown, about 15 minutes.

For the aioli, mix the flax seed powder with 3 tbsp water in a bowl and set aside to thicken for 5 minutes. Whisk in garlic while pouring in the olive oil gradually. Stir in red chili flakes, salt, black pepper, lemon juice, and dairy-free yogurt. Adjust the taste with salt, garlic or yogurt as desired.

For the beet salad, in a salad bowl, combine the beets, red cabbage, cilantro, olive oil, lime juice, salt, and black pepper. Use two spoons to toss the ingredients until properly combined. Serve the eggplant fries with the chili aioli and beet salad.

Chili Bean & Brown Rice Tortillas

Ingredients for 4 servings

1 cups brown rice
Salt and black pepper to taste
1 tbsp olive oil
1 medium red onion, chopped
1 green bell pepper, diced

2 garlic cloves, minced
1 tbsp chili powder
1 tsp cumin powder
1/8 tsp red chili flakes
1 (15 oz) can black beans, rinsed

4 whole-wheat flour tortillas, warmed
1 cup salsa
1 cup coconut cream for topping
1 cup grated plant-based cheddar

Directions and Total Time: 50 minutes

Add 2 cups of water and brown rice to medium pot, season with some salt, and cook over medium heat until the water absorbs and the rice is tender, 15 to 20 minutes.

Heat the olive oil in a medium skillet over medium heat and sauté the onion, bell pepper, and garlic until the softened and fragrant, 3 minutes.

Mix in the chili powder, cumin powder, red chili flakes, and season with salt and black pepper. Cook for 1 minute or until the food releases fragrance. Stir in the brown rice, black beans, and allow warming through, 3 minutes. Lay the tortillas on a clean, flat surface and divide the rice mixture in the center of each. Top with the salsa, coconut cream, and plant cheddar cheese. Fold the sides and ends of the tortillas over the filling to secure. Serve immediately.

Mushroom & Green Bean Biryani

Ingredients for 4 servings

1 cup brown rice
3 tbsp plant butter
3 medium white onions, chopped
6 garlic cloves, minced
1 tsp ginger puree
1 tbsp turmeric powder + for dusting

¼ tsp cinnamon powder
2 tsp garam masala
½ tsp cardamom powder
½ tsp cayenne powder
½ tsp cumin powder
1 tsp smoked paprika

3 large tomatoes, diced
2 green chilies, minced
1 tbsp tomato puree
1 cup chopped cremini mushrooms
1 cup chopped mustard greens
1 cup plant-based yogurt

Directions and Total Time: 50 minutes

Melt the butter in a large pot and sauté the onions until softened, 3 minutes. Mix in the garlic, ginger, turmeric, cardamom powder, garam masala, cardamom powder, cayenne pepper, cumin powder, paprika, and salt. Stir-fry for 1-2 minutes.

Stir in the tomatoes, green chili, tomato puree, and mushrooms. Once boiling, mix in the rice and cover with water. Cover the pot and cook over medium heat until the liquid absorbs and the rice is tender, 15-20 minutes. Open the lid and fluff in the mustard greens and half of the parsley. Dish the food, top with the coconut yogurt, garnish with the remaining parsley, and serve warm.

Quinoa & Veggie Burgers

Ingredients for 4 servings

1 cup quick-cooking quinoa
1 tbsp olive oil
1 shallot, chopped
2 tbsp chopped fresh celery

1 garlic clove, minced
1 (15 oz) can pinto beans, drained
2 tbsp whole-wheat flour
¼ cup chopped fresh basil

2 tbsp pure maple syrup
4 whole-grain hamburger buns, split
4 small lettuce leaves for topping
½ cup tofu mayonnaise for topping

Directions and Total Time: 35 minutes

Cook the quinoa with 2 cups of water in a medium pot until liquid absorbs, 10 to 15 minutes. Heat the olive oil in a medium skillet over medium heat and sauté the shallot, celery, and garlic until softened and fragrant, 3 minutes.

Transfer the quinoa and shallot mixture to a medium bowl and add the pinto beans, flour, basil, maple syrup, salt, and black pepper. Mash and mold 4 patties out of the mixture and set aside.

Heat a grill pan to medium heat and lightly grease with cooking spray. Cook the patties on both sides until light brown, compacted, and cooked through, 10 minutes. Place the patties between the burger buns and top with the lettuce and tofu mayonnaise. Serve.

Black Bean Burgers with BBQ Sauce

Ingredients for 4 servings

3 (15 oz) cans black beans, drained
2 tbsp whole-wheat flour
2 tbsp quick-cooking oats

¼ cup chopped fresh basil
2 tbsp pure barbecue sauce
1 garlic clove, minced

Salt and black pepper to taste
4 whole-grain hamburger buns, split

For topping:

Red onion slices
Tomato slices

Fresh basil leaves
Additional barbecue sauce

Directions and Total Time: 20 minutes

In a medium bowl, mash the black beans and mix in the flour, oats, basil, barbecue sauce, garlic salt, and black pepper until well combined. Mold 4 patties out of the mixture and set aside.

Heat a grill pan to medium heat and lightly grease with cooking spray. Cook the bean patties on both sides until light brown and cooked through, 10 minutes. Place the patties between the burger buns and top with the onions, tomatoes, basil, and some barbecue sauce. Serve warm.

Kale Mushroom Galette

Ingredients for 4 servings

1 tbsp flax seed powder
½ cup grated plant-based mozzarella
1 tbsp plant butter
½ cup almond flour
¼ cup coconut flour
½ tsp onion powder
1 tsp baking powder
3 oz cashew cream cheese, softened
1 garlic clove, finely minced
Salt and black pepper to taste
1 cup kale, chopped
2 oz cremini mushrooms, sliced
2 oz grated plant-based mozzarella
1 oz grated plant-based Parmesan
Olive oil for brushing

Directions and Total Time: 35 minutes

Preheat oven to 375 F, line a baking sheet with parchment paper, and grease with cooking spray.

In a bowl, mix flax seed powder with 3 tbsp water and allow sitting to thicken for 5 minutes. Place a pot over low heat, add in plant-based mozzarella and plant butter, and melt both whiles stirring continuously. Turn the heat off. Stir in almond and coconut flours, onion powder, baking powder, and ¼ tsp of salt. Pour in the flax egg and combine until a quite sticky dough forms. Transfer dough to the baking sheet, cover with another parchment paper and use a rolling pin to flatten into a 12-inch circle.

After, remove the parchment paper and spread the cashew cream cheese on the dough leaving about 2-inch border around the edges. Sprinkle with garlic, salt, and black pepper. Spread kale on top of the cheese, followed by the mushrooms. Sprinkle the plant-based mozzarella and plant-based Parmesan cheese on top. Fold the ends of the crust over the filling and brush with olive oil. Bake until the cheese has melted and the crust golden brown, about 25-30 minutes. Slice and serve with arugula salad.

Jalapeño Quinoa Bowl with Lima Beans

Ingredients for 4 servings

1 tbsp olive oil
1 lb extra firm tofu, cubed
Salt and black pepper to taste
1 medium yellow onion, finely diced
½ cup cauliflower florets
1 jalapeño pepper, minced
2 garlic cloves, minced
1 tbsp red chili powder
1 tsp cumin powder
1 (8 oz) can sweet corn kernels
1 (8 oz) can lima beans, rinsed
1 cup quick-cooking quinoa
1 (14 oz) can diced tomatoes
2 ½ cups vegetable broth
1 cup grated plant-based cheddar
2 tbsp chopped fresh cilantro
2 limes, cut into wedges
1 avocado, pitted, sliced and peeled

Directions and Total Time: 30 minutes

Heat olive oil in a pot and cook the tofu until golden brown, 5 minutes. Season with salt, pepper, and mix in onion, cauliflower, and jalapeño pepper. Cook until the vegetables soften, 3 minutes. Stir in garlic, chili powder, and cumin powder; cook for 1 minute. Mix in sweet corn kernels, lima beans, quinoa, tomatoes, and vegetable broth. Simmer until the quinoa absorbs all the liquid, 10 minutes. Fluff quinoa. Top with the plant-based cheddar cheese, cilantro, lime wedges, and avocado. Serve.

Seitan Cauliflower Gratin

Ingredients for 4 servings

2 oz plant butter
1 leek, coarsely chopped
1 white onion, coarsely chopped
2 cups broccoli florets
1 cup cauliflower florets
2 cups crumbled seitan
1 cup coconut cream
2 tbsp mustard powder
5 oz grated plant-based Parmesan
4 tbsp fresh rosemary
Salt and black pepper to taste

Directions and Total Time: 40 minutes

Preheat oven to 450 F.

Melt half of the plant butter in a pot over medium heat. Add in leek, white onion, broccoli, and cauliflower and cook for about 6 minutes. Transfer the vegetables to a baking dish.

Melt the remaining butter in a skillet over medium heat, and cook the seitan until browned. Mix the coconut cream and mustard powder in a bowl. Then, pour the mixture over the vegetables. Scatter the seitan and plant-based Parmesan cheese on top and sprinkle with the rosemary, salt, and pepper. Bake for 15 minutes. Remove to cool for a few minutes and dish into serving plates.

Tempeh Coconut Curry Bake

Ingredients for 4 servings

1 oz plant butter, for greasing
2 ½ cups chopped tempeh
Salt and black pepper to taste
4 tbsp plant butter
2 tbsp red curry paste
1 ½ cups coconut cream
½ cup fresh parsley, chopped
15 oz cauliflower, cut into florets

Directions and Total Time: 30 minutes

Preheat oven to 400 F and grease a baking dish with 1 ounce of plant butter.

Arrange the tempeh in the baking dish, sprinkle with salt and black pepper, and top each tempeh with a slice of the remaining plant butter. In a bowl, mix the red curry paste with the coconut cream and parsley. Pour the mixture over the tempeh. Bake in the oven for 20 minutes or until the tempeh is cooked. While baking, season the cauliflower with salt, place in a microwave-safe bowl, and sprinkle with some water. Steam in the microwave for 3 minutes or until the cauliflower is soft and tender within. Remove the curry bake and serve with the caulis.

Caprese Casserole

Ingredients for 4 servings

1 cup plant-based mozzarella, cut into pieces
1 cup cherry tomatoes, halved
2 tbsp basil pesto
1 cup tofu mayonnaise
2 oz plant-based Parmesan
1 cup arugula
4 tbsp olive oil

Directions and Total Time: 25 minutes

Preheat oven to 350 F.

In a baking dish, mix the cherry tomatoes, vegan mozzarella, basil pesto, tofu mayonnaise, half of the plant-based Parmesan cheese, salt, and black pepper. Level the ingredients with a spatula and sprinkle the remaining plant-based Parmesan cheese on top. Bake for 20 minutes or until the top of the casserole is golden brown. Remove and allow cooling for a few minutes. Slice and dish into plates, top with some arugula and drizzle with olive oil.

Tempeh Garam Masala Bake

Ingredients for 4 servings

3 tbsp plant butter
3 cups tempeh slices
2 tbsp garam masala
1 green bell pepper, finely diced
1 ¼ cups coconut cream
1 tbsp fresh cilantro, finely chopped

Directions and Total Time: 30 minutes

Preheat oven to 400 F.

Place a skillet over medium heat, add, and melt the plant butter. Meanwhile, season the tempeh with some salt. Fry the tempeh in the plant butter until browned on both sides, about 4 minutes. Stir half of the garam masala into the tempeh until evenly mixed; turn the heat off.

Transfer the tempeh with the spice into a baking dish.

Then, in a small bowl, mix the green bell pepper, coconut cream, cilantro, and remaining garam masala. Pour the mixture over the tempeh and bake in the oven for 20 minutes or until golden brown on top. Garnish with cilantro and serve with some cauli rice.

Vegan Cordon Bleu Casserole

Ingredients for 4 servings

2 cups grilled tofu
1 cup smoked seitan
1 cup cashew cream cheese
1 tbsp mustard powder
1 tbsp plain vinegar
1 ¼ cup grated plant-based cheddar
Salt and black pepper to taste
½ cup baby spinach
4 tbsp olive oil

Directions and Total Time: 30 minutes

Preheat oven to 400 F. Place the tofu and seitan on a chopping board and chop both into small cubes. Mix the cashew cream cheese, mustard powder, plain vinegar, and plant-based cheddar cheese in a baking dish. After, top with the tofu, seitan, and season with salt and black pepper.

Bake in the oven until the casserole is golden brown on top, about 15 to 20 minutes. Serve with some baby spinach and a generous drizzle of olive oil.

Creamy Brussels Sprouts Bake

Ingredients for 4 servings

3 tbsp plant butter
1 cup tempeh, cut into 1-inch cubes
1 ½ lb halved Brussels sprouts
5 garlic cloves, minced
1 ¼ cups coconut cream
10 oz grated plant-based mozzarella
¼ cup grated plant-based Parmesan
Salt and black pepper to taste

Directions and Total Time: 26 minutes

Preheat oven to 400 F.

Melt the plant butter in a large skillet over medium heat and fry the tempeh cubes until browned on both sides, about 6 minutes. Remove onto a plate and set aside. Pour the Brussels sprouts and garlic into the skillet and sauté until nice color forms and fragrant.

Mix in coconut cream and simmer for 4 minutes. Add tempeh cubes and combine well. Pour the sauté into a baking dish, sprinkle with plant-based mozzarella cheese and plant-based Parmesan cheese. Bake for 10 minutes or until golden brown on top. Serve with tomato salad.

Tomato Artichoke Pizza

Ingredients for 4 servings

2 tbsp flax seed powder
4 ¼ oz grated broccoli
6 ¼ oz grated plant-based Parmesan

2 tbsp tomato sauce
2 oz plant-based mozzarella
2 oz canned artichoke wedges

1 garlic clove, thinly sliced
1 tbsp dried oregano
Green olives for garnish

Directions and Total Time: 40 minutes

Preheat oven to 350 F and line a baking sheet with parchment paper. In a bowl, mix flax seed powder and 6 tbsp water and allow thickening for 5 minutes. When the flax egg is ready, add broccoli, 4 ½ ounces of plant-based Parmesan cheese, salt, and stir to combine. Pour the mixture into the baking sheet and spread out with a spatula. Bake until the crust is lightly browned, about 20 minutes. Remove from the oven and spread the tomato sauce on top, sprinkle with the remaining plant-based Parmesan cheese, plant-based mozzarella, add the artichokes, and the slices of garlic. Spread the oregano on top. Bake the pizza further for 5-10 minutes at 420 F. Slice the pizza, garnish with the olives, and serve.

Basil Pesto Seitan Panini

Ingredients for 4 servings

For the seitan:

2/3 cup basil pesto
½ lemon, juiced

1 garlic clove, minced
1/8 tsp salt

1 cup chopped seitan

For the panini:

3 tbsp basil pesto
8 thick slices whole-wheat ciabatta

Olive oil for brushing
8 slices plant-based mozzarella

1 yellow bell pepper, chopped
¼ cup grated plant Parmesan cheese

Directions and Total Time: 15 minutes+ cooling time

In a medium bowl, mix the pesto, lemon juice, garlic, and salt. Add the seitan and coat well with the marinade. Cover with a plastic wrap and marinate in the refrigerator for 30 minutes.

Preheat a large skillet over medium heat and remove the seitan from the fridge. Cook the seitan in the skillet until brown and cooked through, 2-3 minutes. Turn the heat off.

Preheat a panini press to medium heat. In a small bowl, mix the pesto in the inner parts of two slices of bread. On the outer parts, apply some olive oil and place a slice with (the olive oil side down) in the press. Lay 2 slices of plant-based mozzarella cheese on the bread, spoon some seitan on top. Sprinkle with some bell pepper, and some plant-based Parmesan cheese. Cover with another bread slice.

Close the press and grill the bread for 1 to 2 minutes. Flip the bread, and grill further for 1 minute or until the cheese melts and golden brown on both sides. Serve warm.

American-Style Tempeh Bake with Garden Peas

Ingredients for 4 servings

16 oz whole-wheat bow-tie pasta
2 tbsp olive oil, divided
2/3 lb tempeh, cut into 1-inch cubes
Salt and black pepper to taste
1 medium yellow onion, chopped

½ cup sliced white mushrooms
2 tbsp whole-wheat flour
¼ cup white wine
¾ cup vegetable stock
¼ cup oats milk

2 tsp chopped fresh thyme
¼ cup chopped cauliflower
½ cup grated plant-based Parmesan
3 tbsp whole-wheat breadcrumbs

Directions and Total Time: 50 minutes

Cook the pasta in 8 cups of slightly salted water for 10 minutes or until al dente. Drain and set aside. Preheat the oven to 375 F. Heat the 1 tbsp of olive oil in a skillet, season the tempeh with salt and pepper, and cook until golden brown all around. Mix in onion, mushrooms, and cook for 5 minutes. Stir in flour and cook for 1 more minute. Mix in wine and add two-thirds of the vegetable stock. Cook for 2 minutes while occasionally stirring and then add milk; continue cooking until the sauce thickens, 4 minutes. Season with thyme, salt, black pepper, and half of the Parmesan cheese. Once the cheese melts, turn the heat off and allow cooling.

Add the rest of the vegetable stock and cauliflower to a food processor and blend until smooth. Pour the mixture into a bowl, pour in sauce, and mix in pasta until combined. Grease a baking dish with cooking spray and spread in the mixture. Drizzle the remaining olive oil on top, breadcrumbs, some more thyme, and the remaining cheese. Bake until the cheese melts and is golden brown on top, 30 minutes. Remove the dish from the oven, allow cooling for 3 minutes, and serve.

Savoy Cabbage Rolls with Tofu & Buckwheat

Ingredients for 4 servings

2 tbsp plant butter
2 cups extra firm tofu, crumbled
½ medium sweet onion, chopped
2 garlic cloves, minced

Salt and black pepper to taste
1 cup buckwheat groats
1 ¾ cups vegetable stock
1 bay leaf

2 tbsp chopped cilantro
1 head Savoy cabbage, leaves separated (scraps kept)
1 (23 oz) canned chopped tomatoes

Directions and Total Time: 30 minutes

Melt the plant butter in a large bowl and cook the tofu until golden brown, 8 minutes. Stir in the onion and garlic until softened and fragrant, 3 minutes. Season with salt, black pepper and mix in the buckwheat, bay leaf, and vegetable stock. Close the lid, allow boiling, and then simmer until all the liquid is absorbed. Open the lid, remove the bay leaf, and adjust the taste with salt and pepper.

Lay the cabbage leaves on a flat surface and add 3 to 4 tablespoons of the cooked buckwheat onto each leaf. Roll the leaves to firmly secure the filling.

Pour the tomatoes with juices into a medium pot, season with a little salt, black pepper, and lay the cabbage rolls in the sauce. Cook over medium heat until the cabbage softens, 5 to 8 minutes. Turn the heat off and dish the food onto serving plates. Garnish with more cilantro and serve warm.

Green Beans & Grilled Tempeh

Ingredients for 4 servings

1 tbsp plant butter, melted
1 lb tempeh, sliced into 4 pieces
1 lb green beans, trimmed

Salt and black pepper to taste
2 sprigs thyme
2 tbsp olive oil

1 tbsp pure corn syrup
1 lemon, juiced

Directions and Total Time: 15 minutes

Preheat a grill pan over medium heat and brush with the plant butter.

Season the tempeh and green beans with the salt, black pepper, and place the thyme in the pan. Grill the tempeh and green beans on both sides until golden brown and tender, 10 minutes. Transfer to serving plates. In a small bowl, whisk the olive oil, corn syrup, lemon juice, and drizzle all over the food. Serve warm.

Zesty Rice Bowls with Tempeh

Ingredients for 4 servings

2 tbsp olive oil
1 ½ cups crumbled tempeh
1 tsp Creole seasoning
2 red bell peppers, sliced

1 cup brown rice
2 cups vegetable broth
Salt to taste
1 lemon, zested and juiced

1 (8 oz) can black beans, drained
2 chives, chopped
2 tbsp freshly chopped parsley

Directions and Total Time: 50 minutes

Heat the olive oil in a medium pot and cook in the tempeh until golden brown, 5 minutes. Season with the Creole seasoning and stir in the bell peppers. Cook until the peppers slightly soften, 3 minutes. Stir in the brown rice, vegetable broth, salt, and lemon zest. Cover and cook until the rice is tender and all the liquid is absorbed, 15 to 25 minutes. Mix in the lemon juice, beans, and chives. Allow warming for 3 to 5 minutes and dish the food. Garnish with the parsley and serve warm.

Pea & Basil Fettuccine

Ingredients for 4 servings

16 oz whole-wheat fettuccine
Salt and black pepper to taste
¾ cup flax milk

½ cup cashew butter, softened
1 tbsp olive oil
2 garlic cloves, minced

1 ½ cups frozen peas
½ cup chopped fresh basil

Directions and Total Time: 25 minutes

Add the fettuccine and 10 cups of water to a large pot, and cook over medium heat until al dente, 10 minutes. Drain the pasta through a colander and set aside. In a bowl, whisk the flax milk, cashew butter, and salt until smooth. Set aside.

Heat the olive oil in a large skillet and sauté the garlic until fragrant, 30 seconds. Mix in the peas, fettuccine, and basil. Toss well until the pasta is well-coated in the sauce and season with some black pepper. Dish the food and serve warm.

Tofu Loaf with Nuts

Ingredients for 4 servings

2 tbsp olive oil + extra for brushing
2 white onions, finely chopped
4 garlic cloves, minced
1 lb firm tofu, pressed and crumbled
2 tbsp soy sauce

¾ cup chopped mixed nuts
¼ cup flaxseed meal
1 tbsp sesame seeds
1 cup chopped mixed bell peppers
Salt and black pepper to taste

1 tbsp Italian seasoning
½ tsp pure date syrup
½ cup tomato sauce

Directions and Total Time: 65 minutes

Preheat the oven to 350 F and grease a loaf pan with olive oil.

Heat 1 tbsp of olive oil in a small skillet and sauté the onion and garlic until softened and fragrant, 2 minutes. Pour the onion mixture into a large bowl and mix with the tofu, soy sauce, nuts, flaxseed meal, sesame seeds, bell peppers, salt, black pepper, Italian seasoning, and date syrup until well combined. Spoon the mixture into the loaf pan, press to fit and spread the tomato sauce on top. Bake the tofu loaf in the oven for 45 minutes to 1 hour or until well compacted. Remove the loaf pan from the oven, invert the tofu loaf onto a chopping board, and cool for 5 minutes. Slice and serve warm.

Mexican-Style Soy Chorizo & Rice Bowls

Ingredients for 4 servings

2 tbsp olive oil
2 cups chopped soy chorizo
1 tsp taco seasoning
2 green bell peppers, sliced

1 cup brown rice
2 cups vegetable broth
¼ cup salsa
1 lemon, zested and juiced

1 (8 oz) can pinto beans, drained
1 (7 oz) can sweet corn kernels
2 green onions, chopped
2 tbsp freshly chopped parsley

Directions and Total Time: 50 minutes

Heat the olive oil in a medium pot and cook the soy chorizo until golden brown, 5 minutes. Season with the taco seasoning and stir in the bell peppers; cook until the peppers slightly soften, 3 minutes. Stir in the brown rice, vegetable broth, salt, salsa, and lemon zest.

Close the lid and cook the food until the rice is tender and all the liquid is absorbed, 15 to 25 minutes. Mix in the lemon juice, pinto beans, corn kernels, and green onions. Allow warming for 3-5 minutes and dish the food. Garnish with the parsley and serve.

Pesto Mushroom Pizza

Ingredients for 4 servings

2 tbsp flax seed powder
½ cup tofu mayonnaise
¾ cup whole-wheat flour

1 tsp baking powder
1 cup sliced mixed mushrooms
2 tbsp olive oil

1 tbsp basil pesto
½ cup red pizza sauce
¾ cup grated plant-based Parmesan

Directions and Total Time: 40 minutes

Preheat the oven to 350 F.

In a medium bowl, mix the flax seed powder with 6 tbsp water and allow thickening for 5 minutes to make the flax egg. Mix in the tofu mayonnaise, whole-wheat flour, baking powder, and salt until dough forms. Spread the dough on a pizza pan and bake in the oven for 10 minutes or until the dough sets.

In a medium bowl, mix the mushrooms, olive oil, basil pesto, salt, and black pepper. Remove the pizza crust spread the pizza sauce on top. Scatter mushroom mixture on the crust and top with plant-based Parmesan cheese. Bake further until the cheese melts and the mushrooms soften, 10 to 15 minutes. Remove the pizza, slice and serve.

Scallion Sweet Potatoes with Chili Corn Salad

Ingredients for 4 servings

3 tbsp olive oil
4 sweet potatoes, cubed
2 limes, juiced

¼ tsp cayenne pepper
2 scallions, thinly sliced
1 (15 oz) can sweet corn kernels

½ tbsp plant butter, melted
1 large green chili, minced
1 tsp cumin powder

Directions and Total Time: 35 minutes

Preheat the oven to 400 F and lightly grease a baking sheet with cooking spray.

In a medium bowl, add the sweet potatoes, lime juice, salt, black pepper, and cayenne pepper. Toss well and spread the mixture on the baking sheet. Bake until the potatoes soften, 20-25 minutes. Transfer to a serving plate and garnish with scallions. In a bowl, mix corn kernels, butter, green chili, and cumin powder. Serve the sweet potatoes with the corn salad.

Plant-Based Cheddar Broccoli Gratin

Ingredients for 4 servings

1 tbsp olive oil
2 cups broccoli florets
1 (10 oz) can cream mushroom soup

1 cup tofu mayonnaise
3 tbsp coconut cream
1 medium red onion, chopped

2 cups grated plant-based cheddar
¾ cup whole-wheat bread crumbs
3 tbsp plant butter, melted

Directions and Total Time: 50 minutes

Preheat the oven to 350 F.

Heat the olive oil in a medium skillet and sauté the broccoli florets until softened, 8 minutes. Turn the heat off and mix in the mushroom soup, mayonnaise, salt, black pepper, coconut cream, and onion. Spread the mixture into the baking sheet. In a small bowl, mix the breadcrumbs with the plant butter and evenly distribute the mixture on top. Add the cheddar cheese and bake the casserole in the oven until golden on top and the cheese melts. Remove the casserole from the oven, allow cooling for 5 minutes, dish, and serve warm.

Oat & Chickpea Burgers with Avocado Dip

Ingredients for 4 servings

1 large avocado, pitted and peeled
1 tomato, chopped
1 small red onion, chopped
3 (15 oz) cans chickpeas, drained

2 tbsp almond flour
2 tbsp quick-cooking oats
¼ cup chopped fresh parsley
1 tbsp hot sauce

1 garlic clove, minced
¼ tsp garlic salt
1/8 tsp black pepper
4 whole-grain hamburger buns, split

Directions and Total Time: 20 minutes

In a medium bowl, mash avocados and mix in the tomato and onion. Set aside the dip.

In a another bowl, mash the chickpeas and mix in the almond flour, oats, parsley, hot sauce, garlic, garlic salt, and black pepper. Mold 4 patties out of the mixture and set aside.

Heat a grill pan to medium heat and lightly grease with cooking spray. Cook the bean patties on both sides until light brown and cooked through, 10 minutes. Place each patty between each burger bun and top with the avocado dip.

Chickpea & Bean Patties

Ingredients for 4 servings

1 (15 oz) can chickpea, drained
1 (15 oz) can pinto beans, drained
1 (15 oz) can red kidney beans
2 tbsp whole-wheat flour

¼ cup dried mixed herbs
¼ tsp hot sauce
½ tsp garlic powder
Salt and black pepper to taste

4 slices cashew cheese
4 whole-grain hamburger buns, split
4 small lettuce leaves for topping

Directions and Total Time: 30 minutes

In a medium bowl, mash the chickpea, pinto beans, kidney beans and mix in the flour, mixed herbs, hot sauce, garlic powder, salt, and black pepper. Mold 4 patties out of the mixture and set aside.

Heat a grill pan to medium heat and grease with cooking spray. Cook the bean patties on both sides until light brown and cooked through, 10 minutes. Lay a cashew cheese slice on each and allow slight melting, 2 minutes. Remove the patties between the burger buns and top with the lettuce and serve.

Corn & Bean Quesadillas

Ingredients for 4 servings

1 tsp olive oil
1 small onion, chopped
½ red bell pepper, chopped
1 (7 oz) can chopped tomatoes
1 (7 oz) can black beans, drained
1 (7 oz) can sweet corn kernels
4 whole-wheat tortillas
1 cup grated plant-based cheddar

Directions and Total Time: 35 minutes

Heat olive oil in a skillet and sauté onion and bell pepper for 3 minutes. Mix in tomatoes, black beans, sweet corn, and cook until the tomatoes soften, 10 minutes. Season with salt and black pepper.

Heat another medium skillet over medium heat and lay in one tortilla. Spread a quarter of the tomato mixture on top, scatter a quarter of the plant cheese on the sauce, and cover with another tortilla. Cook until the cheese melts. Flip and cook further for 2 minutes. Transfer to a plate and make one more piece using the remaining ingredients. Cut each tortilla set into quarters and serve immediately.

Hot Seitan with Rice

Ingredients for 4 servings

2 tbsp olive oil
1 lb seitan, cut into cubes
Salt and black pepper to taste
1 tsp chili powder
1 tsp onion powder
1 tsp cumin powder
1 tsp garlic powder
1 yellow onion, chopped
2 celery stalks, chopped
2 carrots diced
4-5 cloves garlic
1 cup vegetable broth
1 tsp oregano
1 cup chopped tomatoes
3 green chilies, chopped
1 lime, juiced
1 cup brown rice

Directions and Total Time: 50 minutes

Add brown rice, 2 cups of water, and salt to a pot. Cook for 15-20 minutes.

Heat the olive oil in a large pot, season the seitan with salt, black pepper, and cook in the oil until brown, 10 minutes. Stir in the chili powder, onion powder, cumin powder, garlic powder, and cook until fragrant, 1 minute. Mix in the onion, celery, carrots, garlic, and cook until softened. Pour in the vegetable broth, 1 cup of water, oregano, tomatoes, and green chilies.

Cover the pot and cook until the tomatoes soften and the liquid reduces by half, 10 to 15 minutes. Open the lid, adjust the taste with salt, black pepper, and mix in the lime juice. Dish and serve warm with the brown rice.

Tomato & Alfredo Fettuccine

Ingredients for 4 servings

2 cups almond milk
1 ½ cups vegetable broth
3 tbsp plant butter
1 large garlic clove, minced
16 oz whole-wheat fettuccine
½ cup coconut cream
¼ cup halved cherry tomatoes
¾ cup grated plant-based Parmesan
Chopped fresh parsley to garnish

Directions and Total Time: 20 minutes

Bring almond milk, vegetable broth, butter, and garlic to a boil in a large pot, 5 minutes. Mix in the fettuccine and cook until tender, while frequently tossing around, 10 minutes. Mix in coconut cream, tomatoes, plant Parmesan cheese, salt, and pepper. Cook for 3 minutes or until the cheese melts. Garnish with some parsley and serve warm.

Vegetable & Hummus Pizza

Ingredients for 4 servings

3 ½ cups whole-wheat flour
1 tsp yeast
1 tsp salt
1 pinch sugar

3 tbsp olive oil
1 cup hummus
10 cremini mushrooms, sliced
½ cup fresh baby spinach

½ cup cherry tomatoes, halved
½ cup sliced Kalamata olives
½ medium onion, sliced
2 tsp dried oregano

Directions and Total Time: 30 minutes

Preheat the oven the 350 F and lightly grease a pizza pan with cooking spray.

In a medium bowl, mix the flour, nutritional yeast, salt, sugar, olive oil, and 1 cup warm water until smooth dough forms. Allow rising for an hour or until the dough doubles in size. Spread the dough on the pizza pan and apply the hummus on the dough. Add the mushrooms, spinach, tomatoes, olives, onion, and top with the oregano. Bake for 20 minutes. Cool for 5 minutes, slice, and serve.

Stuffed Zucchini Rolls with Tempeh & Tofu

Ingredients for 4 servings

3 zucchinis, sliced lengthwise
1 tbsp olive oil
¾ lb crumbled tempeh

1 cup crumbled tofu cheese
1/3 cup grated plant-based Parmesan
¼ cup chopped fresh basil leaves

2 garlic cloves, minced
1 ½ cups marinara sauce, divided
2 cups grated plant-based mozzarella

Directions and Total Time: 60 minutes

Line a baking sheet with paper towels and lay the zucchini slices in a single layer on the sheet. Sprinkle each side with some salt and allow releasing of liquid for 15 minutes.

Heat the olive oil in a skillet and cook tempeh for 10 minutes; set aside. In a bowl, mix tempeh, tofu cheese, plant-based Parmesan cheese, basil, and garlic.

Preheat the oven to 400 F. Spread 1 cup of marinara sauce onto the bottom of a baking pan and set aside. Spread 1 tbsp of the cheese mixture evenly along with each zucchini slices; sprinkle with 1 tbsp of plant mozzarella cheese. Roll up the zucchini slices over the filling and arrange in the baking pan. Top with the remaining marinara sauce and sprinkle with the remaining plant-based mozzarella cheese. Bake for 25-30 minutes or until the cheese begins to brown. Serve immediately.

Basil & Tofu Stuffed Portobello Mushrooms

Ingredients for 4 servings

4 large portobello mushrooms, stems removed
Garlic salt and black pepper to taste

½ tsp olive oil
1 small onion, chopped
1 cup chopped fresh kale

¼ cup crumbled tofu cheese
1 tbsp chopped fresh basil

Directions and Total Time: 25 minutes

Preheat the oven to 350 F and grease a baking sheet with cooking spray.

Lightly oil the mushrooms with some cooking spray and season with the black pepper and garlic salt. Arrange the mushrooms on the baking sheet and bake in the oven until tender, 10 to 15 minutes.

Heat olive oil in a skillet and sauté onion until tender, 3 minutes. Stir in kale until wilted, 3 minutes. Spoon the mixture into the mushrooms and top with the tofu cheese and basil. Serve.

Kale Pizza with Grilled Zucchini

Ingredients for 4 servings

¼ cup capers
½ cup grated plant Parmesan cheese
3 ½ cups whole-wheat flour
1 tsp yeast

1 tsp salt
1 pinch sugar
3 tbsp olive oil
1 cup marinara sauce

2 large zucchinis, sliced
½ cup chopped kale
1 tsp oregano

Directions and Total Time: 30 minutes

Preheat the oven the 350 F and lightly grease a pizza pan with cooking spray. In a bowl, mix flour, nutritional yeast, salt, sugar, olive oil, and 1 cup of warm water until smooth dough forms. Allow rising for an hour or until the dough doubles in size. Spread the dough on the pizza pan and apply marinara sauce and oregano on top. Heat a grill pan, season the zucchinis with salt, black pepper, and cook in the pan until slightly charred on both sides. Sit the zucchini on the pizza crust and top with kale, capers, and plant-based Parmesan cheese. Bake for 20 minutes. Cool for 5 minutes, slice, and serve.

Amazing Tofu Burgers

Ingredients for 4 servings

1 tbsp flax seed powder
2/3 lb crumble tofu
1 tbsp quick-cooking oats

1 tbsp toasted almond flour
½ tsp garlic powder
½ tsp onion powder

¼ tsp curry powder
3 tbsp whole-grain breadcrumbs
4 whole-wheat burger buns, halved

Directions and Total Time: 20 minutes

In a small bowl, mix the flax seed powder with 3 tbsp water and allow thickening for 5 minutes to make the flax egg. Set aside. In a bowl, mix tofu, oats, almond flour, garlic powder, onion powder, salt, pepper, and curry powder. Mold 4 patties out of the mixture and lightly brush both sides with the flax egg. Pour the breadcrumbs onto a plate and coat the patties in the crumbs until well covered.

Heat a pan over medium heat and grease with cooking spray. Cook the patties on both sides for 10 minutes. Place each patty between each burger bun and top with the guacamole. Serve immediately.

Bell Pepper & Tempeh Balls with Asparagus

Ingredients for 4 servings

1 tbsp flax seed powder
1 lb tempeh, crumbled
¼ cup chopped red bell pepper
Salt and black pepper to taste

1 tbsp almond flour
1 tsp garlic powder
1 tsp onion powder
1 tsp tofu mayonnaise

2 tbsp plant butter
1 lb asparagus, hard part trimmed
2 tbsp pure maple syrup
1 tbsp freshly squeezed lemon juice

Directions and Total Time: 40 minutes

Preheat the oven to 400 F and line a baking sheet with parchment paper. In a bowl, mix flax seed powder with 3 tbsp water and allow thickening for 5 minutes. Add in tempeh, bell pepper, salt, pepper, almond flour, garlic powder, onion powder, and tofu mayonnaise. Mix and form 1-inch balls from the mixture. Arrange on the baking sheet, brush with cooking spray and bake for 15-20 minutes; set aside.

Melt butter in a skillet and sauté asparagus until softened with some crunch, 7 minutes. Mix in maple syrup and lemon juice. Cook for 2 minutes and plate the asparagus. Serve warm with the tempeh balls.

Black Olive & Chickpea Lunch

Ingredients for 4 servings

2 tbsp olive oil
2 cups chopped onion
2 garlic cloves, minced
2 carrots, cut into thick slices

1/3 cup white wine
3 cups cherry tomatoes
2/3 cup vegetable stock
1 1/3 cups canned chickpeas

½ cup pitted black olives
1 tbsp chopped fresh oregano
Salt and black pepper to taste

Directions and Total Time: 15 minutes

Heat the olive oil in a medium pot and sauté the onion, garlic, and carrots until softened, 5 minutes. Mix in the white wine, allow reduction by one-third and mix in the tomatoes, and vegetable stock. Cover the lid and cook until the tomatoes break, soften, and the liquid reduces by half. Stir in the chickpeas, olives, oregano and season with salt and pepper. Cook for 3 minutes to warm the chickpeas.

Gingery Pea & Potato Skillet

Ingredients for 4 servings

4 medium potatoes, diced
2 tbsp olive oil
1 medium onion, chopped

1 tsp red chili powder
1 tsp fresh ginger-garlic paste
1 tsp cumin powder

¼ tsp turmeric powder
Salt and black pepper to taste
1 cup fresh green peas

Directions and Total Time: 21 minutes

Steam potatoes in a safe microwave bowl in the microwave for 8-10 minutes or until soften. Heat the olive oil in a wok and sauté the onion until softened, 3 minutes. Mix in the chili powder, ginger-garlic paste, cumin powder, turmeric powder, salt, and black pepper. Cook until the fragrant releases, 1 minute. Stir in the green peas, potatoes, and cook until softened, 2 to 3 minutes. Serve warm.

Broccoli Stuffed Cremini Mushrooms

Ingredients for 4 servings

½ head broccoli, cut into florets
1 lb cremini mushroom caps
2 tbsp olive oil

1 onion, finely chopped
1 tsp garlic, minced
1 bell pepper, chopped

1 tsp Cajun seasoning mix
Salt and black pepper, to taste
¼ cup plant-based mozzarella

Directions and Total Time: 35 minutes

Preheat oven to 360 F. Bake mushroom caps in a greased baking dish for 10-12 minutes. In a food processor place broccoli and pulse until become like small rice-like granules. In a heavy-bottomed skillet, warm olive oil; stir in bell pepper, garlic, and onion and sauté until fragrant. Place in pepper, salt, and Cajun seasoning mix. Fold in broccoli rice. Divide the filling mixture among mushroom caps. Top with plant-based mozzarella cheese and bake for 17 more minutes. Serve warm.

Saucy Seitan with Sesame Seeds

Ingredients for 4 servings

4 tsp olive oil
½ tsp freshly grated ginger
3 garlic cloves, minced
1/3 tsp red chili flakes

1/3 tsp allspice
1/2 cup soy sauce
½ cup + 2 tbsp pure date sugar
2 tsp cornstarch

1 ½ tbsp olive oil
1 lb seitan, cut into 1-inch pieces
1 tbsp toasted sesame seeds
1 tbsp sliced scallions

Directions and Total Time: 20 minutes

Heat half of the olive oil in a wok and sauté ginger and garlic until fragrant, 30 seconds. Mix in red chili flakes, allspice, soy sauce, and date sugar. Allow the sugar to melt and set aside. In a small bowl, mix cornstarch and 2 tbsp of water. Stir the cornstarch mixture into the sauce and allow thickening for 1 minute. Heat the remaining olive oil in a medium skillet over medium heat and fry the seitan on both sides until crispy, 10 minutes, Mix the seitan into the sauce and warm over low heat. Dish the food, garnish with the sesame seeds and scallions. Serve warm.

Tempeh & Vegetable Stir-Fry

Ingredients for 4 servings

- 1 can (28 oz) whole plum tomatoes
- 1 lb crumbled tempeh
- 1 large yellow onion, chopped
- 1 can (8 oz) tomato sauce
- 2 tbsp plain vinegar
- 1 tbsp pure date sugar
- 1 tsp dried mixed herbs
- 1 small head cabbage, thinly sliced
- 1 green bell pepper, cut into strips

Directions and Total Time: 30 minutes

Drain the tomatoes and reserve its liquid. Chop the tomatoes and set aside.

Add the tempeh to a large skillet and cook until brown, 10 minutes. Mix in the onion, tomato sauce, vinegar, date sugar, mixed herbs, and chopped tomatoes. Close the lid and cook until the liquid reduces, 10 minutes. Stir in the cabbage and bell pepper; cook until softened, 5 minutes. Serve.

Watercress & Mushroom Spaghetti

Ingredients for 4 servings

- 1 lb whole-wheat spaghetti
- 3 tbsp plant butter
- 2 tbsp olive oil
- 2 shallots, finely chopped
- 2 garlic cloves, minced
- ½ lb chopped button mushrooms
- 1 tbsp sake
- 3 tbsp soy sauce
- 1 tsp hot sauce
- A handful fresh watercress
- ¼ cup chopped fresh parsley
- Black pepper to taste

Directions and Total Time: 30 minutes

Cook spaghetti in slightly salted water in a large pot over medium heat until al dente, 10 minutes. Drain and set aside. Heat butter and olive oil in a skillet and sauté shallots, garlic, and mushrooms for 5 minutes. Stir in sake, soy sauce, and hot sauce. Cook for 1 minute. Toss spaghetti in the sauce along with watercress and parsley. Season with the black pepper. Dish the food and serve warm.

Pasta Primavera with Cherry Tomatoes

Ingredients for 4 servings

- 2 tbsp olive oil
- 8 oz whole-wheat fidelini pasta
- ½ tsp paprika
- 1 small red onion, sliced
- 2 garlic cloves, minced
- 1 cup dry white wine
- Salt and black pepper to taste
- 2 cups cherry tomatoes, halved
- 3 tbsp plant butter, cubed
- 1 lemon, zested and juiced
- 1 cup packed fresh basil leaves

Directions and Total Time: 25 minutes

Heat olive oil in a pot and mix in fidelini, paprika, onion, garlic, and stir-fry for 2-3 minutes.Mix in white wine, salt, and pepper. Cover with water. Cook until the water absorbs and the fidelini al dente, 5 minutes. Mix in the cherry tomatoes, butter, lemon zest, lemon juice, and basil leaves. Serve warm.

Rice with Green Lentil & Celery

Ingredients for 4 servings

2 tbsp olive oil	1 tsp cumin powder	1 tsp oregano
1 lb tempeh, cut into cubes	2 celery stalks, chopped	1 cup green lentils, rinsed
1 yellow onion, chopped	2 carrots diced	¼ cup chopped tomatoes
Salt and black pepper to taste	4 garlic cloves, minced	1 lime, juiced
1 tsp chili powder	3 cups vegetable broth	1 cup brown rice

Directions and Total Time: 50 minutes

Heat the olive oil in a large pot, season the tempeh with salt, pepper, and cook for 10 minutes. Stir in chili powder, cumin powder, onion, celery, carrots, garlic, and cook for 5 minutes. Pour in vegetable broth, oregano, green lentils, tomatoes, brown rice, and green chilies. Cover the pot and cook for 18-20 minutes. Open the lid, adjust the taste with salt, black pepper, and mix in the lime juice. Serve.

Quinoa a la Puttanesca

Ingredients for 4 servings

1 cup brown quinoa	4 pitted green olives, sliced	1 tbsp olive oil
2 cups water	4 pitted kalamata olives, sliced	1 tbsp chopped fresh parsley
1/8 tsp salt	1 ½ tbsp capers, rinsed and drained	¼ cup chopped fresh basil
4 cups plum tomatoes, chopped	2 garlic cloves, minced	1/8 tsp red chili flakes

Directions and Total Time: 30 minutes

Add quinoa, water, and salt to a medium pot and cook for 15 minutes. In a bowl, mix tomatoes, green olives, olives, capers, garlic, olive oil, parsley, basil, and red chili flakes. Allow sitting for 5 minutes. Serve the puttanesca with the quinoa.

Cherry & Quinoa Tacos

Ingredients for 4 servings

½ cup brown quinoa	1 ¼ cups fresh cherries, halved	2 tbsp soy sauce
2 tsp olive oil	4 scallions, chopped	1 tbsp pure maple syrup
1 ½ cups shredded carrots	2 tbsp plain vinegar	4 (8-inch) tortilla wraps

Directions and Total Time: 25 minutes

Cook the quinoa in 1 cup of slightly salted water in a pot for 15 minutes. Fluff and set aside. Heat olive oil in a skillet and sauté carrots, cherries, and scallions. In a small bowl, mix vinegar, soy sauce, and maple syrup. Stir the mixture into the vegetable mixture. Simmer for 5 minutes. Spread the tortillas on a flat surface, spoon the mixture at the center, fold the sides and ends to wrap in the filling. Serve.

Herby Quinoa with Walnuts

Ingredients for 4 servings

1 cup quinoa, well-rinsed	2 tbsp finely chopped parsley	1 tbsp olive oil
2 cups vegetable broth	2 tbsp finely chopped basil	½ tsp lemon zest
2 garlic cloves, minced, divided	2 tbsp finely chopped mint	1 tbsp fresh lemon juice
¼ cup chopped chives	2 tbsp chopped sundried tomatoes	2 tbsp minced walnuts

Directions and Total Time: 20 minutes

In a pot, combine quinoa, vegetable broth, and garlic. Boil until the quinoa is tender and the liquid absorbs, 10-15 minutes. Fuff with a fork and stir in chives, parsley, basil, mint, tomatoes, olive oil, zest, lemon juice, and walnuts. Warm for 5 minutes. Serve.

Spinach & Chickpea Pizza with Avocado

Ingredients for 4 servings

3 tbsp olive oil
1tsp oregano
3 ½ cups whole-wheat flour
1 tsp yeast

1 tsp salt
1 pinch sugar
1 cup red pizza sauce
1 cup baby spinach

1 (15 oz) can chickpeas, drained
1 avocado, chopped
¼ cup grated plant-based Parmesan

Directions and Total Time: 40 minutes

Preheat the oven the 350 F and lightly grease a pizza pan with cooking spray. In a bowl, mix flour, nutritional yeast, salt, sugar, olive oil, and 1 cup of warm water until smooth dough forms. Allow rising for an hour or until the dough doubles in size. Spread the dough on the pizza pan and apply the pizza sauce on top. Top with oregano, baby spinach, chickpeas, avocado, and plant Parmesan cheese. Bake for 20 minutes or until the cheese melts. Remove from the oven, cool for 5 minutes, slice, and serve.

Acorn Squash Stuffed with Beans & Spinach

Ingredients for 4 servings

2 pounds large acorn squash
2 tbsp olive oil
3 garlic cloves, minced

1 (15 oz) can white beans, drained
1 cup chopped spinach leaves
½ cup vegetable stock

Salt and black pepper to taste
½ tsp cumin powder
½ tsp chili powder

Directions and Total Time: 60 minutes

Preheat the oven to 350 F. Cut the squash into half and scoop out the seeds. Season with salt and pepper and place face down on a sheet pan. Bake for 45 minutes.

Heat olive oil in a pot over medium heat. Sauté garlic until fragrant, 30 seconds and mix in beans and spinach, allow wilting for 2 minutes and season with salt, black pepper, cumin powder, and chili powder. Cook for 2 minutes and turn the heat off. When the squash is fork-tender, remove from the oven and fill the holes with the bean and spinach mixture. Serve.

Cabbage & Bean Stir-Fry

Ingredients for 2 servings

1 cup canned white beans
1 tsp olive oil
2 carrots, julienned
1 cup sliced red cabbage

1 red bell pepper, sliced
2 scallions, chopped
3 tbsp fresh mint, chopped
1 cup bean sprouts

¼ cup peanut sauce
¼ cup fresh cilantro, chopped
2 tbsp roasted peanuts, chopped
Fresh lime wedges

Directions and Total Time: 20 minutes

Heat oil in a skillet and cook carrots, cabbage, and bell pepper for 10-15 minutes. Stir in scallions, mint and bean sprouts, cook for 1-2 minutes. Remove to a bowl. Mix in white beans and peanut sauce; toss to combine. Garnish with cilantro and peanuts. Serve with lime wedges on the side.

Lemony Green Bean Risotto

Ingredients for 4 servings

2 tsp plant butter
2 cloves minced garlic
1 cup brown rice
2 cups vegetable broth
2 cups green beans
2 tbsp parsley, chopped

Directions and Total Time: 25 minutes

Melt the butter in a skillet over medium heat. Place in garlic and cook for 1 minute. Stir in rice, broth, salt, and pepper. Bring to a boil, then lower the heat and simmer for 10 minutes. Put in the green beans and cook for another 10 minutes. Fluff the rice with a fork, sprinkle with parsley and serve.

Chipotle Kidney Bean Chili

Ingredients for 4 servings

2 tbsp olive oil
1 onion, chopped
2 garlic cloves, minced
1 (16-oz) can tomato sauce
1 (4-oz) can chopped green chilies
1 tbsp chili powder
1 canned chipotle chili, minced
1 tsp ground cumin
½ tsp dried marjoram
1 (15.5-oz) can kidney beans
Salt and black pepper to taste
½ tsp cayenne pepper

Directions and Total Time: 30 minutes

Heat the oil in a pot over medium heat. Place in onion and garlic and sauté for 3 minutes. Put in tomato sauce, green chilies, chili powder, cumin, cayenne pepper, marjoram, salt, and pepper and cook for 5 minutes. Stir in kidney beans and 2 cups of water. Bring to a boil, then lower the heat and simmer for 15 minutes, stirring often. Serve immediately.

Carrot & Black Bean Chili

Ingredients for 4 servings

2 tbsp olive oil
1 onion, finely chopped
2 carrots, chopped
1 tsp grated fresh ginger
1 green bell pepper, chopped
2 tbsp chili powder
1 (28-oz) can diced tomatoes
1 (15.5-oz) can black beans
3 minced green onions

Directions and Total Time: 25 minutes

Heat the oil in a pot over medium heat. Place in onion, carrot, ginger, bell pepper, and chili powder and sauté for 5 minutes until tender. Stir in tomatoes, 2 cups of water, black beans, salt, and pepper. Bring to a boil, then lower the heat and simmer for 15 minutes. Serve topped with green onions.

Special Butternut Squash Chili

Ingredients for 4 servings

1 butternut squash, cubed
2 tbsp olive oil
1 onion, chopped
3 cups tomato salsa
1 (15.5-oz) can garbanzo beans
1 cup frozen green peas
1 cup corn kernels
½ tsp cayenne pepper
½ tsp ground allspice

Directions and Total Time: 60 minutes

Heat the oil in a saucepan over medium heat. Place in onion and squash and cook for 10 minutes until tender. Add in tomato salsa, garbanzo beans, green peas, corn, cayenne pepper, allspice, salt, and pepper. Pour in 2 cups of water. Bring to a boil, then lower the heat and simmer for 15 minutes. Serve.

Bean Gyros

Ingredients for 6 servings

1 (14-oz) can white beans
2 scallions, minced
¼ cup fresh parsley, chopped
2 tbsp kalamata olives, chopped
1 tbsp tahini

1 tbsp lemon juice
½ tsp ground cumin
¼ tsp paprika
4 tsp olive oil
6 whole-grain wraps, warm

1 cup hummus
1 cup arugula, chopped
2 tomatoes, chopped
1 cucumber, chopped
¼ cup chopped avocado

Directions and Total Time: 60 minutes

In a blender, place the white beans, scallions, parsley, and olives. Pulse until finely chopped. In a bowl, beat the tahini with lemon juice. Add in cumin, paprika and salt. Transfer into beans mixture and mix well to combine. Shape the mixture into balls; flatten to make 6 patties.

In a skillet over medium heat, warm the oil and cook the patties for 8-10 minutes on both sides; reserve. Spread each wrap with hummus and top with patties, tomatoes, cucumber, and avocado. Roll the wraps up to serve.

Mediterranean Chickpeas with Vegetables

Ingredients for 6 servings

3 tbsp olive oil
1 red onion, chopped
2 carrots, chopped
1 celery stalk, chopped
2 garlic cloves, minced

1 tsp grated fresh ginger
1 tsp ground cumin
½ tsp turmeric
2 parsnips, peeled and chopped
8 oz green beans, chopped

1 (15.5-oz) can chickpeas, drained
1 (14.5-oz) can diced tomatoes
1 ½ cups vegetable broth
2 tbsp minced cilantro
1 tsp fresh lemon juice

Directions and Total Time: 40 minutes

Heat the oil in a pot over medium heat. Place in onion, carrots, celery, garlic, and ginger. Sauté for 5 minutes. Add in cumin, turmeric, parsnips, green beans, chickpeas, tomatoes and juices, and broth. Bring to a boil, then lower the heat and sprinkle with salt and pepper. Simmer for 30 minutes. Sprinkle with lemon juice and cilantro and serve.

Bean & Spinach Casserole

Ingredients for 6 servings

3 tbsp olive oil
1 onion, chopped
2 carrots, chopped
1 celery stalk, chopped
2 garlic cloves, minced

1 (15.5-oz) can Navy beans
1 (15.5-oz) can Great Northern beans
1 cup baby spinach
3 tomatoes, chopped
1 cup vegetable broth

1 tbsp fresh parsley, chopped
1 tsp dried thyme
Salt and black pepper to taste
½ cup breadcrumbs

Directions and Total Time: 35 minutes

Preheat oven to 380 F.

Heat the oil in a skillet over medium heat. Place in onion, carrots, celery, and garlic. Sauté for 5 minutes. Remove into a greased casserole. Add in beans, spinach, tomatoes, broth, parsley, thyme, salt, and pepper and stir to combine. Cover with foil and bake in the oven for 15 minutes.

Next, take out the casserole from the oven, remove the foil and spread the breadcrumbs all over. Bake for another 10 minutes until the top is crispy and golden. Serve warm.

Southern Bean Salad

Ingredients for 4 servings

1 tomato, chopped
1 red bell pepper, chopped
1 green bell pepper, chopped
1 small red onion, sliced
1 (14.5-oz) can black-eyed peas
1 (14.5-oz) can black beans
¼ cup capers
2 avocados, pitted
1 tbsp lemon juice
¼ cup sake
1 tsp dried oregano
Salt to taste
2 tbsp olive oil
1 cup leafy greens, chopped

Directions and Total Time: 15 minutes

In a bowl, mix the tomato, peppers, onion, black-eyed peas, beans, and capers. Put the avocados, lemon juice, sake, olive oil, oregano, and salt in a food processor and blitz until smooth. Add the dressing to the bean bowl and toss to combine. Transfer to a plate and top with leafy greens to serve.

Hot Coconut Beans with Vegetables

Ingredients for 4 servings

2 tbsp olive oil
1 onion, chopped
1 red bell pepper, chopped
2 garlic cloves, minced
1 tbsp hot powder
2 tbsp plant butter
1 (13.5-oz) can coconut milk
2 (15.5-oz) cans white beans
1 (14.5-oz) can diced tomatoes
3 cups fresh baby spinach
Salt and black pepper to taste
Chopped toasted walnuts

Directions and Total Time: 18 minutes

Heat the oil in a pot over medium heat. Place in onion, garlic, hot powder, and bell pepper and sauté for 5 minutes, stirring occasionally. Put in butter and coconut milk and whisk until well mixed. Add in white beans, tomatoes, spinach, salt, and pepper and cook for 5 minutes until the spinach wilts. Transfer to a platter, garnish with walnuts and serve.

Hot Bean Salad

Ingredients for 4 servings

1 cup pinto beans, soaked overnight
4 tomatoes, halved and sliced
2 celery stalks, sliced
2 hot chilies, seeded and minced
1/3 cup chopped green onions
1 tbsp chopped fresh parsley
2 tbsp olive oil
2 tbsp balsamic vinegar
Salt and black pepper to taste

Directions and Total Time: 45 minutes

Cook pinto beans in salted water for 40 minutes. Drain and remove to a bowl. Let cool for a few minutes. Stir in tomatoes, celery, chilies, and green onions. In another bowl, mix olive oil, vinegar, salt, and pepper. Add the dressing to the bean bowl and toss to coat. Transfer to a serving plate. Top with parsley and serve.

Seitan & Lentil Chili

Ingredients for 4 servings

2 tbsp olive oil
1 onion, chopped
8 oz seitan, chopped
1 cup lentils
1 (14.5-oz) can diced tomatoes
1 tbsp soy sauce
1 tbsp chili powder
1 tsp ground cumin
1 tsp ground allspice
½ tsp ground oregano
¼ tsp ground cayenne
Salt and black pepper to taste

Directions and Total Time: 35 minutes

Heat the oil in a pot over medium heat. Place in onion and seitan and cook for 10 minutes. Add in lentils, diced tomatoes, 2 cups of water, soy sauce, chili powder, cumin, allspice, sugar, oregano, cayenne pepper, salt, and pepper. Bring to a boil, then lower the heat and simmer for 20 minutes.

White Salad with Walnut Pesto

Ingredients for 4 servings-6

- 1 pound potatoes, cut into chunks
- 3 cups cauliflower florets
- 1 (15.5-oz) can cannellini beans
- ½ cup kalamata olives, halved
- ½ cup walnuts
- 2 garlic cloves, minced
- ½ cup chopped fresh parsley
- ¼ cup walnut oil
- ¼ cup olive oil
- ¼ cup white wine vinegar
- Salt to taste
- ¼ tsp crushed red pepper

Directions and Total Time: 25 minutes

Cook the potatoes for 15 minutes in salted water. Add in the cauliflower and cook another 5 minutes until the veggies are tender. Drain and remove to a bowl. Stir in beans, olives and half of the walnuts.

In a food processor, mix the remaining walnuts, garlic, parsley, walnut oil, olive oil, vinegar, salt, sugar, and red pepper. Blitz until well blended. Pour the dressing over the salad and toss to combine. Serve.

Hot Lentil Tacos with Guacamole

Ingredients for 4 servings

- ½ cup red lentils, rinsed, and drained
- 2 tbsp olive oil
- ½ cup minced onion
- 1 potato, peeled and shredded
- ½ cup roasted cashews
- ¼ cup chickpea flour
- 1 tbsp minced fresh parsley
- 2 tsp hot powder
- Salt to taste
- 4 corn tortillas, warmed and halved
- Shredded romaine lettuce
- Guacamole

Directions and Total Time: 35 minutes

Place the lentils in a pot and cover with cold water. Bring to a boil and simmer for 15-20 minutes. Heat the oil in a skillet over medium heat. Place in onion and potato and cook for 5 minutes. Set aside.

In a blender, mince cashews, add in cooked lentils and onion mixture. Pulse to blend. Transfer to a bowl and stir in flour, parsley, hot powder, and salt. Mix to combine. Mould 8 patties out of the mixture. Heat the remaining oil in a skillet over medium heat. Brown the patties for 10 minutes on both sides. To assemble, put one patty in each tortilla, top with shredded lettuce and guacamole.

Curried Indian Rolls

Ingredients for 4 servings

- 3 tbsp tahini
- Zest and juice of 1 lime
- 1 tbsp curry powder
- Sea salt to taste
- 3 tbsp water
- 1 (14-oz) can chickpeas, drained
- 1 cup diced peaches
- 1 red bell pepper, diced small
- ½ cup fresh cilantro, chopped
- 4 large whole-grain wraps
- 2 cups shredded Iceberg lettuce

Directions and Total Time: 15 minutes

In a bowl, beat tahini, lime zest, lime juice, curry powder, 3-4 tbsp of water, and salt until creamy. In another bowl, combine the chickpeas, peaches, bell pepper, cilantro, and tahini dressing. Divide the mixture between the wraps and top with lettuce. Roll up and serve.

Rice, Lentil & Spinach Pilaf

Ingredients for 4 servings

½ cup wild rice	1 (14.5-oz) can diced tomatoes	Salt and black pepper to taste
1 (15.5-oz) can lentils, drained	1 tsp dried thyme	3 cups fresh baby spinach

Directions and Total Time: 25 minutes

In a pot over medium heat, bring the rice and 1 ½ cups of salted water to a boil. Reduce the heat, cover, and simmer for 20 minutes. Add in lentils, tomatoes, thyme, salt, and pepper. Stir and cook until heated through. Mix in the spinach, cook for 2 minutes until the spinach wilts. Serve warm.

Dijon Faro & Walnut Salad

Ingredients for 4 servings

1 cup faro	1 tbsp Dijon mustard	½ cup chopped red bell peppers
1 red onion, sliced	¼ cup olive oil	1/3 cup chopped toasted walnuts
1 garlic clove, minced	½ tsp dried oregano	2 tbsp minced fresh parsley
2 tbsp white wine vinegar	Salt and black pepper to taste	

Directions and Total Time: 50 minutes

Cook faro in salted water for 25 minutes. Drain and set aside to cool. In a bowl, put the onion, garlic, vinegar, mustard, oil, oregano, salt, and pepper. Mix to combine. To the cooled faro, add bell peppers, walnuts and parsley; stir. Transfer to a serving plate, drizzle with the onion mixture and serve.

Awesome Barley Jambalaya

Ingredients for 4 servings

2 tbsp olive oil	2 garlic cloves, minced	1 tsp dried rosemary
1 onion, chopped	1 cup pearl barley	2 ½ cups vegetable broth
2 celery stalks, chopped	2 (15.5-oz) cans kidney beans	1 tbsp chopped fresh parsley
1 green bell pepper, chopped	1 (14.5-oz) can diced tomatoes	Sriracha sauce

Directions and Total Time: 25 minutes

Heat the oil in a pot over medium heat. Place in onion, celery, bell pepper, and garlic. Sauté for 5 minutes. Add in barley, beans, tomatoes, rosemary, salt, and pepper. Stir in broth and simmer for 15 minutes. Top with parsley and drizzle with sriracha sauce to serve.

Parsley Bean & Olives Salad

Ingredients for 4 servings

1 cup green olives, pitted and sliced	¼ cup red onions, sliced	Salt and black pepper to taste
2 (15.5-oz) cans black beans	2 garlic cloves, crushed	2 tbsp fresh lime juice
½ cup chopped red bell pepper	¼ cup chopped fresh parsley	¼ cup olive oil

Directions and Total Time: 15 minutes

Combine the olives, beans, bell pepper, and onion in a bowl. Set aside. In a food processor, put garlic, lime juice, 2 tbsp water, olive oil, parsley, salt and pepper. Pulse until blended. Add to the salad bowl and mix to combine. Serve immediately.

Habanero Pinto Beans with Bell Pepper Pot

Ingredients for 6 servings

1 tsp olive oil
2 red bell peppers, diced
1 habanero pepper, minced
2 (14.5-oz) cans pinto beans
½ cup vegetable broth
1 tsp ground cumin
1 tsp chili powder
Salt and black pepper to taste

Directions and Total Time: 20 minutes

Heat the oil in a pot over medium heat. Place in bell and habanero peppers, sauté for 5 minutes until tender. Add in beans, broth, cumin, chili powder, salt, and pepper. Bring to a boil, then lower the heat and simmer for 10 minutes. Serve.

Baked Mustard Beans

Ingredients for 4 servings

2 tbsp olive oil
1 onion, minced
2 garlic cloves, minced
1 (14.5-oz) can crushed tomatoes
½ cup pure date syrup
1 ½ tsp dry mustard
¼ tsp ground cayenne pepper
Salt and black pepper to taste
2 (15.5-oz) cans Great Northern beans

Directions and Total Time: 25 minutes

Preheat oven to 350 F.

Heat the oil in a pot over medium heat. Place in onion and garlic and sauté for 3 minutes. Add in tomatoes, date syrup, mustard, cayenne pepper, salt, and pepper. Cook for 5 minutes. Pour the beans in a baking dish and stir in the sauce to coat. Bake for 10 minutes. Serve warm.

Cucumber & Carrot Pizza with Pesto

Ingredients for 2 servings

1 prebaked pizza crust
½ cup vegan pesto
1 tomato, sliced
1 carrot, grated
1 red onion, sliced
1 cucumber, sliced

Directions and Total Time: 30 minutes

Preheat oven to 390 F.

Spread half of the pesto over the pizza crust and top with tomato slices. Combine the grated carrot with salt, toss to coat. Put the carrot over the tomato and top with onion. Transfer to a baking tray and put in the oven. Bake for 15-20 minutes until golden. Serve topped with cucumber slices.

Hot Paprika Lentils

Ingredients for 6 servings

1 onion, chopped
3 tbsp olive oil
1 tbsp hot paprika
2 ¼ cups lentils, drained
3 garlic cloves, minced
½ tsp dried thyme

Directions and Total Time: 20 minutes

Heat the oil in a pot over medium heat. Place the onion and garlic and sauté for 3 minutes. Add in paprika, salt, pepper, 5 cups water, lentils, and thyme. Bring to a boil, then lower the heat and simmer for 15 minutes until tender, stirring often. Serve.

DINNER

Black-Eyed Pea Oat Bake

Ingredients for 4 servings

1 carrot, shredded	¾ cup whole-wheat flour	1 tbsp soy sauce
1 onion, chopped	¾ cup quick-cooking oats	½ tsp dried sage
2 garlic cloves, minced	½ cup breadcrumbs	Salt and black pepper to taste
1 (15.5-oz) can black-eyed peas	¼ cup minced fresh parsley	

Directions and Total Time: 25 minutes

Preheat oven to 360 F.

In a blender, combine the carrot, onion, garlic and peas and pulse until creamy and smooth. Add in flour, oats, breadcrumbs, parsley, soy sauce, sage, salt, and pepper. Blend until ingredients are evenly mixed. Spoon the mixture into a greased loaf pan. Bake for 40 minutes until golden. Allow it to cool down for a few minutes before slicing. Serve immediately.

Paprika Fava Bean Patties

Ingredients for 4 servings

4 tbsp olive oil	1 tbsp minced fresh parsley	½ tsp dried thyme
1 minced onion	½ cup breadcrumbs	4 burger buns, toasted
1 garlic clove, minced	¼ cup almond flour	4 lettuce leaves
1 (15.5-oz) can fava beans	1 tsp smoked paprika	1 ripe tomato, sliced

Directions and Total Time: 15 minutes

In a blender, add onion, garlic, beans, parsley, breadcrumbs, flour, paprika, thyme, salt, and pepper. Pulse until uniform but not smooth. Shape 4 patties out of the mixture. Refrigerate for 15 minutes.

Heat olive oil in a skillet over medium heat. Fry the patties for 10 minutes on both sides until golden brown. Serve in toasted buns with lettuce and tomato slices.

Walnut Lentil Burgers

Ingredients for 4 servings

2 tbsp olive oil	1 onion, diced	¾ cup almond flour
1 cup dry lentils, rinsed	½ cup walnuts	2 tsp curry powder
2 carrots, grated	1 tbsp tomato puree	4 whole grain buns

Directions and Total Time: 70 minutes

Place lentils in a pot and cover with water. Bring to a boil and simmer for 15-20 minutes.

Meanwhile, combine the carrots, walnuts, onion, tomato puree, flour, curry powder, salt, and pepper in a bowl. Toss to coat.

Once the lentils are ready, drain and transfer into the veggie bowl. Mash the mixture until get sticky. Shape the mixture into balls; flatten to make patties.

Heat the oil in a skillet over medium heat. Brown the patties for 8 minutes on both sides.

To assemble, put the patties on the buns and top with your desired toppings.

Bean & Pecan Sandwiches

Ingredients for 4 servings

1 onion, chopped
1 garlic clove, crushed
¾ cup pecans, chopped
¾ cup canned black beans
¾ cup almond flour
2 tbsp minced fresh parsley
1 tbsp soy sauce
1 tsp Dijon mustard + to serve
Salt and black pepper to taste
½ tsp ground sage
½ tsp sweet paprika
2 tbsp olive oil
Bread slices
Lettuce leaves and sliced tomatoes

Directions and Total Time: 20 minutes

Put the onion, garlic, and pecans in a blender and pulse until roughly ground. Add in the beans and pulse until until everything is well combined. Transfer to a large mixing bowl and stir in the flour, parsley, soy sauce, mustard, salt, sage, paprika, and pepper. Mould patties out of the mixture.

Heat the oil in a skillet over medium heat. Brown the patties for 10 minutes on both sides. To assemble, lay patties on the bread slices and top with mustard, lettuce and tomato slices.

Homemade Kitchari

Ingredients for 5 servings

4 cups chopped cauliflower and broccoli florets
½ cup split peas
½ cup brown rice
1 red onion, chopped
1 (14.5-oz) can diced tomatoes
3 garlic cloves, minced
1 jalapeño pepper, seeded
½ tsp ground ginger
1 tsp ground turmeric
1 tsp olive oil
1 tsp fennel seeds
Juice of 1 large lemon
Salt and black pepper to taste

Directions and Total Time: 40 minutes

In a food processor, place the onion, tomatoes with juices, garlic, jalapeño pepper, ginger, turmeric, and 2 tbsp of water. Pulse until ingredients are evenly mixed.

Heat the oil in a pot over medium heat. Cook the cumin and fennel seeds for 2-3 minutes, stirring often. Pour in the puréed mixture, split peas and rice and 3 cups of water. Bring to a boil, then lower the heat and simmer for 10 minutes. Stir in cauliflower, broccoli and cook for another 10 minutes. Mix in lemon juice and adjust seasoning.

Faro & Black Bean Loaf

Ingredients for 6 servings

3 tbsp olive oil
1 onion, minced
1 cup faro
2 (15.5-oz) cans black beans, mashed
½ cup quick-cooking oats
1/3 cup whole-wheat flour
2 tbsp nutritional yeast
1 ½ tsp dried thyme
½ tsp dried oregano

Directions and Total Time: 50 minutes

Heat the oil in a pot over medium heat. Place in onion and sauté for 3 minutes. Add in faro, 2 cups of water, salt, and pepper. Bring to a boil, lower the heat and simmer for 20 minutes. Remove to a bowl.

Preheat oven to 350 F.

Add the mashed beans, oats, flour, yeast, thyme, and oregano to the faro bowl. Toss to combine. Taste and adjust the seasoning. Shape the mixture into a greased loaf. Bake for 20 minutes. Let cool for a few minutes. Slice and serve.

Cuban-Style Millet

Ingredients for 4 servings

2 tbsp olive oil
1 onion, chopped
2 zucchinis, chopped
2 garlic cloves, minced
1 tsp dried thyme
½ tsp ground cumin
1 (15.5-oz) can black-eyed peas
1 cup millet
2 tbsp chopped fresh cilantro

Directions and Total Time: 40 minutes

Heat the oil in a pot over medium heat. Place in onion and sauté for 3 minutes until translucent. Add in zucchinis, garlic, thyme, and cumin and cook for 10 minutes. Put in peas, millet and 2 ½ cups hot water. Bring to a boil, then lower the heat and simmer for 20 minutes. Fluff the millet using a fork. Serve garnished with cilantro.

Traditional Cilantro Pilaf

Ingredients for 6 servings

3 tbsp olive oil
1 onion, minced
1 carrot, chopped
2 garlic cloves, minced
1 cup wild rice
1 ½ tsp ground fennel seeds
½ tsp ground cumin
Salt and black pepper to taste
3 tbsp minced fresh cilantro

Directions and Total Time: 30 minutes

Heat the oil in a pot over medium heat. Place in onion, carrot, and garlic and sauté for 5 minutes. Stir in rice, fennel seeds, cumin, and 2 cups water. Bring to a boil, then lower the heat and simmer for 20 minutes. Remove to a bowl and fluff using a fork. Serve topped with cilantro and black pepper.

Oriental Bulgur & White Beans

Ingredients for 4 servings

2 tbsp olive oil
3 green onions, chopped
1 cup bulgur
1 cups water
1 tbsp soy sauce
Salt to taste
1 ½ cups cooked white beans
1 tbsp nutritional yeast
1 tbsp dried parsley

Directions and Total Time: 55 minutes

Heat the oil in a pot over medium heat. Place in green onions and sauté for 3 minutes. Stir in bulgur, water, soy sauce, and salt. Bring to a boil, then lower the heat and simmer for 20-22 minutes. Mix in beans and yeast. Cook for 5 minutes. Serve topped with parsley.

One-Pot Red Lentils with Mushrooms

Ingredients for 4 servings

2 tsp olive oil
2 cloves garlic, minced
2 tsp grated fresh ginger
½ tsp ground cumin
½ tsp fennel seeds
1 cup mushrooms, chopped
1 large tomato, chopped
1 cup dried red lentils
2 tbsp lemon juice

Directions and Total Time: 25 minutes

Heat the oil in a pot over medium heat. Place in the garlic and ginger and cook for 3 minutes. Stir in cumin, fennel, mushrooms, tomato, lentils, and 2 ¼ cups water. Bring to a boil, then lower the heat and simmer for 15 minutes. Mix in lemon juice and serve.

Picante Green Rice

Ingredients for 4 servings

1 roasted bell pepper, chopped
3 small hot green chilies, chopped
2 ½ cups vegetable broth
½ cup chopped fresh parsley
1 onion, chopped
2 garlic cloves, chopped
Salt and black pepper to taste
½ tsp dried oregano
3 tbsp canola oil
1 cup long-grain brown rice
1 ½ cups cooked black beans
2 tbsp minced fresh cilantro

Directions and Total Time: 35 minutes

In a food processor, place bell pepper, chilies, 1 cup of broth, parsley, onion, garlic, pepper, oregano, salt, and pepper and blend until smooth. Heat oil in a skillet over medium heat. Add in rice and veggie mixture. Cook for 5 minutes, stirring often. Add in the remaining broth and bring to a boil, lower the heat, and simmer for 15 minutes. Mix in beans and cook for another 5 minutes. Serve with cilantro.

Sherry Shallot Beans

Ingredients for 5 servings

1 tsp olive oil
4 shallots, chopped
1 tsp ground cumin
1 (14.5-oz) cans black beans
1 cup vegetable broth
2 tbsp sherry vinegar

Directions and Total Time: 25 minutes

Heat the oil in a pot over medium heat. Place in shallots and cumin and cook for 3 minutes until soft. Stir in beans and broth. Bring to a boil, then lower the heat and simmer for 10 minutes. Add in sherry vinegar, increase the heat and cook for an additional 3 minutes. Serve warm.

Celery Buckwheat Croquettes

Ingredients for 6 servings

¾ cup cooked buckwheat groats
½ cup cooked brown rice
3 tbsp olive oil
¼ cup minced onion
1 celery stalk, chopped
¼ cup shredded carrots
1/3 cup whole-wheat flour
¼ cup chopped fresh parsley
Salt and black pepper to taste

Directions and Total Time: 25 minutes

Combine the groats and rice in a bowl. Set aside. Heat 1 tbsp of oil in a skillet over medium heat. Place in onion, celery and carrot and cook for 5 minutes. Transfer to the rice bowl. Mix in flour, parsley, salt, and pepper. Place in the fridge for 20 minutes. Mould the mixture into cylinder-shaped balls.

Heat the remaining oil in a skillet over medium heat. Fry the croquettes for 8 minutes, turning occasionally until golden. Serve warm.

Oregano Chickpeas

Ingredients for 6 servings

1 tsp olive oil
1 onion, cut into half-moon slices
2 (14.5-oz) cans chickpeas
½ cup vegetable broth
2 tsp dried oregano
Salt and black pepper to taste

Directions and Total Time: 5 minutes

Heat the oil in a skillet over medium heat. Cook the onion for 3 minutes. Stir in chickpeas, broth, oregano, salt, and pepper. Bring to a boil, then lower the heat and simmer for 10 minutes. Serve.

Matcha-Infused Tofu Rice

Ingredients for 4 servings

4 matcha bags	8 oz extra-firm tofu, chopped	1 tbsp fresh lemon juice
1 ½ cups brown rice	3 green onions, minced	1 tsp grated lemon zest
2 tbsp canola oil	2 cups snow peas, cut diagonally	Salt and black pepper to taste

Directions and Total Time: 35 minutes

Boil 3 cups water in a pot. Place in the tea bags and turn the heat off. Let sit for 7 minutes. Discard the bags. Wash the rice and put into the tea. Cook for 20 minutes over medium heat. Drain and set aside. Heat the oil in a skillet over medium heat. Fry the tofu for 5 minutes until golden. Stir in green onions and snow peas and cook for another 3 minutes. Mix in lemon juice and lemon zest. Place the rice in a serving bowl and mix in the tofu mixture. Adjust the seasoning with salt and pepper. Serve right away.

Chinese Fried Rice

Ingredients for 4 servings

2 tbsp canola oil	2 garlic cloves, minced	1 cup frozen peas, thawed
1 onion, chopped	2 tsp grated fresh ginger	3 tbsp soy sauce
1 large carrot, chopped	3 green onions, minced	2 tsp dry white wine
1 head broccoli, cut into florets	3 ½ cups cooked brown rice	1 tbsp toasted sesame oil

Directions and Total Time: 20 minutes

Heat the oil in a skillet over medium heat. Place in onion, carrot and broccoli, sauté for 5 minutes until tender. Add in garlic, ginger and green onions, sauté for another 3 minutes. Stir in rice, peas, soy sauce, and white wine and cook for 5 minutes. Add in sesame oil, toss to combine. Serve right away.

Green Pea & Lemon Couscous

Ingredients for 6 servings

1 cup green peas	Juice and zest of 1 lemon	1 ½ cups couscous
2 ¾ cups vegetable stock	2 tbsp chopped fresh thyme	¼ cup chopped fresh parsley

Directions and Total Time: 15 minutes

Pour the vegetable stock, lemon juice thyme, salt, and pepper in a pot. Bring to a boil, then add in green peas and couscous. Turn the heat off and let sit covered for 5 minutes, until the liquid has absorbed. Fluff the couscous using a fork and mix in the lemon and parsley. Serve immediately.

Chimichurri Fusili with Navy Beans

Ingredients for 4 servings

8 oz whole-wheat fusilli	½ cup chimichurri salsa	1 red onion, chopped
1 ½ cups canned navy beans	1 cup chopped tomatoes	½ cup chopped pitted black olives

Directions and Total Time: 25 minutes

In a large pot over medium heat, pour 8 cups of salted water. Bring to a boil and add in the pasta. Cook for 8-10 minutes, drain and let cool. Combine the pasta, beans and chimichurri in a bowl. Toss to coat. Stir in tomato, red onion and olives. Serve.

Buckwheat Pilaf with Pine Nuts

Ingredients for 4 servings

1 cup buckwheat groats
2 cups vegetable stock
¼ cup pine nuts
2 tbsp olive oil
½ onion, chopped
⅓ cup chopped fresh parsley

Directions and Total Time: 25 minutes

Put the groats and vegetable stock in a pot. Bring to a boil, then lower the heat and simmer for 15 minutes. Heat a skillet over medium heat. Place in the pine nuts and toast for 2-3 minutes, shaking often. Heat the oil in the same skillet and sauté the onion for 3 minutes until translucent.

Once the groats are ready, fluff them using a fork. Mix in pine nuts, onion and parsley. Sprinkle with salt and pepper. Serve immediately.

Korean-Style Millet

Ingredients for 4 servings

1 cup dried millet, drained
1 tsp gochugaru flakes
Salt and black pepper to taste

Directions and Total Time: 30 minutes

Place the millet and gochugaru flakes in a pot. Cover with enough water and bring to a boil. Lower the heat and simmer for 20 minutes. Drain and let cool. Transfer to a serving bowl and season with salt and pepper. Serve.

Savory Seitan & Bell Pepper Rice

Ingredients for 4 servings

2 cups water
1 cup long-grain brown rice
2 tbsp olive oil
1 onion, chopped
2 garlic cloves, minced
8 oz seitan, chopped
1 green bell pepper, chopped
1 tsp dried basil
½ tsp ground fennel seeds
¼ tsp crushed red pepper
Salt and black pepper to taste

Directions and Total Time: 35 minutes

Bring water to a boil in a pot. Place in rice and lower the heat. Simmer for 20 minutes.

Heat the oil in a skillet over medium heat. Sauté the onion for 3 minutes until translucent. Add in the seitan and bell pepper and cook for another 5 minutes. Stir in basil, fennel, red pepper, salt, and black pepper. Once the rice is ready, remove to a bowl. Add in seitan mixture and toss to combine. Serve.

Mushroom Fried Rice

Ingredients for 6 servings

2 tbsp sesame oil
1 onion, chopped
1 carrot, chopped
1 cup okra, chopped
1 cup sliced shiitake mushrooms
2 garlic cloves, minced
¼ cup soy sauce
1 cups cooked brown rice
2 green onions, chopped

Directions and Total Time: 25 minutes

Heat the oil in a skillet over medium heat. Place in onion and carrot and cook for 3 minutes. Add in okra and mushrooms, cook for 5-7 minutes. Stir in garlic and cook for 30 seconds. Put in soy sauce and rice. Cook until hot. Add in green onions and stir. Serve warm.

Veggie Paella with Lentils

Ingredients for 4 servings

2 tbsp olive oil
1 onion, chopped
1 green bell pepper, chopped
2 garlic cloves, minced

1 (14.5-oz) can diced tomatoes
1 tbsp capers
¼ tsp crushed red pepper
1 ½ cups long-grain brown rice

3 cups vegetable broth
1 ½ cups cooked lentils, drained
¼ cup sliced pitted black olives
2 tbsp minced fresh parsley

Directions and Total Time: 50 minutes

Heat oil in a pot and sauté onion, bell pepper and garlic for 5 minutes. Stir in tomatoes, capers red pepper, and salt. Cook for 5 minutes. Pour in the rice and broth. Bring to a boil, then lower the heat. Simmer for 20 minutes. Turn the heat off and mix in lentils. Serve garnished with olives and parsley.

Bean & Brown Rice with Artichokes

Ingredients for 4 servings

2 tbsp olive oil
3 garlic cloves, minced
1 cup artichokes hearts, chopped
1 tsp dried basil

1 ½ cups cooked navy beans
1 ½ cups long-grain brown rice
3 cups vegetable broth
Salt and black pepper to taste

2 ripe grape tomatoes, quartered
2 tbsp minced fresh parsley

Directions and Total Time: 35 minutes

Heat the oil in a pot over medium heat. Sauté the garlic for 1 minute. Stir in artichokes, basil, navy beans, rice, and broth. Sprinkle with salt and pepper. Lower the heat and simmer for 20-25 minutes. Remove to a bowl and mix in tomatoes and parsley. Using a fork, fluff the rice and serve right away.

Cherry & Pistachio Bulgur

Ingredients for 4 servings

1 tbsp plant butter
1 white onion, chopped
1 carrot, chopped

1 celery stalk, chopped
1 cup chopped mushrooms
1 ½ cups bulgur

4 cups vegetable broth
1 cup chopped dried cherries, soaked
½ cup chopped pistachios

Directions and Total Time: 45 minutes

Preheat oven to 375 F.

Melt butter in a skillet over medium heat. Sauté the onion, carrot and celery for 5 minutes until tender. Add in mushrooms and cook for 3 more minutes. Pour in bulgur and broth. Transfer to a casserole and bake covered for 30 minutes. Once ready, uncovered and stir in cherries. Top with pistachios to serve.

Quinoa & Chickpea Pot

Ingredients for 2 servings

2 tsp olive oil
1 cup cooked quinoa

1 (15-oz) can chickpeas
1 bunch arugula chopped

1 tbsp soy
Sea salt and black pepper to taste

Directions and Total Time: 15 minutes

Heat the oil in a skillet over medium heat. Stir in quinoa, chickpeas and arugula, cook for 3-5 minutes until the arugula wilts. Pour in soy sauce, salt and pepper. Toss to coat. Serve immediately.

Italian Holiday Stuffing

Ingredients for 4 servings

¼ cup plant butter
1 onion, chopped
2 celery stalks, sliced
1 cup button mushrooms, sliced
3 garlic cloves, minced
½ cup vegetable broth
½ cup raisins
½ cup chopped walnuts
2 cups cooked quinoa
1 tsp Italian seasoning
Sea salt to taste
Chopped fresh parsley

Directions and Total Time: 25 minutes

In a skillet over medium heat, melt the butter. Sauté the onion, garlic, celery and mushrooms for 5 minutes until tender, stirring occasionally. Pour in broth, raisins and walnuts. Bring to a boil, then lower the heat and simmer for 5 minutes. Stir in quinoa, Italian seasoning and salt. Cook for another 4 minutes. Serve garnished with parsley.

Curry Bean with Artichokes

Ingredients for 4 servings

1 (14.5-oz) can artichoke hearts, drained and quartered
1 tsp olive oil
1 small onion, diced
2 garlic cloves, minced
1 (14.5-oz) can cannellini beans
2 tsp curry powder
½ tsp ground coriander
1 (5.4-oz) can coconut milk
Salt and black pepper to taste

Directions and Total Time: 25 minutes

Heat the oil in a skillet over medium heat. Sauté the onion and garlic for 3 minutes until translucent. Stir in beans, artichoke, curry powder, and coriander. Add in coconut milk. Bring to a boil, then lower the heat and simmer for 10 minutes. Serve.

Pressure Cooker Green Lentils

Ingredients for 6 servings

3 tbsp coconut oil
2 tbsp curry powder
1 tsp ground ginger
1 onion, chopped
2 garlic cloves, sliced
1 cup dried green lentils
3 cups water
Salt and black pepper to taste

Directions and Total Time: 30 minutes

Set your IP to Sauté. Add in coconut oil, curry powder, ginger, onion, and garlic. Cook for 3 minutes. Stir in green lentils. Pour in water.

Lock the lid and set the time to 10 minutes on High. Once ready, perform a natural pressure release for 10 minutes. Unlock the lid and season with salt and pepper. Serve.

Simple Pesto Millet

Ingredients for 4 servings

1 cup millet
2 ½ cups vegetable broth
½ cup vegan basil pesto

Directions and Total Time: 50 minutes

Place the millet and broth in a pot. Bring to a boil, then lower the heat and simmer for 25 minutes. Let cool for 5 minutes and fluff the millet. Mix in the pesto and serve.

Peppered Pinto Beans

Ingredients for 6 servings

1 serrano pepper, cut into strips
1 red bell pepper, cut into strips
1 green bell pepper, cut into strips
1 onion, chopped
2 carrots, chopped
2 garlic cloves, minced
3 (15-oz) cans pinto beans
18-ounce bottle barbecue sauce
½ tsp chipotle powder

Directions and Total Time: 30 minutes

In a blender, place the serrano and bell peppers, onion, carrot, and garlic. Pulse until well mixed.

Place the mixture in a pot with the beans, BBQ sauce and chipotle powder. Cook for 15 minutes. Season with salt and pepper. Serve warm.

Black-Eyed Peas with Sun-Dried Tomatoes

Ingredients for 4 servings

1 cup black-eyed peas, soaked overnight
¼ cup sun-dried tomatoes, chopped
2 tbsp olive oil
2 tsp ground chipotle pepper
1 ½ tsp ground cumin
1 ½ tsp onion powder
1 tsp dried oregano
¾ tsp garlic powder
½ tsp smoked paprika

Directions and Total Time: 35 minutes

Place the black-eyed peas in a pot and add in 2 cups of water, olive oil, chipotle pepper, cumin, onion powder, oregano, garlic powder, salt, and paprika. Cook for 20 minutes over medium heat. Mix in sun-dried tomatoes, let sit for a few minutes, and serve.

Pressure Cooker Celery & Spinach Chickpeas

Ingredients for 5 servings

1 cup chickpeas, soaked overnight
1 onion, chopped
2 garlic cloves, minced
1 celery stalk, chopped
2 tbsp olive oil
3 tsp ground cinnamon
½ tsp ground nutmeg
1 tbsp coconut oil
1 cup spinach, chopped

Directions and Total Time: 50 minutes

Place chickpeas in your IP with the onion, garlic, celery, olive oil, 2 cups water, cinnamon, and nutmeg.

Lock the lid in place; set the time to 30 minutes on High. Once ready, perform a natural pressure release for 10 minutes. Unlock the lid and drain the excess water. Put back the chickpeas and stir in coconut oil and spinach. Set the pot to Sauté and cook for another 5 minutes.

Vegetarian Quinoa Curry

Ingredients for 4 servings

4 tsp olive oil
1 onion, chopped
2 tbsp curry powder
1 ½ cups quinoa
1 cup canned diced tomatoes
4 cups chopped spinach
½ cup non-dairy milk
2 tbsp soy sauce
Salt to taste

Directions and Total Time: 35 minutes

Heat the oil in a pot over medium heat. Sauté the onion and ginger for 3 minutes until tender. Pour in curry powder, quinoa and 3 cupwater. Bring to a boil, then lower the heat and simmer for 15-20 minutes. Mix in tomatoes, spinach, milk, soy sauce, and salt. Simmer for an additional 3 minutes.

Alfredo Rice with Green Beans

Ingredients for 3 servings

1 cup Alfredo arugula vegan pesto   1 cup frozen green beans, thawed   2 cups brown rice

Directions and Total Time: 25 minutes

Cook the rice in salted water in a pot over medium heat for 20 minutes. Drain and let it cool completely. Place the Alfredo sauce and beans in a skillet. Cook over low heat for 3-5 minutes. Stir in the rice to coat. Serve immediately.

Couscous & Quinoa Burgers

Ingredients for 4 servings

- 2 tbsp olive oil
- ¼ cup couscous
- ¼ cup boiling water
- 2 cups cooker quinoa
- 2 tbsp balsamic vinegar
- 3 tbsp chopped olives
- ½ tsp garlic powder
- Salt to taste
- 4 burger buns
- Lettuce leaves, for serving
- Tomato slices, for serving

Directions and Total Time: 20 minutes

Preheat oven to 350 F.

In a bowl, place the couscous with boiling water. Let sit covered for 5 minutes. Once the liquid is absorbed, fluff with a fork. Add in quinoa and mash them to form a chunky texture. Stir in vinegar, olive oil, olives, garlic powder, and salt. Shape the mixture into 4 patties. Arrange them on a greased tray and bake for 25-30 minutes. To assemble, place the patties on the buns and top with lettuce, tomato and desired condiments.

Lemony Chickpeas with Kale

Ingredients for 4 servings

- 4 tbsp olive oil
- 1 (15-oz) can chickpeas
- 1 onion, chopped
- 2 garlic cloves, minced
- 1 tbsp Italian seasoning
- 2 cups kale, chopped
- Sea salt and black pepper to taste
- Juice and zest of 1 lemon

Directions and Total Time: 20 minutes

Heat the oil in a skillet over medium heat. Place in chickpeas and cook for 5 minutes. Add in onion, garlic, Italian seasoning and kale cook for 5 minutes until the kale wilts. Stir in salt, lemon juice, lemon zest and pepper. Serve warm.

Endive Slaw with Olives

Ingredients for 6 servings

- 1 pound curly endive, chopped
- ⅓ cup vegan mayonnaise
- ¼ cup rice vinegar
- 2 tbsp vegan yogurt
- 1 tbsp pure date sugar
- 10 black olives for garnish
- ¼ tsp freshly ground black pepper
- ¼ tsp smoked paprika
- ¼ tsp chipotle powder

Directions and Total Time: 10 minutes

In a bowl, mix the mayonnaise, vinegar, yogurt, sugar, salt, pepper, paprika, and chipotle powder. Gently add in the curly endive and mix with a wood spatula to coat. d. Top with black olives and serve.

Dinner Rice & Lentils

Ingredients for 4 servings

2 tbsp olive oil
4 scallions, chopped
1 carrot, diced
1 celery stalk, chopped
2 (15-oz) cans lentils, drained
1 (15-oz) can diced tomatoes
1 tbsp dried rosemary
1 tsp ground coriander
1 tbsp garlic powder
2 cups cooked brown rice
Sea salt and black pepper to taste

Directions and Total Time: 25 minutes

Heat the oil in a pot over medium heat. Place in scallions, carrot and celery, cook for 5 minutes until tender. Stir in lentils, tomatoes, rosemary, coriander, and garlic powder. Lower the heat and simmer for 5-7 minutes. Mix in rice, salt, and pepper and cook another 2-3 minutes. Serve.

Asparagus & Mushrooms with Mashed Potatoes

Ingredients for 4 servings

5 large portobello mushrooms, stems removed
6 potatoes, chopped
4 garlic cloves, minced
2 tsp olive oil
½ cup non-dairy milk
2 tbsp nutritional yeast
Sea salt to taste
7 cups asparagus, chopped
3 tsp coconut oil
2 tbsp nutritional yeast

Directions and Total Time: 60 minutes

Place the chopped potatoes in a pot and cover with salted water. Cook for 20 minutes.

Heat oil in a skillet and sauté garlic for 1 minute. Once the potatoes are ready, drain them and reserve the water. Transfer to a bowl and mash them with some of the hot water, garlic, milk, yeast, and salt.

Preheat your grill to medium. Grease the mushrooms with cooking spray and season with salt. Arrange the mushrooms face down and grill for 10 minutes. After, grill the asparagus for about 10 minutes, turning often. Arrange the veggies in a serving platter. Add in the potato mash and serve.

Sesame Kale Slaw

Ingredients for 4 servings-6

¼ cup tahini
2 tbsp white miso paste
1 tbsp rice vinegar
1 tbsp toasted sesame oil
2 tsp soy sauce
1 (12-oz) bag kale slaw
2 scallions, minced
¼ cup toasted sesame seeds

Directions and Total Time: 15 minutes

In a bowl, combine the tahini, miso, vinegar, oil, and soy sauce. Stir in kale slaw, scallions and sesame seeds. Let sit for 20 minutes. Serve immediately.

Spicy Steamed Broccoli

Ingredients for 6 servings

1 large head broccoli, into florets
Salt to taste
1 tsp red pepper flakes

Directions and Total Time: 15 minutes

Boil 1 cup water in a pot over medium heat. Place in a steamer basket and put in the florets. Steam covered for 5-7 minutes. In a bowl, toss the broccoli with red pepper flakes and salt. Serve.

Paprika Cauliflower Tacos

Ingredients for 6 servings

1 head cauliflower, cut into pieces
2 tbsp olive oil
2 tbsp whole-wheat flour
2 tbsp nutritional yeast
2 tsp paprika
1 tsp cayenne pepper
Salt to taste
1 cups shredded watercress
2 cups cherry tomatoes, halved
2 carrots, grated
½ cup mango salsa
½ cup guacamole
8 small corn tortillas, warm
1 lime, cut into wedges

Directions and Total Time: 40 minutes

Preheat oven to 350 F.

Brush the cauliflower with oil in a bowl. In another bowl, mix the flour, yeast, paprika, cayenne pepper, and salt. Pour into the cauliflower bowl and toss to coat. Spread the cauliflower on a greased baking sheet. Bake for 20-30 minutes.

In a bowl, combine the watercress, cherry tomatoes, carrots, mango salsa, and guacamole. Once the cauliflower is ready, divide it between the tortillas, add the mango mixture, roll up and serve with lime wedges on the side.

Garlic Roasted Carrots

Ingredients for 4 servings

2 pounds carrots, chopped into ¾ inch cubes
2 tsp olive oil
½ tsp chili powder
½ tsp smoked paprika
½ tsp dried oregano
½ tsp dried thyme
½ tsp garlic powder
Salt to taste

Directions and Total Time: 35 minutes

Preheat oven to 400 F. Line with parchment paper a baking sheet. Rinse the carrots and pat dry. Chop into ¾ inch cubes. Place in a bowl and toss with olive oil.

In a bowl, mix chili powder, paprika, oregano, thyme, olive oil, salt, and garlic powder. Pour over the carrots and toss to coat. Transfer to a greased baking sheet and bake for 30 minutes, turn once by half.

Asian Quinoa Sauté

Ingredients for 4 servings

1 cup quinoa
Salt to taste
1 head cauliflower, break into florets
2 tsp untoasted sesame oil
1 cup snow peas, cut in half
1 cup frozen peas
2 cups chopped Swiss chard
2 scallions, chopped
2 tbsp water
1 tsp toasted sesame oil
1 tbsp soy sauce
2 tbsp sesame seeds

Directions and Total Time: 30 minutes

Place the quinoa with 2 cups water and salt in a bowl. Bring to a boil, then lower the heat and simmer for 15 minute. Do not stir.

In the meantime, heat the oil in a skillet over medium heat and sauté the cauliflower for 4-5 minutes. Add in snow peas and stir until thaw. Stir in Swiss chard, scallions, and 2 tbsp of water; cook until wilted, about 5 minutes. Season with salt. Drizzle with sesame oil and soy sauce and cook for 1 minute.

Divide the quinoa in bowls and top with the cauliflower mixture. Garnish with sesame seeds and soy sauce to serve.

Eggplant & Hummus Pizza

Ingredients for 2 servings

½ eggplant, sliced
½ red onion, sliced
1 cup cherry tomatoes, halved
3 tbsp chopped black olives
Salt to taste
Drizzle olive oil
2 prebaked pizza crusts
½ cup hummus
2 tbsp oregano

Directions and Total Time: 25 minutes

Preheat oven to 390 F,

In a bowl, combine the eggplant, onion, tomatoes, olives and salt. Toss to coat. Sprinkle with some olive oil. Arrange the crusts on a baking sheet and spread the hummus on each pizza. Top with the eggplant mixture. Bake for 20-30 minutes. Serve warm.

Miso Green Cabbage

Ingredients for 4 servings

1 pound green cabbage, halved
2 tsp olive
3 tsp miso paste
1 tsp dried oregano
½ tsp dried rosemary
1 tbsp balsamic vinegar

Directions and Total Time: 50 minutes

Preheat oven to 390 F. Line with parchment paper a baking sheet.

Put the green cabbage in a bowl. Coat with olive oil, miso, oregano, rosemary, salt, and pepper. Remove to the baking sheet and bake for 35-40 minutes, shaking every 5 minutes until tender. Remove from the oven to a plate. Drizzle with balsamic vinegar and serve.

Cilantro Okra

Ingredients for 4 servings

2 tbsp olive oil
4 cups okra, halved
Sea salt and black pepper to taste
3 tbsp chopped fresh cilantro

Directions and Total Time: 10 minutes

Heat the oil in a skillet over medium heat. Place in the okra, cook for 5 minutes. Turn the heat off and mix in salt, pepper and cilantro. Serve immediately.

Citrus Asparagus

Ingredients for 4 servings

1 onion, minced
2 tsp lemon zest
1/3 cup fresh lemon juice
1 tbsp olive oil
Salt and black pepper to taste
1 pound asparagus, trimmed

Directions and Total Time: 15 minutes

Combine the onion, lemon zest, lemon juice, and oil in a bowl. Sprinkle with salt and pepper. Let sit for 5-10 minutes.

Insert a steamer basket and 1 cup of water in a pot over medium heat. Place the asparagus on the basket and steam for 4-5 minutes until tender but crispy. Leave to cool for 10 minutes, then arrange on a plate. Serve drizzled with the dressing.

Japanese-Style Tofu with Haricots Vert

Ingredients for 4 servings

- 1 cup haricots vert
- 1 tbsp grapeseed oil
- 1 onion, minced
- 5 shiitake mushroom caps, sliced
- 1 tsp grated fresh ginger
- 3 green onions, minced
- 8 oz firm tofu, crumbled
- 2 tbsp soy sauce
- 3 cups hot cooked rice
- 1 tbsp toasted sesame oil
- 1 tbsp toasted sesame seeds

Directions and Total Time: 25 minutes

Place the haricots in boiled salted water and cook for 10 minutes until tender. Drain and set aside.

Heat the oil in a skillet over medium heat. Place in onion and cook for 3 minutes until translucent. Add in mushrooms, ginger, green onions, tofu, and soy sauce. Cook for 10 minutes. Share into 4 bowls and top with haricot and tofu mixture. Sprinkle with sesame oil. Serve garnished with sesame seeds.

Raisin & Orzo Stuffed Tomatoes

Ingredients for 4 servings

- 2 cups cooked orzo
- Salt and black pepper to taste
- 3 green onions, minced
- 1/3 cup golden raisins
- 1 tsp orange zest
- 4 large ripe tomatoes
- 1/3 cup toasted pine nuts
- ¼ cup minced fresh parsley
- 2 tsp olive oil

Directions and Total Time: 40 minutes

Preheat oven to 380 F.

Mix the orzo, green onions, raisins, and orange zest in a bowl. Set aside. Slice the top of the tomato by ½-inch and take out the pulp. Cut the pulp and place in a bowl. Stir in orzo mixture, pine nuts, parsley, salt, and pepper. Spoon the mixture into the tomatoes and arrange on a greased baking tray. Sprinkle with oil and cover with foil. Bake for 15 minutes. Uncover and bake for another 5 minutes until golden.

Rosemary Baked Potatoes with Cherry Tomatoes

Ingredients for 5 servings

- 5 russet potatoes, sliced
- ½ cup cherry tomatoes, halved
- 2 tbsp rosemary
- 2 tbsp olive oil
- Salt and black pepper to taste

Directions and Total Time: 65 minutes

Preheat oven to 390 F. Make several incisions with a fork in each potato. Rub each potato and cherry tomatoes with olive oil and sprinkle with salt, rosemary and pepper. Arrange on a baking dish and bake for 50-60 minutes. Once ready, transfer to a rack and allow to completely cool before serving.

Squash & Zucchini Stir-Fry

Ingredients for 4 servings

- 2 tbsp olive oil
- 1 red onion, sliced
- 3 garlic cloves, sliced
- 2 green zucchinis, sliced half moons
- 2 yellow squashes, sliced half moons
- 1 tsp herbs de Provence

Directions and Total Time: 20 minutes

Heat oil in a skillet over medium heat. Sauté the onion and garlic for 3 minutes. Mix in zucchini, squashes, herbs de Provence, salt, and pepper. Cook for 4-6 minutes, stirring often. Serve.

Steamed Broccoli with Hazelnuts

Ingredients for 4 servings

1 pound broccoli, cut into florets
2 tbsp olive oil
3 garlic cloves, minced
1 cup sliced white mushrooms
¼ cup dry white wine
2 tbsp minced fresh parsley
Salt and black pepper to taste
½ cup slivered toasted hazelnuts

Directions and Total Time: 20 minutes

Steam the broccoli for 8 minutes or until tender. Remove and set aside.

Heat 1 tbsp of oil in a skillet over medium heat. Add in garlic and mushrooms and sauté for 5 minutes until tender. Pour in the wine and cook for 1 minute. Stir in broccoli, parsley, salt and pepper. Cook for 3 minutes, until the liquid has reduced. Remove to a bowl and add in the remaining oil and hazelnuts and toss to coat. Serve warm.

Sweet Potatoes with Curry Glaze

Ingredients for 6 servings

1 pound sweet potatoes, sliced
2 tbsp olive oil
2 tbsp curry powder
2 tbsp pure date syrup
Juice of ½ lemon
Sea salt and black pepper to taste

Directions and Total Time: 20 minutes

Cook the sweet potatoes covered with salted water for 10 minutes. Drain and return the potatoes to the pot. Lower the heat. Add in oil, curry powder, date syrup, and lemon juice. Cook for 5 minutes. Season with salt and pepper. Serve warm.

Spaghetti Squash in Tahini Sauce

Ingredients for 4 servings

1 (3-pound) spaghetti squash, halved lengthwise
1 tbsp rice vinegar
1 tbsp tahini
Salt and black pepper to taste

Directions and Total Time: 50 minutes

Preheat oven to 390 F. Line with parchment paper a baking sheet. Slice the squash half lengthwise and arrange on the baking sheet skin-side up. Bake for 35-40 minutes. Let cool before scraping the flesh to make "noodles". Place the spaghetti in a bowl. In another bowl whisk 1 tbsp hot water, vinegar, tahini, salt, and pepper. Add into the spaghetti bowl and toss to coat. Serve.

Cumin Red & White Cabbage with Apples

Ingredients for 6 servings

2 tbsp olive oil
1 onion, sliced
1 head red cabbage, shredded
1 head white cabbage, shredded
2 apples, sliced
2 tbsp pure date sugar
¼ cup cider vinegar
1 tsp cumin seeds, crushed
Salt and black pepper to taste

Directions and Total Time: 30 minutes

Heat the oil in a pot over medium heat. Place in onion, shredded cabbages and apples and sauté for 5 minutes until tender. Stir in date sugar, 1 cup water, vinegar, cumin seeds, salt, and pepper. Lower the heat and simmer for 20 minutes. Serve right away.

Parsley Carrots & Parsnips

Ingredients for 4 servings

2 tbsp plant butter
½ pound carrots, cut lengthways
½ pound parsnips, cut lengthways
Salt and black pepper to taste
½ cup Port wine
¼ cup chopped fresh parsley

Directions and Total Time: 25 minutes

Melt the butter in a skillet over medium heat. Place in carrots and parsnips and cook for 5 minutes, stirring occasionally. Sprinkle with salt and pepper. Pour in Port wine and ¼ cup water. Lower the heat and simmer for 15 minutes. Uncover and increase the heat. Cook until forms a syrupy sauce. Remove to a bowl and serve garnished with parsley.

Basil Beet Pasta

Ingredients for 4 servings

1 tsp olive oil
1 garlic clove, minced
4 medium beets, spiralized
½ tsp dried basil
½ tsp dried oregano
½ tsp red pepper flakes

Directions and Total Time: 20 minutes

Heat the oil in a skillet over medium heat. Place in garlic, beets, basil, oregano, pepper flakes, salt, and pepper. Cook for 15 minutes. Serve.

Sherry Eggplants with Cherry Tomatoes

Ingredients for 4 servings

1 garlic cloves, minced
2 tbsp tamari sauce
1 tbsp dry sherry
1 tsp toasted sesame oil
½ tsp pure date sugar
1 tbsp canola oil
2 eggplants, unpeeled and sliced
2 green onions, minced
10 pitted black olives, chopped

Directions and Total Time: 20 minutes

Combine the garlic, tamari, sherry, sesame oil, and sugar in a bowl. Set aside.

Heat the oil in a skillet over medium heat. Place in the eggplant slices, fry for 4 minutes per side. Spread the tamari sauce on the eggplants. Pour in ¼ cup water and cook for 15 minutes. Remove to a plate and sprinkle with green onions and black olives. Serve right away.

Date Caramelized Vegetables

Ingredients for 4 servings

1 tbsp olive oil
2 garlic cloves, minced
4 medium shallots, halved
3 sweet potatoes, cut into chunks
2 large carrots, cut into chunks
2 large parsnips, cut into chunks
2 small turnips, cut into chunks
½ cup pure date sugar
¼ cup water
¼ cup sherry vinegar
Salt and black pepper to taste

Directions and Total Time: 30 minutes

Heat oil in a skillet over medium heat. Place in garlic and shallots and sauté for 3 minutes. Stir in sweet potatoes, carrots, parsnips, and turnips; cook for 5 minutes until tender. Pour in sugar and 2 tbsp of water, cook for 5 minutes until the sugar dissolves. Stir in the remaining water and vinegar, simmer for 2-3 minutes. Season with salt and pepper. Lower the heat and cook for 25 minutes, stirring often.

Sesame Roasted Broccoli with Brown Rice

Ingredients for 4 servings

1 head broccoli, cut into florets
2 tbsp olive oil
¾ cup pure date sugar
⅔ cup water
⅓ cup apple cider vinegar
1 tbsp ketchup
¼ cup soy sauce
2 tbsp cornstarch
4 cups cooked brown rice
2 scallions, chopped
Sesame seeds

Directions and Total Time: 30 minutes

Preheat oven to 420 F. Line with parchment paper a baking sheet. Coat the broccoli with oil in a bowl. Spread on the baking sheet and roast for 20 minutes, turning once.

Add the sugar, water, vinegar, and ketchup in a skillet and bring to a boil. Lower the heat and simmer for 5 minutes. In a bowl, whisk the soy sauce with cornstarch and pour into the skillet. Stir for 2-4 minutes. Once the broccoli is ready, transfer into the skillet and toss to combine. Share the rice into 4 bowls and top with the broccoli. Serve garnished with scallions and sesame seeds.

Tofu Eggplant Pizza

Ingredients for 4 servings

2 eggplants, sliced lengthwise
1/3 cup melted plant butter
2 garlic cloves, minced
1 red onion
12 oz crumbled tofu
7 oz tomato sauce
½ tsp cinnamon powder
1 cup grated plant-based Parmesan
¼ cup chopped fresh oregano

Directions and Total Time: 45 minutes

Preheat oven to 400 F and line a baking sheet with parchment paper. Brush eggplants with some plant butter. Transfer to the baking sheet and bake until lightly browned, about 20 minutes.

Heat the remaining butter in a skillet and sauté the garlic and onion until fragrant and soft, about 3 minutes. Stir in the tofu and cook for 3 minutes. Add the tomato sauce and season with salt and black pepper. Simmer for 10 minutes.

Remove the eggplant from the oven and spread the tofu sauce on top. Sprinkle with the plant-based Parmesan cheese and oregano. Bake further for 10 minutes or until the cheese has melted. Serve.

Raisin & Pine Nut Zucchini Rolls

Ingredients for 4 servings

4 zucchinis, sliced lengthwise
Salt and black pepper to taste
2 tbsp olive oil
1 garlic cloves, minced
4 green onions, chopped
¼ cup ground pine nuts
2 tbsp chopped sun-dried tomatoes
3 tbsp golden raisins
3 tbsp plant-based Parmesan
1 tbsp minced fresh parsley
2 cups marinara sauce

Directions and Total Time: 50 minutes

Preheat oven to 360 F. Arrange the zucchini slices on a greased baking sheet. Season with salt and pepper and bake for 15 minutes. Set aside.

Heat the oil in a skillet over medium heat. Place in garlic, green onions, and pine nuts and cook for 1 minute. Stir in tomatoes, raisins, Parmesan cheese, parsley, salt, and pepper. Spread the mixture onto the zucchini slices. Roll up and transfer to the baking dish. Top with marinara sauce. Cover with foil and bake for 30 minutes. Serve hot.

Almond & Chickpea Patties

Ingredients for 6 servings

1 roasted red bell pepper, chopped
1 (19-oz) can chickpeas
1 cup ground almonds
2 tsp Dijon mustard
2 tsp date syrup
1 garlic clove, pressed
Juice of ½ lemon
1 cup kale, chopped
1 ½ cups rolled oats

Directions and Total Time: 50 minutes

Preheat oven to 360 F. Line with parchment paper a baking sheet.

In a blender, place the chickpeas, almonds, bell pepper, mustard, date syrup, garlic, lemon juice, and kale. Pulse until ingredients are finely chopped but not over blended. Add in the oats. Pulse until everything is well combined. Shape the mixture into 12 patties and arrange on the baking sheet. Bake for 30 minutes until light brown. Serve.

Korean-Style Buckwheat

Ingredients for 4 servings

2 cups water
1 cup buckwheat groats, rinsed
¼ cup unseasoned rice vinegar
¼ cup Mirin wine

Directions and Total Time: 25 minutes

Boil water in a pot. Put in the buckwheat groats, lower the heat and simmer covered for 15-20 minutes, until the liquid absorbs. Let cool for a few minutes. Using a fork, fluff the groats and stir in vinegar and Mirin wine. Serve.

Basil Bell Pepper & Mushroom Medley

Ingredients for 4 servings

3 tbsp olive oil
1 cup mushrooms, sliced
1 red bell pepper, sliced
1 orange bell pepper, sliced
1 yellow bell pepper, sliced
1 green bell pepper, sliced
2 garlic cloves, minced
3 tbsp red wine vinegar
2 tbsp chopped fresh basil

Directions and Total Time: 25 minutes

Heat the oil in a skillet over medium heat. Place in mushrooms, garlic, and bell peppers and sauté for 7-10 minutes. Pour in vinegar and scrape any bit from the bottom. Cook for 2-3 minutes until the vinegar is reduced. Sprinkle with salt and pepper. Serve topped with basil.

Peanut Quinoa & Chickpea Pilaf

Ingredients for 4 servings

1 tbsp olive oil
1 medium red onion, minced
1 ½ cups quinoa, rinsed
3 cups vegetable broth
2 (15.5-oz) cans chickpeas
¼ tsp ground cayenne
1 tbsp minced fresh chives
1 tangerine, chopped
½ cup peanuts

Directions and Total Time: 30 minutes

Heat the oil in a pot over medium heat. Place the onion and cook for 3 minutes until softened. Add in quinoa and broth. Bring to a boil, then lower the heat and sprinkle with salt. Simmer for 20 minutes. Stir in chickpeas, cayenne pepper, chives, tangerine, and peanuts. Serve warm.

Spicy Vegetable Paella

Ingredients for 4 servings

2 tbsp olive oil
2 medium carrots, sliced
1 celery stalk, sliced
1 medium yellow onion, chopped
1 medium red bell pepper, diced

3 garlic cloves, chopped
8 oz green peas
1 cup Spanish brown rice
1 (14.5-oz) can diced tomatoes
2 ½ cups vegetable broth

½ tsp crushed red pepper
½ tsp ground fennel seed
¼ tsp saffron
2 cups oyster mushrooms
1 cup asparagus, chopped

Directions and Total Time: 35 minutes

Heat the oil in a pot over medium heat. Place in carrots, celery, onion, bell pepper, and garlic. Cook for 5 minutes until tender. Stir in green peas, rice, tomatoes, broth, salt, red pepper, fennel seeds, and saffron. Cook for 20 minutes. Mix in mushrooms and asparagus. Cook covered another 10 minutes.

Baked Potatoes & Asparagus & Pine Nuts

Ingredients for 4 servings

1 bunch of asparagus, sliced
2 tbsp olive oil
2 garlic cloves, minced
5 cups fresh baby spinach

Salt and black pepper to taste
1 tsp dried basil
½ tsp dried thyme
2 potatoes, sliced

½ cup vegetable broth
2 tbsp nutritional yeast
½ cup ground pine nuts

Directions and Total Time: 50 minutes

Preheat oven to 370 F.

Heat half of the oil in a skillet over medium heat. Place in garlic, spinach, salt, and pepper and cook for 4 minutes until the spinach wilts. Add in basil and thyme. Set aside.

Arrange half of potato slices on a greased casserole and season with salt and pepper. Top with the asparagus slices and finish with the spinach mixture. Cover with the remaining potato slices.

Whisk the broth with nutritional yeast in a bowl. Pour over the vegetables. Sprinkle with remaining oil and pine nuts. Cover with foil and bake for 40 minutes. Uncover and bake for another 10 minutes until golden brown. Serve warm.

Italian Potato & Swiss Chard Au Gratin

Ingredients for 4 servings

3 tbsp olive oil
1 medium yellow onion, minced
3 garlic cloves, minced

1 cup Swiss chard, chopped
Salt and black pepper to taste
2 lb new potatoes, unpeeled, sliced

1 tsp Italian seasoning
2 tbsp plant-based Parmesan

Directions and Total Time: 1 hour 15 minutes

Preheat oven to 360 F.

Warm half of the oil in a skillet over medium heat. Place in onion and garlic and sauté for 3 minutes until translucent. Add in Swiss chard to wilt for 3-4 minutes. Season with salt and pepper. Set aside.

Arrange half of potato slices on a greased baking dish. Sprinkle with Italian seasoning, salt and pepper. Sprinkle with the remaining olive oil. Top with Swiss chard mixture and cover with the remaining potatoes. Cover with foil and bake for 1 hour. Scatter Parmesan cheese over and bake another 10 minutes. Serve immediately.

French Vegetable Byaldi

Ingredients for 6 servings

2 potatoes, sliced
2 eggplants, sliced diagonally
3 tbsp olive oil
1 onion, chopped
3 garlic cloves, minced
3 cups spinach, chopped
2 cups kale, chopped
2 cups collard greens, chopped
1 cup loosely packed basil leaves
6 ripe plum tomatoes, sliced
¾ cup breadcrumbs
3 tbsp plant-based Parmesan

Directions and Total Time: 75 minutes

Preheat oven to 390 F.

Arrange the potato slices on a greased baking sheet and the eggplant slices in a separated baking sheet. Sprinkle the vegetables with oil, salt and pepper. Bake the eggplants for 10 minutes and the potato for 20 minutes. Set aside.

Heat oil in a skillet over medium heat. Place in onion and garlic and sauté for 3 minutes until soft. Add in spinach, kale, collard greens, salt, and pepper. Cook for 7 minutes until the greens wilt. Remove the mixture to a blender. Add in basil and remaining oil, salt and pepper and blend until smooth.

On a grease baking dish, arrange half of potato slices and cover with some greens mixture. Then add a layer of eggplant slices and cover with more greens mixture. Then add a layer of tomato slices and cover with more greens mixture. Repeat the process until any ingredients left. Sprinkle each layer with salt and pepper. Finally, scatter with breadcrumbs and Parmesan cheese. Sprinkle the remaining oil. Bake for another 10 minutes. Serve warm.

Sautéed Veggies with Rice

Ingredients for 4 servings

1 ½ cups brown rice, rinsed
2 tbsp olive oil
4 shallots, chopped
1 medium red bell pepper, chopped
1 medium zucchini, chopped
2 cups cooked shelled edamame
2 cups corn kernels
2 tomatoes, chopped
3 tbsp chopped parsley

Directions and Total Time: 40 minutes

Boil 3 cups of salted water in a pot over high heat. Place in rice, lower the heat and cook for 20 minutes. Set aside.

Heat the oil in a skillet over medium heat. Add in shallots, zucchini, and bell pepper and sauté for 5 minutes until tender. Mix in edamame, corn, tomatoes, salt, and pepper. Cook for 5 minutes, stirring often. Put in cooked rice and parsley, toss to combine. Serve warm.

Melon & Cucumber Gazpacho

Ingredients for 8 servings

2 large tomatoes
1 jalapeño pepper, seeded
4 cups cubed fresh melon, divided
2 tsp rice vinegar
¼ cup extra-virgin olive oil
1 large cucumber, peeled, chopped
1 small red onion, chopped
1 small red bell pepper, chopped
¼ cup minced fresh dill

Directions and Total Time: 10 minutes

Put the tomatoes, jalapeño pepper, vinegar, olive oil, and half of the melon in a food processor and blitz. Place in cucumber, onion, bell pepper, and dill and blend until uniform and smooth. Adjust seasoning with salt and pepper. Place the remaining melon in a bowl and top with the gazpacho.

Artichoke & Tomato Tart with Peanuts

Ingredients for 4 servings

1 (10-oz) package artichoke hearts
1 frozen puff pastry sheet, thawed
½ cup toasted peanuts
8 oz extra-firm tofu, crumbled
3 green onions, minced
2 tsp fresh lemon juice
2 tbsp minced fresh parsley
1 tbsp minced fresh marjoram
2 tomatoes, sliced

Directions and Total Time: 55 minutes

Preheat oven to 390 F.

Boil salted water in a pot over high heat. Place in artichoke hearts and cook for 12 minutes. Drain and set aside. Lay the pastry on a floured flat surface and roll out. Transfer to a tart dish and trim the edges. Bake for 10 minutes. Set aside.

Cut finely 2 artichoke hearts and set aside. In a blender, place the remaining hearts, half of the peanuts, tofu, and green onions and pulse until finely chopped. Add in lemon juice, parsley, marjoram, salt, and pepper. Blitz until smooth. Remove to a bowl and mix in remaining peanuts and reserved artichokes.

Spread the mixture over the tart pastry and top with tomato slices. Sprinkle with salt and pepper. Bake for 25 minutes until golden brown. Let cool 10-15 minutes before slicing.

Chili Broccoli & Beans with Almonds

Ingredients for 4 servings

1 ½ pounds potatoes
4 cups broccoli florets
3 tbsp olive oil
3 garlic cloves, minced
¾ cup chopped almonds
¼ tsp crushed red pepper
1 (15.5-oz) can white beans
1 tsp dried thyme
1 tbsp fresh lemon juice

Directions and Total Time: 40 minutes

Place the potatoes in water and cook for 20 minutes. Set aside. Place the broccoli in water and steam for 7 minutes. Set aside.

Heat 2 tbsp of oil in a skillet over medium heat. Place in garlic, almonds and red pepper and cook for 1 minute. Add in potatoes, broccoli, beans, thyme, salt, and pepper. Cook for 5 minutes. Drizzle with the lemon juice and remaining oil. Serve right away.

Bean & Pecan Stuffed Mushrooms

Ingredients for 4 servings

4 mushroom caps
2 tbsp olive oil
1 onion, minced
2 garlic cloves, minced
1 carrot, chopped
1 (15.5-oz) can white beans, mashed
1 cup finely chopped pecans
2 tbsp minced fresh parsley
½ cup dry breadcrumbs

Directions and Total Time: 45 minutes

Preheat oven to 360 F.

Heat the oil in a skillet over medium heat. Place the onion, garlic, and carrot and sauté for 5 minutes until tender. Stir in beans, pecans, parsley, and half of the breadcrumbs. Sprinkle with salt and pepper.

Stuff the mushrooms with the mixture and arrange on a greased baking dish. Cover with foil and bake for 20 minutes. Uncover and scatter with the remaining breadcrumbs. Bake another 10 minutes until golden brown. Serve warm.

Dilly Potatoes

Ingredients for 4 servings

1 ½ lb baby red potatoes, halved
2 tbsp plant butter
3 garlic cloves, minced
1 tbsp minced fresh dill
Sea salt to taste

Directions and Total Time: 35 minutes

Preheat oven to 430 F. Line with parchment paper a baking sheet. Mix in the potatoes, butter, garlic, dill, and salt and spread evenly. Bake for 30 minutes until golden brown. Serve.

Balsamic Artichoke Hearts

Ingredients for 4 servings

1 ½ pounds artichoke hearts
2 tbsp olive oil
Sea salt and black pepper to taste
⅓ cup balsamic vinegar
Juice and zest of 1 lemon

Directions and Total Time: 35 minutes

Preheat oven to 360 F. Brush the artichoke hearts with olive oil, salt and pepper. Arrange on a baking sheet. Roast for 20-25 minutes, turning once.

Meanwhile, put the vinegar in a skillet over medium heat and bring to a boil. Lower the heat and simmer for 8 minutes, until gets a syrupy texture. Once the artichokes are ready, coat them with lemon juice and lemon zest. Serve topped with the balsamic reduction.

Roasted Sweet Potato Porridge

Ingredients for 4 servings

2 sweet potatoes, chopped
2 tbsp olive oil
1 onion, finely chopped
1 cup buckwheat groats
2 cups vegetable broth
1 cup green beans, chopped

Directions and Total Time: 25 minutes

Preheat oven to 420 F.

Arrange the sweet potatoes on a greased baking dish and coat with half of the oil. Sprinkle with salt and pepper. Roast for 25 minutes, turning once. Set aside.

Heat the remaining oil in a skillet over medium heat. Place the onion and sauté for 3 minutes, stirring often. Stir in buckwheat groats and broth. Bring to a boil, then lower the heat and simmer for 15 minutes. Mix in green beans, sweet potatoes, salt, and pepper. Serve right away.

Orange Kale Stir-Fry

Ingredients for 4 servings

2 tbsp olive oil
1 shallot, chopped
2 garlic cloves, minced
10 oz kale
Zest and juice of 1 orange
Sea salt and black pepper to taste

Directions and Total Time: 20 minutes

Heat the oil in a skillet over medium heat. Place the shallot and garlic and sauté for 3 minutes until translucent. Stir in kale, orange juice and orange zest. Cook for 2-3 minutes until the kale wilts. Sprinkle with salt and pepper. Serve immediately.

Parsley Faro & Bean Casserole

Ingredients for 6 servings

2 ¾ cups water
1 cup faro
3 tbsp olive oil
1 medium yellow onion, chopped
1 medium red bell pepper, chopped

2 garlic cloves, minced
3 cups chopped Swiss chard
Salt and black pepper to taste
1 (15.5-oz) can Great Northern beans
1 cup cherry tomatoes, quartered

2 tbsp fresh lemon juice
¼ cup nutritional yeast
2 tbsp minced fresh dill weed
2 tbsp minced fresh parsley
1/3 cup dry breadcrumbs

Directions and Total Time: 50 minutes

Boil salted water in a pot over high heat. Place in faro, the lower the heat and simmer for 30 minutes. Set aside.

Preheat oven to 360 F.

Heat the oil in a skillet over medium heat. Add in onion and bell pepper and sauté for 5 minutes. Stir in garlic, Swiss chard, salt, and pepper. Cook for 5 minutes until the chard wilts. Remove to the faro pot. Put in beans, tomatoes, lemon juice, yeast, dill weed, and parsley; stir.

Transfer into a greased baking pan and scatter breadcrumbs over. Bake for 10-15 minutes. Serve immediately.

Creamy Bell Pepper Goulash

Ingredients for 4 servings

2 tbsp olive oil
1 onion, chopped
2 garlic cloves, minced
1 potato, chopped

1 pound bell peppers, chopped
1 tbsp tomato paste
½ cup dry white wine
1 ½ tbsp sweet paprika

1 tsp caraway seeds
1 ½ cups sauerkraut, drained
1 ½ cups vegetable broth
½ cup vegan sour cream

Directions and Total Time: 50 minutes

Heat the oil in a pot over medium heat. Place in onion, garlic, bell peppers, and potato and sauté for 8-10 minutes. Mix in tomato paste, wine, paprika, caraway seeds, sauerkraut, and broth. Bring to a boil, then lower the heat and sprinkle with salt and pepper. Simmer for 30 minutes.

Whisk 1 cup of cooking liquid with sour cream in a bowl. Pour into the pot and adjust the seasonings if needed. Serve hot.

Pomegranate Bell Peppers & Eggplants

Ingredients for 4 servings

½ cup olive oil
1 onion, chopped
3 eggplants, cut into chunks
1 red pepper, chopped

1 yellow bell pepper, chopped
2 garlic cloves, minced
1 hot chili, seeded and minced
2 tbsp pomegranate molasses

½ cup orange juice
2 tsp pure date sugar
1 ripe peach, chopped
½ cup finely chopped fresh cilantro

Directions and Total Time: 40 minutes

Heat the oil in a skillet over medium heat. Place the onion and sauté for 5 minutes. Add in eggplants, bell peppers, garlic, and chili. Cook for 10 minutes. Stir in pomegranate molasses, orange juice, sugar, salt, and pepper. Bring to a boil, then lower the heat and simmer for 20 minutes, until the liquid reduce. Top with peach and cilantro and serve right away.

Thyme Black Bean Loaf with Artichokes

Ingredients for 6 servings

1 potato, chopped
1 (10-oz) package artichoke hearts
¼ cup olive oil
1 onion, chopped
1 (15.5-oz) can black beans
¼ cup vegetable broth
2 tbsp tahini
1 ½ tbsp soy sauce
1 ½ tbsp fresh lemon juice
1 cup whole-wheat flour
½ cup nutritional yeast
1 tsp dried thyme
Salt and black pepper to taste
½ cup chopped sun-dried tomatoes
¼ cup minced fresh parsley

Directions and Total Time: 60 minutes

Preheat oven to 360 F.

Place the potatoes and artichokes in hot water and steam for 15 minutes. Drain and set aside. Cut 2 artichoke hearts and set aside.

Heat the oil in a skillet. Place onion and sauté for 3 minutes. Add in potatoes and artichokes. Remove to a blender and add in beans, broth, tahini, soy sauce, and lemon juice. Pulse until smooth.

In a bowl, combine the flour, yeast, thyme, salt, and pepper. Pour the potato mixture into the flour mixture. Add in sun-dried tomatoes, parsley and reserved artichokes. Toss to coat. Shape the mixture into a loaf and place in a greased loaf pan to bake for 40 minutes, until golden brown. Allow to cool for 15 minutes. Slice and serve.

Leek & Mushroom Stroganoff

Ingredients for 6 servings

2 tbsp plant butter
1 leek, chopped
1 cup button mushrooms, sliced
3 garlic cloves, minced
1 red bell pepper, chopped
¼ cup vegetable broth
1 tsp paprika
Sea salt and black pepper to taste
¼ cup vegan sour cream
2 tbsp chopped parsley
1 pound pasta, cooked

Directions and Total Time: 15 minutes

In a skillet over medium heat, melt the butter. Place in leek, mushrooms, garlic, and bell pepper and cook for 5 minutes until tender. Stir in broth, paprika, salt and pepper and cook for another 5 minutes. Turn the heat off and mix in sour cream and pasta. Share into 6 bowls and serve topped with parsley.

Couscous & Lentil Curry

Ingredients for 4 servings

2 tbsp olive oil
3 green onions, chopped
1 eggplant, diced
Salt to taste
1-inch piece fresh ginger, minced
1 (15-oz) can green lentils, drained
1 tomato, chopped
1 ½ cups couscous
2 ¼ cups boiling water
6 tbsp curry sauce
Chopped cilantro

Directions and Total Time: 20 minutes

Place the couscous in a bowl with hot water. Cover and let sit until the liquid absorbs.

Warm the oil in a skillet over medium heat. Place in green onion, eggplant, ginger, lentils, tomato, and salt. Cook for 8-10 minutes.

Mix the curry sauce with the vegetables. Using a fork, fluff the couscous and divide between 4 bowls. Top with the lentil mixture. Garnish with cilantro and serve.

Sicilian Spaghetti Squash

Ingredients for 4 servings

- 1 (4-pound) spaghetti squash, halved and seeded
- 3 tbsp olive oil
- 1 onion, chopped
- 2 cups chopped artichoke hearts
- ½ cup pitted and sliced green olives
- 1 cup halved cherry tomatoes
- 3 garlic cloves, minced
- 1 ½ tsp Italian seasoning
- Sea salt and black pepper to taste
- Pine nuts
- Plant-based Parmesan cheese
- Red pepper flakes

Directions and Total Time: 50 minutes

Preheat oven to 390 F. Line with parchment paper a baking sheet. Rub each squash half with some oil on all sides. Arrange on the sheet cut-sides down and bake for 40-45 minutes until tender. Let cool.

Meanwhile, heat oil in a skillet over medium heat. Place in onion, garlic, and artichoke and cook for 5 minutes. Add in olives and tomatoes and cook for another 3-5 minutes. Set aside.

Take out the squash flesh, using a fork and separate into strands. Transfer to the veggie skillet. Season with Italian seasoning, salt, and pepper; toss to combine. Share into bowls and serve garnished with pine nuts, Parmesan cheese, and pepper flakes.

Sesame Tempeh Sauté

Ingredients for 4 servings

- 8 oz tempeh
- Salt and black pepper to taste
- 2 tsp cornstarch
- 3 cups cauliflower florets
- 2 tbsp canola oil
- 3 tbsp soy sauce
- 2 tbsp water
- 1 tbsp Mirin wine
- ½ tsp crushed red pepper
- 2 tsp toasted sesame oil
- 1 medium red bell pepper, sliced
- 8 oz white mushrooms, sliced
- 2 garlic cloves, minced
- 3 tbsp minced green onions
- 1 tsp grated fresh ginger

Directions and Total Time: 50 minutes

Combine the soy sauce, water, Mirin wine, red pepper, and sesame oil in a bowl. Boil water in a pot and place in tempeh. Simmer for 30 minutes. Drain and let cool. Chop tempeh into cubes. Transfer to a bowl and sprinkle with salt, pepper and cornstarch. Set aside.

Steam the cauliflower for 5 minutes; reserve. Heat the canola oil in a skillet over medium heat. Place in tempeh and fry for 5 minutes. Remove to a plate.

To the same skillet, add bell pepper, mushrooms, garlic, green onions, and ginger and sauté for 5 minutes. Stir in cauliflower and tempeh and stir-fry for 1 minute. Pour in the Mirin wine mixture and stir to coat. Serve warm.

Cayenne Kale

Ingredients for 4 servings

- Sea salt and black pepper to taste
- 2 Bunches kale, chopped
- 3 tbsp olive oil
- 3 garlic cloves, minced
- 1 tsp cayenne pepper
- Zest of 1 lemon

Directions and Total Time: 20 minutes

Boil 8 cups of water in a pot. Add salt and kale. Cook for 2 minutes. Drain and reserve. Heat the oil in a skillet over medium heat. Place in garlic and sauté for 30 seconds. Stir in kale, cayenne pepper, lemon zest, salt, and pepper. Serve right away.

Parsley Pumpkin Noodles

Ingredients for 4 servings

¼ cup plant butter
½ cup chopped onion
1 pound pumpkin, spiralized
1 bunch kale, sliced
¼ cup chopped fresh parsley
Salt and black pepper to taste

Directions and Total Time: 15 minutes

Mel the butter in a skillet over medium heat. Place the onion and cook for 3 minutes. Add in pumpkin and cook for another 7-8 minutes. Stir in kale and cook for another 2 minutes, until the kale wilts. Sprinkle with parsley, salt and pepper and serve.

Cinnamon-Brandy Acorn Squash

Ingredients for 4 servings

1 acorn squash, sliced
½ cup brandy
⅓ cup pure date syrup
¼ cup plant butter
¼ tsp ground cinnamon
Sea salt to taste

Directions and Total Time: 40 minutes

Preheat oven to 430 F. Line with parchment paper a baking sheet. Arrange the squash slices on the sheet and bake for 20 minutes.

In the meantime, pour the brandy, date syrup, and butter in a pot over medium heat. Cook for 2-3 minutes.

Turn the squash slices over and sprinkle the brandy mixture on top. Season with cinnamon and salt. Bake another 8-10 minutes, until the squash is tender and caramelized on top.

Maple Green Cabbage Hash

Ingredients for 4 servings

3 tbsp olive oil
2 shallots, thinly sliced
1 ½ lb green cabbage, shredded
3 tbsp apple cider vinegar
1 tbsp pure maple syrup
½ tsp sriracha sauce

Directions and Total Time: 25 minutes

Heat the oil in a skillet over medium heat. Place in shallots and cabbage and cook for 10 minutes until tender. Pour in vinegar and scrape any bits from the bottom. Mix in maple syrup and sriracha sauce. Cook for 3-5 minutes, until the liquid absorbs. Sprinkle with salt and pepper. Serve right away.

Eggplant with Tofu

Ingredients for 2 servings

½ cup non-dairy milk
½ cup breadcrumbs
2 tbsp nutritional yeast
Salt to taste
2 eggplants, sliced
2 tbsp olive oil
4 tbsp tomato sauce
½ cup tofu, crumbled

Directions and Total Time: 25 minutes

Pour the milk in a bowl. In another bowl, mix the breadcrumbs, yeast and salt. Dip the eggplant slices in the milk, then coat in the breadcrumbs. Remove to a plate. In a skillet over medium heat, warm the oil. Fry the eggplant slices for 10 minutes on both sides. Remove to a baking sheet. Top with tomato sauce and tofu. Place the sheet under the broiler for 6 minutes until the tofu begins to brown. Serve.

Lemony Arugula with Pine Nuts

Ingredients for 4 servings

2 bunches arugula, chopped
3 tbsp olive oil
3 garlic cloves, minced
1 tsp cayenne pepper
Zest of 1 lemon
¼ cup toasted pine nuts for garnish

Directions and Total Time: 20 minutes

Steam the arugula in a pot over medium heat for 2-3 minutes. Drain and set aside.

Heat the oil in a skillet over medium heat. Add in garlic and cook for 30 seconds. Mix in arugula, cayenne pepper, lemon zest, salt, pepper. Serve garnished with toasted pine nuts.

Bell Pepper & Spinach with Walnuts

Ingredients for 4 servings

2 pounds spinach, chopped
3 tbsp olive oil
1 onion, chopped
2 red bell peppers, cut into strips
2 garlic cloves, minced
¼ tsp red pepper flakes
Sea salt and black pepper to taste
¼ cup toasted walnuts for garnish

Directions and Total Time: 15 minutes

Place the spinach in a steamer basket and cook for 5 minutes until tender. Set aside.

Warm oil in a skillet over medium heat. Add in onion, garlic, and bell peppers and sauté for 5 minutes. Turn the heat off and mix in spinach, pepper flakes, salt, and pepper. Serve topped with walnuts.

Mustard Tofu & Cauliflower

Ingredients for 6 servings

4 cups cauliflower florets
1 ½ cups almond milk
¼ cup soft tofu
Juice of ½ lemon
1 tbsp English mustard
1 ½ tsp onion powder
Sea salt and black pepper to taste
1 tsp garlic powder
1 lb whole-wheat macaroni, cooked
Plant-based Parmesan cheese
Chopped fresh parsley

Directions and Total Time: 20 minutes

Steam the cauliflower for 10 minutes. Remove to a blender. Put in milk, tofu, lemon juice, mustard, onion powder, salt, garlic powder, and pepper. Pulse until smooth. Remove to a bowls and add in the pasta; toss to coat. Sprinkle with plant-based Parmesan cheese, parsley and pepper to serve.

Lentil Stuffed Avocados

Ingredients for 4 servings

2 avocados, halved and pitted
1 (15-oz) can lentils, drained
1 cup corn kernels
½ cup diced tomato
Juice of ½ lime
1 tbsp maple syrup
1 tsp olive oil
Sea salt and black pepper to taste
1 tbsp chopped fresh cilantro

Directions and Total Time: 10 minutes

Take out the avocado flesh, leaving ½-inch of flesh in the shell.

Place the avocado flesh in a bowl and stir the lentils, corn, tomato, lime juice, maple syrup, oil, salt, pepper, and cilantro. Scoop the mixture into the shells and serve immediately.

Lentil & Sweet Potato Tortillas

Ingredients for 2 servings

2 tsp olive oil
¼ onion, chopped
1 cooked sweet potato
½ cup canned lentils, drained
1 tsp chili powder
1 tsp lime juice
2 corn tortillas
¼ cup grated plant-based mozzarella
1 tbsp cilantro, chopped for serving

Directions and Total Time: 20 minutes

Warm the oil in a skillet over medium heat. Place the onion and cook for 5 minutes until softened. Remove to a bowl. Add in sweet potato, lentils, chili powder, lime juice, and salt and mash well. Divide the mixture between the tortillas, top with plant-based mozzarella cheese and fold them. Heat the oil in the skillet and put in the tortillas. Cook for 4 minutes on both sides, until golden brown. Cut in thirds and top with cilantro. Serve immediately.

Spicy Broccoli in Pecan Pesto

Ingredients for 4 servings

1 pound broccoli florets
2 cups chopped fresh basil
¼ cup olive oil
4 garlic cloves
½ cup pecans
1 tsp chili powder

Directions and Total Time: 15 minutes

Place water in a pot and add the broccoli. Bring to a boil and steam for 5 minutes. In a blender, put basil, olive oil, garlic, pecans, and chili powder. Pulse until everything is blended. Drain the broccoli and mix in the basil sauce; toss to coat. Serve right away.

Grilled Tofu Mayo Sandwiches

Ingredients for 2 servings

¼ cup tofu mayonnaise
2 slices whole-grain bread
¼ cucumber, sliced
½ cup lettuce, chopped
½ tomato, sliced
1 tsp olive oil, divided

Directions and Total Time: 15 minutes

Spread the vegan mayonnaise over a bread slice, top with the cucumber, lettuce and tomato and finish with the other slice. Heat the oil in a skillet over medium heat. Place the sandwich and grill for 3 minutes, then flip over and cook for a further 3 minutes. Cut the sandwich in half and serve.

Bulgur & Bean Bowls with Tortilla Chips

Ingredients for 4 servings

Juice of 2 limes
1 tbsp olive oil
1 tbsp maple syrup
2 cups cooked bulgur
1 tbsp Taco seasoning
2 heads romaine lettuce, chopped
1 (15-oz) can black beans
1 cup cherry tomatoes, halved
1 cup corn kernels
1 avocado, peeled, pitted, and diced
4 scallions, thinly sliced
12 tortilla chips, crushed

Directions and Total Time: 15 minutes

Mix the lime juice, olive oil, maple syrup, and salt in a bowl. Set aside. In a bowl, combine the bulgur and taco seasoning. In another bowl, mix the lettuce with the vinaigrette. Separate into 4 bowls and add on each bowl the bulgur, beans, tomatoes, corn, avocado, scallions, and tortilla chips. Serve.

SNAKS AND SIDES

Kentucky Cauliflower with Mashed Parsnips

Ingredients for 6 servings

½ cup unsweetened almond milk
¼ cup coconut flour
¼ tsp cayenne pepper
½ cup whole-grain breadcrumbs

½ cup grated plant-based mozzarella
30 oz cauliflower florets
1 lb parsnips, peeled and quartered
3 tbsp melted plant butter

A pinch of nutmeg
1 tsp cumin powder
1 cup coconut cream
2 tbsp sesame oil

Directions and Total Time: 35 minutes

Preheat oven to 425 F and line a baking sheet with parchment paper.

In a small bowl, combine almond milk, coconut flour, and cayenne pepper. In another bowl, mix salt, breadcrumbs, and plant-based mozzarella cheese. Dip each cauliflower floret into the milk mixture, coating properly, and then into the cheese mixture. Place the breaded cauliflower on the baking sheet and bake in the oven for 30 minutes, turning once after 15 minutes.

Make slightly salted water in a saucepan and add the parsnips. Bring to boil over medium heat for 15 minutes or until the parsnips are fork tender. Drain and transfer to a bowl. Add in melted plant butter, cumin powder, nutmeg, and coconut cream. Puree the ingredients using an immersion blender until smooth. Spoon the parsnip mash into serving plates and drizzle with some sesame oil. Serve with the baked cauliflower when ready.

Spinach Chips with Guacamole Hummus

Ingredients for 4 servings

½ cup baby spinach
1 tbsp olive oil
½ tsp plain vinegar
3 large avocados, chopped

½ cup chopped parsley + for garnish
½ cup melted plant butter
¼ cup pumpkin seeds
¼ cup sesame paste

Juice from ½ lemon
1 garlic clove, minced
½ tsp coriander powder
Salt and black pepper to taste

Directions and Total Time: 30 minutes

Preheat oven to 300 F. Put spinach in a bowl and toss with olive oil, vinegar, and salt. Place in a parchment paper-lined baking sheet and bake until the leaves are crispy but not burned, about 15 minutes.

Place avocado into the bowl of a food processor. Add in parsley, plant butter, pumpkin seeds, sesame paste, lemon juice, garlic, coriander powder, salt, and black pepper. Puree until smooth. Spoon the hummus into a bowl and garnish with parsley. Serve with the spinach chips.

Parmesan Croutons with Rosemary Tomato Soup

Ingredients for 6 servings

3 tbsp flax seed powder
1 ¼ cups almond flour
2 tsp baking powder
5 tbsp psyllium husk powder
2 tsp plain vinegar
3 oz plant butter

2 oz grated plant-based Parmesan
2 lb fresh ripe tomatoes
4 cloves garlic, peeled only
1 small white onion, diced
1 small red bell pepper, diced
3 tbsp olive oil

1 cup coconut cream
½ tsp dried rosemary
½ tsp dried oregano
2 tbsp chopped fresh basil
Salt and black pepper to taste
Basil leaves to garnish

Directions and Total Time: 1 hour 25 minutes

In a medium bowl, mix the flax seed powder with 9 tbsp of water and set aside to soak for 5 minutes. Preheat oven to 350 F and line a baking sheet with parchment paper.

In another bowl, combine almond flour, baking powder, psyllium husk powder, and salt. When the flax egg is ready, mix in 1 ¼ cups boiling water and plain vinegar. Add in the flour mixture and whisk for 30 seconds. Form 8 flat pieces out of the dough. Place the flattened dough on the baking sheet while leaving enough room between each to allow rising. Bake for 40 minutes. Remove the croutons to cool and break them into halves. Mix the plant butter with plant-based Parmesan cheese and spread the mixture in the inner parts of the croutons. Increase the oven's temperature to 450 F and bake the croutons further for 5 minutes or until golden brown and crispier.

In a baking pan, add tomatoes, garlic, onion, red bell pepper, and drizzle with olive oil. Roast in the oven for 25 minutes and after broil for 3 to 4 minutes until some of the tomatoes are slightly charred. Transfer to a blender and add coconut cream, rosemary, oregano, basil, salt, and black pepper. Puree until smooth and creamy. Pour the soup into serving bowls, drop some croutons on top, garnish with basil leaves, and serve.

Buttered Carrot Noodles with Kale

Ingredients for 4 servings

2 large carrots	4 tbsp plant butter	1 cup chopped kale
¼ cup vegetable broth	1 garlic clove, minced	Salt and black pepper to taste

Directions and Total Time: 15 minutes

Peel the carrots with a slicer and run both through a spiralizer to form noodles.

Pour the vegetable broth into a saucepan and add the carrot noodles. Simmer (over low heat) the carrots for 3 minutes. Strain through a colander and set the vegetables aside.

Place a large skillet over medium heat and melt the plant butter. Add the garlic and sauté until softened and put in the kale; cook until wilted.

Pour the carrots into the pan, season with the salt and black pepper, and stir-fry for 3 to 4 minutes. Spoon the vegetables into a bowl and serve with pan-grilled tofu.

Baked Spicy Eggplant

Ingredients for 4 servings

2 large eggplants	2 tbsp plant butter	4 oz raw ground almonds
Salt and black pepper to taste	1 tsp red chili flakes	

Directions and Total Time: 30 minutes

Preheat oven to 400 F.

Cut off the head of the eggplants and slice the body into 2-inch rounds. Season with salt and black pepper and arrange on a parchment paper-lined baking sheet.

Drop thin slices of the plant butter on each eggplant slice, sprinkle with red chili flakes, and bake in the oven for 20 minutes.

Slide the baking sheet out and sprinkle with the almonds. Roast further for 5 minutes or until golden brown. Dish the eggplants and serve with arugula salad.

Mashed Broccoli with Roasted Garlic

Ingredients for 4 servings

½ head garlic
2 tbsp olive oil + for garnish
1 head broccoli, cut into florets
1 tsp salt
4 oz plant butter
¼ tsp dried thyme
Juice and zest of half a lemon
4 tbsp coconut cream

Directions and Total Time: 45 minutes

Preheat oven to 400 F.

Use a knife to cut a ¼ inch off the top of the garlic cloves, drizzle with olive oil, and wrap in aluminum foil. Place on a baking sheet and roast for 30 minutes. Remove and set aside when ready.

Pour the broccoli into a pot, add 3 cups of water, and 1 teaspoon of salt. Bring to a boil until tender, about 7 minutes. Drain and transfer the broccoli to a bowl. Add the plant butter, thyme, lemon juice and zest, coconut cream, and olive oil. Use an immersion blender to puree the ingredients until smooth and nice. Spoon the mash into serving bowls and garnish with some olive oil. Serve.

Spicy Pistachio Dip

Ingredients for 4 servings

3 oz toasted pistachios + for garnish
3 tbsp coconut cream
¼ cup water
Juice of half a lemon
½ tsp smoked paprika
Cayenne pepper to taste
½ tsp salt
½ cup olive oil

Directions and Total Time: 10 minutes

Pour the pistachios, coconut cream, water, lemon juice, paprika, cayenne pepper, and salt. Puree the ingredients on high speed until smooth. Add the olive oil and puree a little further. Manage the consistency of the dip by adding more oil or water. Spoon the dip into little bowls, garnish with some pistachios, and serve with julienned celery and carrots.

Paprika Roasted Nuts

Ingredients for 4 servings

8 oz walnuts and pecans
1 tsp salt
1 tbsp coconut oil
1 tsp cumin powder
1 tsp paprika powder

Directions and Total Time: 10 minutes

In a bowl, mix walnuts, pecans, salt, coconut oil, cumin powder, and paprika powder until the nuts are well coated with spice and oil. Pour the mixture into a pan and toast while stirring continually. Once the nuts are fragrant and brown, transfer to a bowl. Allow to cool and serve with a chilled berry juice.

Onion Rings & Kale Dip

Ingredients for 4 servings

1 onion, sliced into rings
1 tbsp flax seed meal + 3 tbsp water
1 cup almond flour
½ cup grated plant-based Parmesan
2 tsp garlic powder
½ tbsp sweet paprika powder
2 oz chopped kale
2 tbsp olive oil
2 tbsp dried cilantro
1 tbsp dried oregano
Salt and black pepper to taste
1 cup tofu mayonnaise
4 tbsp coconut cream
Juice of ½ a lemon

Directions and Total Time: 35 minutes

Preheat oven to 400 F. In a bowl, mix the flax seed meal and water and leave the mixture to thicken and fully absorb for 5 minutes. In another bowl, combine almond flour, plant-based Parmesan cheese, half of the garlic powder, sweet paprika, and salt. Line a baking sheet with parchment paper in readiness for the rings. When the flax egg is ready, dip in the onion rings one after another, and then into the almond flour mixture. Place the rings on the baking sheet and oil with cooking spray. Bake for 15-20 minutes or until golden brown and crispy. Remove the onion rings into a serving bowl.

Put kale in a food processor. Add in olive oil, cilantro, oregano, remaining garlic powder, salt, black pepper, tofu mayonnaise, coconut cream, and lemon juice; puree until nice and smooth. Allow the dip to sit for about 10 minutes for the flavors to develop. After, serve the dip with the crispy onion rings.

Soy Chorizo Stuffed Cabbage Rolls

Ingredients for 4 servings

¼ cup coconut oil, divided
1 large white onion, chopped
3 cloves garlic, minced, divided
1 cup crumbled soy chorizo
1 cup cauliflower rice
1 can tomato sauce
1 tsp dried oregano
1 tsp dried basil
8 full green cabbage leaves

Directions and Total Time: 35 minutes

Heat half of the coconut oil in a saucepan over medium heat.

Add half of the onion, half of the garlic, and all of the soy chorizo. Sauté for 5 minutes or until the chorizo has browned further and the onion softened.

Stir in the cauli rice, season with salt and black pepper, and cook for 3 to 4 minutes. Turn the heat off and set the pot aside.

Heat the remaining oil in a saucepan over medium heat, add, and sauté the remaining onion and garlic until fragrant and soft. Pour in the tomato sauce, and season with salt, black pepper, oregano, and basil. Add ¼ cup water and simmer the sauce for 10 minutes.

While the sauce cooks, lay the cabbage leaves on a flat surface, and spoon the soy chorizo mixture into the middle of each leaf. Roll the leaves to secure the filling. Place the cabbage rolls in the tomato sauce and cook further for 10 minutes. When ready, serve the cabbage rolls with sauce over mashed broccoli or with mixed seed bread.

Tofu Stuffed Peppers

Ingredients for 4 servings

1 cup red and yellow bell peppers
1 oz tofu, chopped into small bits
1 cup cashew cream cheese
1 tbsp chili paste, mild
2 tbsp melted plant butter
1 cup grated plant-based Parmesan

Directions and Total Time: 25 minutes

Preheat oven to 400 F. Use a knife to cut the bell peppers into two (lengthwise) and remove the core.

In a bowl, mix tofu, cashew cream cheese, chili paste, and melted butter until smooth.

Spoon the cheese mixture into the bell peppers and use the back of the spoon to level the filling in the peppers. Grease a baking sheet with cooking spray and arrange the stuffed peppers on the sheet.

Sprinkle the plant-based Parmesan cheese on top and bake the peppers for 15-20 minutes until the peppers are golden brown and the cheese melted. Remove onto a serving platter and serve warm.

Curry Cauli Rice with Mushrooms

Ingredients for 4 servings

8 oz baby bella mushrooms, stemmed and sliced
2 large heads cauliflower
2 tbsp toasted sesame oil, divided
1 onion, chopped
3 garlic cloves, minced
Salt and black pepper to taste
½ tsp curry powder
1 tsp freshly chopped parsley
2 scallions, thinly sliced

Directions and Total Time: 15 minutes

Use a knife to cut the entire cauliflower head into 6 pieces and transfer to a food processor. With the grater attachment, shred the cauliflower into a rice-like consistency.

Heat half of the sesame oil in a large skillet over medium heat, and then add the onion and mushrooms. Sauté for 5 minutes or until the mushrooms are soft.

Add the garlic and sauté for 2 minutes or until fragrant. Pour in the cauliflower and cook until the rice has slightly softened about 10 minutes.

Season with salt, black pepper, and curry powder; then, mix the ingredients to be well combined. After, turn the heat off and stir in the parsley and scallions. Dish the cauli rice into serving plates and serve warm as a compliment for salads, barbecues, and soups.

Mushroom Broccoli Faux Risotto

Ingredients for 4 servings

4 oz plant butter
1 cup cremini mushrooms, chopped
2 garlic cloves, minced
1 small red onion, finely chopped
1 large head broccoli, grated
¾ cup white wine
1 cup coconut whipping cream
¾ cup grated plant-based Parmesan
Freshly chopped thyme

Directions and Total Time: 25 minutes

Place a pot over medium heat, add, and melt the plant butter. Sauté the mushrooms in the pot until golden, about 5 minutes. Add the garlic and onions and cook for 3 minutes or until fragrant and soft. Mix in the broccoli, 1 cup water, and half of the white wine. Season with salt and black pepper and simmer the ingredients (uncovered) for 8 to 10 minutes or until the broccoli is soft.

Mix in the coconut whipping cream and simmer until most of the cream has evaporated. Turn the heat off and stir in the parmesan cheese and thyme until well incorporated. Dish the risotto and serve warm as itself or with grilled tofu.

Crispy Squash Nacho Chips

Ingredients for 4 servings

1 large yellow squash
1 ½ cups coconut oil
1 tbsp taco seasoning

Directions and Total Time: 26 minutes

With a mandolin slicer, cut the squash into thin, round slices and place in a colander.

Sprinkle the squash with a lot of salt and allow sitting for 5 minutes. After, press the water out of the squash and pat dry with a paper towel. Pour the coconut oil in a deep skillet and heat the oil over medium heat. Carefully, add the squash slices in the oil, about 20 pieces at a time and fry until crispy and golden brown. Use a slotted spoon to remove the squash onto a paper towel-lined plate. Sprinkle the slices with taco seasoning and serve.

Pepita Cheese Tomato Chips

Ingredients for 6 servings

5 tomatoes, sliced
¼ cup olive oil
½ cup pepitas seeds
1 tbsp nutritional yeast
Salt and black pepper, to taste
1 tsp garlic puree

Directions and Total Time: 15 minutes

Preheat oven to 400 F. Over the sliced tomatoes, drizzle olive oil. In a food processor, add pepitas seeds, nutritional yeast, garlic, salt, and pepper and pulse until the desired consistency is attained. Toss in tomato slices to coat. Set the tomato slices on a baking pan and bake for 10 minutes.

Mixed Seed Crackers

Ingredients for 6 servings

1/3 cup sesame seed flour
1/3 cup pumpkin seeds
1/3 cup sunflower seeds
1/3 cup sesame seeds
1/3 cup chia seeds
1 tbsp psyllium husk powder
1 tsp salt
¼ cup plant butter, melted
1 cup boiling water

Directions and Total Time: 57 minutes

Preheat oven to 300 F.

Combine the sesame seed flour with the pumpkin seeds, sunflower seeds, sesame seeds, chia seeds, psyllium husk powder, and salt.

Pour in the plant butter and hot water and mix the ingredients until a dough forms with a gel-like consistency.

Line a baking sheet with parchment paper and place the dough on the sheet. Cover the dough with another parchment paper and with a rolling pin flatten the dough into the baking sheet. Remove the parchment paper on top.

Tuck the baking sheet in the oven and bake for 45 minutes Allow the crackers to cool and dry in the oven, about 10 minutes. After, remove the sheet and break the crackers into small pieces. Serve.

Mixed Vegetables with Basil

Ingredients for 4 servings

2 medium zucchinis, chopped
2 medium yellow squash, chopped
1 red onion, cut into 1-inch wedges
1 red bell pepper, diced
1 cup cherry tomatoes, halved
4 tbsp olive oil
Salt and black pepper to taste
3 garlic cloves, minced
2/3 cup whole-wheat breadcrumbs
1 lemon, zested
¼ cup chopped fresh basil

Directions and Total Time: 40 minutes

Preheat the oven to 450 F and lightly grease a large baking sheet with cooking spray.

In a medium bowl, add the zucchini, yellow squash, red onion, bell pepper, tomatoes, olive oil, salt, black pepper, and garlic. Toss well and spread the mixture on the baking sheet. Roast in the oven for 25 to 30 minutes or until the vegetables are tender, while stirring every 5 minutes.

Meanwhile, heat the olive oil in a medium skillet and sauté the garlic until fragrant. Mix in the breadcrumbs, lemon zest, and basil. Cook for 2 to 3 minutes. Remove the vegetables from the oven and toss in the breadcrumb's mixture. Serve warm.

Four-Seed Crackers

Ingredients for 4 servings

1/3 cup coconut flour
1/3 cup sesame seeds
1/3 cup sunflower seeds
1/3 cup chia seeds
1/3 cup pumpkin seeds
¼ cup plant butter, melted

Directions and Total Time: 50 minutes

Preheat an oven to 300 F and line a baking sheet with parchment paper.

In a medium bowl, mix the coconut flour, sesame seeds, sunflower seeds, chia seeds, pumpkin seeds, and salt. Add the plant butter, 1 cup of boiling water, and mix until well combined. Spread the mixture on the baking sheet and bake in the oven until the batter is firm, 45 minutes. Remove the crackers and allow cooling for 10 minutes. Break the crackers into pieces and serve.

Bell Pepper & Seitan Balls

Ingredients for 4 servings

1 tbsp flax seed powder
1 lb seitan, crumbled
¼ cup chopped mixed bell peppers
Salt and black pepper to taste
1 tbsp almond flour
1 tsp garlic powder
1 tsp onion powder
1 tsp tofu mayonnaise
Olive oil for brushing

Directions and Total Time: 25 minutes

Preheat the oven to 400 F and line a baking sheet with parchment paper.

In a bowl, mix flax seed powder with 3 tbsp water and allow thickening for 5 minutes. Add in seitan, bell peppers, salt, pepper, almond flour, garlic powder, onion powder, and tofu mayonnaise. Mix and form 1-inch balls from the mixture. Arrange on the baking sheet, brush with cooking spray and bake in the oven for 15 to 20 minutes or until brown and compacted. Remove from the oven and serve.

Chocolate Bars with Walnuts

Ingredients for 4 servings

1 cup walnuts
3 tbsp sunflower seeds
2 tbsp unsweetened chocolate chips
1 tbsp unsweetened cocoa powder
1 ½ tsp vanilla extract
¼ tsp cinnamon powder
2 tbsp melted coconut oil
2 tbsp toasted almond meal
2 tsp pure maple syrup

Directions and Total Time: 60 minutes

In a food processor, add the walnuts, sunflower seeds, chocolate chips, cocoa powder, vanilla extract, cinnamon powder, coconut oil, almond meal, maple syrup, and blitz a few times until combined.

Line a flat baking sheet with plastic wrap, pour the mixture onto the sheet, and place another plastic wrap on top. Use a rolling pin to flatten the batter and then remove the top plastic wrap. Freeze the snack until firm, 1 hour. Remove from the freezer, cut into 1 ½-inch bars and enjoy immediately.

Baked Brussels Sprouts with Cranberries

Ingredients for 4 servings

1 pound Brussels sprouts, halved
3 tbsp olive oil
1 medium white onion, chopped
½ cup dried cranberries
1 lemon, juiced
1 tbsp chopped fresh basil

Directions and Total Time: 50 minutes

Preheat the oven to 425 F.

Spread the Brussels sprouts on a roasting sheet, drizzle with the olive oil, and season with salt and black pepper. Mix the seasoning onto the vegetables and roast in the oven until light brown and tender, 20 to 25 minutes. Transfer the Brussels sprouts to a large salad bowl and mix in the onion, cranberries, lemon juice, and basil. Serve immediately.

Dijon Roasted Asparagus

Ingredients for 4 servings

2 tbsp plant butter
1 lb asparagus, hard part trimmed
2 garlic cloves, minced
1 tsp Dijon mustard
1 tbsp freshly squeezed lemon juice

Directions and Total Time: 35 minutes

Melt the butter in a large skillet and sauté the asparagus until softened with some crunch, 7 minutes. Mix in the garlic and cook until fragrant, 30 seconds.

Meanwhile, in a small bowl, quickly whisk the mustard, lemon juice and pour the mixture over the asparagus. Cook for 2 minutes and plate the asparagus. Serve warm.

Paprika Tofu & Zucchini Skewers

Ingredients for 4 servings

1 (14 oz) block tofu, pressed cubed
1 medium zucchini, cut into rounds
1 tbsp olive oil
2 tbsp freshly squeezed lemon juice
1 tsp smoked paprika
1 tsp cumin powder
1 tsp garlic powder
Salt and black pepper to taste

Directions and Total Time: 10 minutes

Preheat a grill to medium heat.

Meanwhile, thread the tofu and zucchini alternately on the wooden skewers.

In a small bowl, whisk the olive oil, lemon juice, paprika, cumin powder, and garlic powder. Brush the skewers all around with the mixture and place on the grill grate. Cook on both sides until golden brown, 5 minutes. Season with salt and pepper and serve afterwards.

Sesame Cabbage Sauté

Ingredients for 4 servings

2 tbsp soy sauce
1 tbsp toasted sesame oil
1 tbsp hot sauce
½ tbsp pure date sugar
½ tbsp olive oil
1 head green cabbage, shredded
2 carrots, julienned
3 green onions, thinly sliced
2 garlic cloves, minced
1 tbsp fresh grated ginger
Salt and black pepper to taste
1 tbsp sesame seeds

Directions and Total Time: 15 minutes

In a small bowl, mix the soy sauce, sesame oil, hot sauce, and date sugar.

Heat the olive oil in a large skillet and sauté the cabbage, carrots, green onion, garlic, and ginger until softened, 5 minutes. Mix in the prepared sauce and toss well. Cook for 1 to 2 minutes. Dish the food and garnish with the sesame seeds.

Parmesan Broccoli Tots

Ingredients for 4 servings

1 tbsp flax seed powder
1 head broccoli, cut into florets
2/3 cup toasted almond flour
2 garlic cloves, minced
2 cups grated plant-based Parmesan
Salt to taste

Directions and Total Time: 30 minutes

Preheat the oven to 350 F and line a baking sheet with parchment paper.

In a small bowl, mix the flax seed powder with the 3 tbsp water and allow thickening for 5 minutes to make the flax egg. Place the broccoli in a safe microwave bowl, sprinkle with 2 tbsp of water, and steam in the microwave for 1 minute or until softened. Transfer the broccoli to a food processor and add the flax egg, almond flour, garlic, plant cheese, and salt. Blend until coarsely smooth.

Pour the mixture into a bowl and form 2-inch oblong balls from the mixture. Place the tots on the baking sheet and bake in the oven for 15 to 20 minutes or until firm and compacted. Remove the tots from the oven and serve warm with tomato dipping sauce.

Tomatoes Stuffed with Chickpeas & Quinoa

Ingredients for 4 servings

8 medium sized tomatoes
¾ cup quinoa, rinsed and drained
1 ½ cups water
1 tbsp olive oil
1 small onion, diced
3 garlic cloves, minced
1 cup chopped spinach
1 (7 oz) can chickpeas, drained
½ cup chopped fresh basil

Directions and Total Time: 50 minutes

Preheat the oven to 400 F.

Cut off the heads of tomatoes and use a paring knife to scoop the inner pulp of the tomatoes. Season with some olive oil, salt, and black pepper. Add the quinoa and water to a medium pot, season with salt and cook until the quinoa is tender and the water absorbs, 10 to 15 minutes. Fluff and set aside.

Heat the remaining olive oil in a skillet and sauté th onion and garlic for 30 seconds. Mix in the spinach and cook until wilted, 2 minutes. Stir in the basil, chickpeas, and quinoa; allow warming from 2 minutes.

Spoon the mixture into the tomatoes, place the tomatoes into the baking dish and bake in the oven for 20 minutes or until the tomatoes soften. Remove the tomatoes from the oven and dish the food.

Herbed Vegetable Traybake

Ingredients for 4 servings

2 tbsp plant butter
1 large onion, diced
1 cup celery, diced
½ cup carrots, diced
½ tsp dried marjoram
2 cups chopped cremini mushrooms
1 cup vegetable broth
¼ cup chopped fresh parsley
1 whole-grain bread loaf, cubed

Directions and Total Time: 85 minutes

Melt the butter in large skillet and sauté onion, celery, mushrooms, and carrots for 5 minutes. Mix in marjoram, salt, and pepper. Pour in the vegetable broth and mix in parsley and bread. Cook until the broth reduces by half, 10 minutes. Pour the mixture into a baking dish and cover with foil. Bake in the oven at 375 F for 30 minutes. Uncover and bake further for 30 minutes or until golden brown on top and the liquid absorbs. Remove the dish from the oven and serve the stuffing.

Louisiana-Style Sweet Potato Chips

Ingredients for 4 servings

2 sweet potatoes, peeled and sliced   2 tbsp melted plant butter   1 tbsp Cajun seasoning

Directions and Total Time: 55 minutes

Preheat the oven to 400 F and line a baking sheet with parchment paper.

In a medium bowl, add the sweet potatoes, salt, plant butter, and Cajun seasoning. Toss well. Spread the chips on the baking sheet making sure not to overlap and bake in the oven for 50 minutes to 1 hour or until crispy. Remove the sheet and pour the chips into a large bowl. Allow cooling and enjoy.

Cinnamon-Maple Popcorn

Ingredients for 4 servings

½ cup popcorn kernels
¼ tsp cinnamon powder
½ tsp pure maple syrup
1 tsp plant butter, melted
Salt to taste

Directions and Total Time: 15 minutes

Pour the popcorn kernels in a large pot and set over medium heat. Cover the lid and allow the kernels pop completely. Shake the pot a few times to ensure even popping, 10 minutes.

Meanwhile, in a small bowl, mix the cinnamon powder, maple syrup, butter, and salt. When the popcorn is ready, turn the heat off, and toss in the cinnamon mixture until well distributed. Pour the popcorn into serving bowls, allow cooling and enjoy.

Strawberries Stuffed with Banana Cream

Ingredients for 4 servings

12 strawberries, heads removed
¼ cup cashew cream
¼ tsp banana extract
1 tbsp unsweetened coconut flakes

Directions and Total Time: 10 minutes

Use a teaspoon to scoop out some of the strawberries pulp to create a hole within. In a small bowl, mix the cashew cream, banana extract, and maple syrup. Spoon the mixture into the strawberries and garnish with the coconut flakes. Serve.

Mediterranean Tahini Beans

Ingredients for 4 servings

1 tbsp sesame oil
1 cup string beans, trimmed
Salt to taste
2 tbsp pure tahini
2 tbsp coarsely chopped mint leaves
¼ tsp red chili flakes for topping

Directions and Total Time: 10 minutes

Pour the string beans into medium safe microwave dish, sprinkle with 1 tbsp of water and steam in the microwave until softened, 1 minute.

Heat the sesame oil in a large skillet and toss in the string beans until well coated in the butter. Season with salt and mix in the tahini and mint leaves. Cook for 1 to 2 minutes and turn the heat off. Serve.

Hot Crunchy Nuts

Ingredients for 4 servings

1 cup mixed nuts
1 tbsp plant butter, melted
¼ tsp hot sauce
¼ tsp garlic powder
¼ tsp onion powder

Directions and Total Time: 35 minutes

Preheat the oven to 350 F and line a baking sheet with baking paper.

In a medium bowl, mix the nuts, butter, hot sauce, garlic powder, and onion powder. Spread the mixture on the baking sheet and toast in the oven for 10 minutes. Remove the sheet, allow complete cooling, and serve.

Maple-Glazed Butternut Squash

Ingredients for 4 servings

1 butternut squash, cubed
2 tbsp olive oil
4 garlic cloves, minced
¼ cup pure maple syrup
1 tsp red chili flakes
1 tsp coriander seeds

Directions and Total Time: 40 minutes

Preheat the oven to 375 F.

In a medium bowl, toss the squash with the olive oil, garlic, maple syrup, salt, black pepper, red chili flakes, and coriander seeds. Spread the mixture on a baking sheet and roast in the oven for 25 to 30 minutes or until the potatoes soften and golden brown. Remove from the oven, plate, and serve.

Beet & Carrot Stir-Fry

Ingredients for 4 servings

2 beets, peeled and cut into wedges
3 small carrots, cut crosswise
2 tbsp plant butter
1 red onion, cut into wedges
½ tsp dried oregano
1/8 tsp salt

Directions and Total Time: 20 minutes

Steam the beets and carrots in a medium safe microwave bowl until softened, 6 minutes.

Meanwhile, melt the butter in a large skillet and sauté the onion until softened, 3 minutes. Stir in the carrots, beets, oregano, and salt. Mix well and cook for 5 minutes. Serve warm.

Parmesan Baby Potatoes

Ingredients for 4 servings

4 tbsp plant butter, melted
4 garlic cloves, minced
3 tbsp chopped chives
Salt and black pepper to taste
2 tbsp grated plant-based Parmesan
1 ½ lb baby potatoes

Directions and Total Time: 40 minutes

Preheat the oven to 400 F.

In a bowl, mix butter, garlic, chives, salt, pepper, and plant Parmesan cheese. Toss the potatoes in the butter mixture until coated. Spread the mixture into a baking sheet, cover with foil, and roast for 30 minutes. Remove the potatoes from the oven and toss in the remaining butter mixture. Serve.

Lemon-Maple Glazed Carrots

Ingredients for 4 servings

1 lb baby carrots
2 tbsp plant butter
2 tbsp pure maple syrup
1 tbsp freshly squeezed lemon juice
½ tsp black pepper
¼ cup chopped fresh parsley

Directions and Total Time: 15 minutes

Boil some water in a medium pot. Add some salt and cook the carrots until tender, 5 to 6 minutes. Drain the carrots. Melt the butter in a large skillet and mix in the maple syrup and lemon juice. Toss in the carrots, season with black pepper, and toss in the parsley. Serve the carrots.

Carrot Nori Rolls

Ingredients for 4 servings ROLLS

2 tbsp almond butter
2 tbsp tamari
4 standard nori sheets
1 green bell pepper, sliced
1 tbsp pickled ginger
½ cup grated carrots

Directions and Total Time: 15 minutes

Preheat oven to 350 F.

Whisk the almond butter and tamari until smooth and thick.

Place a nori sheet on a flat surface with the rough side facing up. Spoon a bit of the tamari mixture at the other side of the nori sheet, and spread on all sides. Put bell pepper slices, carrots and ginger in a layer at the other end of the sheet. Fold up in the tahini direction to seal. Repeat the process with the remaining sheets. Arrange on a baking tray and bake for about 10 minutes, until browned and crispy. Allow to cool for a few minutes before slicing into 4 pieces.

Guacamole with Daikon

Ingredients for 4 servings

Juice of 1 lime
1 avocados, cubed
½ red onion, sliced
1 garlic clove, minced
¼ cup chopped cilantro
1 daikon, cut into matchsticks

Directions and Total Time: 15 minutes

Place the avocado in a bowl and squeeze the lime juice. Sprinkle with salt. Mash the avocado using a fork, stir in onion, garlic and cilantro. Serve with daikon slices.

Tofu & Tomato Sandwiches

Ingredients for 4 servings

1 lb extra-firm tofu, crumbled
1 medium carrot, chopped
1 celery stalk, chopped
3 green onions, minced
¼ cup shelled sunflower seeds
½ cup tofu mayonnaise
8 slices whole grain bread
4 slices ripe tomato
4 lettuce leaves

Directions and Total Time: 15 minutes

Place the tofu in a bowl. Stir in carrot, celery, green onions, and sunflower seeds. Mix in mayonnaise, salt, and pepper. Toast the bread slices. Spread the tofu mixture onto 4 bread slices. Layer a tomato slice and lettuce leaf. Top each sandwich with a bread slice and cut diagonally. Serve immediately.

Mustard Tofu-Avocado Wraps

Ingredients for 4 servings

6 tbsp olive oil
1 lb extra-firm tofu, cut into strips
1 tbsp soy sauce
¼ cup apple cider vinegar
1 tsp yellow mustard
3 cups shredded romaine lettuce
3 ripe Roma tomatoes, chopped
1 large carrot, shredded
1 medium avocado, chopped
⅓ cup minced red onion
¼ cup sliced pitted green olives
4 whole-grain flour tortillas

Directions and Total Time: 25 minutes

Heat 2 tbsp of olive oil in a skillet over medium heat. Place the tofu, cook for 10 minutes until golden brown. Drizzle with soy sauce. Let cool.

In a bowl, whisk the vinegar, mustard, salt, pepper, and the remaining oil. In another bowl, mix the lettuce, tomatoes, carrot, avocado, onion, and olives. Pour the dressing over the salad and toss to coat. Lay out a tortilla on a clean flat surface, and spoon ¼ of the salad, some tofu, and then roll up. Cut in half. Repeat the process with the remaining tortillas. Serve immediately.

Walnut & Tempeh Ball

Ingredients for 8 servings

8 oz tempeh, cut into ½-inch pieces
1 (2-oz) jar chopped pimientos
¼ cup nutritional yeast
¼ cup tofu mayonnaise
2 tbsp soy sauce
¾ cup chopped walnuts

Directions and Total Time: 35 minutes

Place the tempeh in a pot with boiling water and cook for 30 minutes. Let cool. In a blender, put the tempeh, pimientos, yeast, mayo, and soy sauce. Pulse until smooth. Remove to a bowl and let chill in the fridge for 2 hours.

Heat a skillet over medium heat. Add the walnuts and toast for 5 minutes, shaking constantly. Remove to a large plate and leave to cool. Mould the tempeh mixture into a ball and roll in the walnuts' plate; be sure it's coated through. Serve chilled.

Yummy Vegetarian Burritos

Ingredients for 2 servings

3 tbsp soy sauce
3 tbsp fresh lemon juice
1 ½ tbsp toasted sesame oil
2 portobello mushroom caps, sliced
1 ripe avocado, pitted and peeled
2 whole-grain flour tortillas
2 cups kale, chopped
1 red bell pepper, cut into strips
1 ripe tomato, chopped

Directions and Total Time: 15 minutes

Whisk soy sauce, 2 tbsp of lemon juice and oil in a bowl. Toss in portobello strips and marinate for 45 minutes. Drain and set aside. Using a fork, mash the avocado with the remaining lemon juice. Spread avocado mash over tortillas and top with kale, mushrooms, bell pepper strips, and tomato. Sprinkle with salt and pepper. Fold the outside edges over the filling to make burritos. Cut in half and serve.

Paprika Baked Beans

Ingredients for 1 servings

1 (14-oz) can white beans
2 tbsp soy sauce
1 tbsp nutritional yeast
1 tsp smoked paprika
1 tsp onion powder
½ tsp garlic powder

Directions and Total Time: 30 minutes

Preheat oven to 390 F.

Mix the beans, soy sauce, yeast, paprika, onion powder, and garlic powder. Arrange on a greased baking sheet and bake for 20-25 minutes, turning once. Lower the heat and bake until dried and crispy.

Pecan Tempeh Cakes

Ingredients for 4 servings

8 oz tempeh, chopped
1 chopped onion
2 garlic cloves, minced
¾ cup chopped pecans
½ cup old-fashioned oats
1 tbsp minced fresh parsley
½ tsp dried oregano
½ tsp dried thyme
Salt and black pepper to taste
3 tbsp olive oil
1 tbsp Dijon mustard
4 whole grain burger buns
Sliced red onion, tomato, lettuce, and avocado

Directions and Total Time: 20 minutes

Place the tempeh in a pot with hot water. Cook for 30 minutes. Drain and let cool.

In a blender, add onion, garlic, tempeh, pecans, oats, parsley, oregano, thyme, salt, and pepper. Pulse until everything is well combined. Form the mixture into 4 balls; flatten to make burgers.

Heat the oil in a skillet over medium heat. Place the burgers and fry for 10-12 minutes on both sides. Spread a layer of the mustard over each bun half. Top the bottom buns with the lettuce, tomato, onion, avocado, and burgers and cover with the remaining bun half. Serve right away.

Homemade Seedy Bars

Ingredients for 6 servings

¾ cup pumpkin seeds
½ cup sunflower seeds
½ cup sesame seeds
¼ cup poppy seeds
1 tsp minced garlic
1 tsp tamari sauce
1 tsp vegan Worcestershire sauce
½ tsp ground cayenne pepper
½ tsp dried oregano

Directions and Total Time: 55 minutes

Preheat oven to 320 F. Line with parchment paper a baking sheet.

Mix the pumpkin seeds, sunflower seeds, sesame seeds, poppy seeds, garlic, tamari, Worcestershire sauce, cayenne, oregano, and ½ cup water in a bowl. Spread on the baking sheet and bake for 25 minutes. Turn the seeds and bake for another 20-25 minutes. Allow to cool before slicing into bars.

Curry Mango-Tofu Pitas

Ingredients for 4 servings

1 pound extra-firm tofu, crumbled
½ cup tofu mayonnaise
¼ cup chopped mango chutney
2 tsp Dijon mustard
1 tbsp curry powder
Salt to taste
⅛ tsp ground cayenne
¾ cup shredded carrots
1 fennel bulb, sliced
¼ cup minced red onion
4 lettuce leaves
4 whole-wheat pita breads, halved

Directions and Total Time: 15 minutes

In a bowl, place tofu, mayonnaise, chutney, mustard, curry powder, salt, and cayenne pepper and stir to combine. Mix in the carrots, fennel and onion. Let sit in the fridge for 20 minutes. Cover the pita breads with lettuce leaves and scoop some of the tofu mixture in. Serve immediately.

Spicy Nut Burgers

Ingredients for 4 servings

¾ cup chopped walnuts
¾ cup chopped cashews
1 medium carrot, grated
1 small onion, chopped
1 garlic clove, minced

1 serrano pepper, minced
¾ cup old-fashioned oats
¾ cup breadcrumbs
2 tbsp minced fresh cilantro
½ tsp ground coriander

Salt and black pepper to taste
2 tsp fresh lime juice
Canola oil, for frying
4 sandwich rolls
Lettuce leaves for garnish

Directions and Total Time: 20 minutes

Pulse walnuts, cashews, carrot, onion, garlic, serrano pepper, oats, breadcrumbs, cilantro, coriander, lime juice, salt, and pepper in a food processor until well mixed. Remove and form into 4 burgers.

Warm the oil in a skillet over medium heat. Cook the burgers for 5 minutes per side, until golden brown. Serve in sandwich rolls with lettuce and a dressing of your choice.

Soy Chorizo & Avocado Tacos

Ingredients for 4 servings

2 tbsp olive oil
8 oz soy chorizo
4 soft flour tortillas

¼ cup tofu mayonnaise
4 large lettuce leaves
2 ripe avocados, sliced

1 tomato, sliced

Directions and Total Time: 20 minutes

Warm the oil in a skillet over medium heat. Place the soy chorizo and cook for 6 minutes on all sides, until browned. Set aside. Spread mayonnaise over tortillas and top with lettuce leaves and tomato siles. Cover with avocado slices and finish with soy chorizo. Roll up the tortillas and serve immediately.

Paprika Hummus with Mushrooms

Ingredients for 4 servings

1 (15-oz) can chickpeas
Juice of 1 lemon
¼ cup tahini

3 tbsp olive oil
½ tsp ground cumin
1 tbsp water

¼ tsp paprika
1 pound sautéed mushrooms

Directions and Total Time: 15 minutes

In a blender, put the chickpeas, lemon juice, tahini, 2 tbsp of olive oil, cumin, and water. Pulse for 30 seconds until ingredients are evenly mixed. Remove to a bowl and sprinkle with the remaining olive oil and paprika. Serve with mushrooms.

Hazelnut Snack

Ingredients for 1 servings

½ cup raw hazelnuts

2 tbsp tamari sauce

1 tsp toasted sesame oil

Directions and Total Time: 10 minutes

Heat a skillet over medium heat. Place in hazelnuts and toast for 7-8 minutes, moving continually with a spatula. Stir in tamari sauce and sesame oil to coat. Remove from the heat and allow the tamari mixture to dry on the hazelnuts.

Crispy Mushroom Wontons

Ingredients for 12 servings

12 vegan wonton wrappers
3 tbsp toasted sesame oil
2 tbsp olive oil
12 shiitake mushrooms, sliced
4 green beans, chopped crosswise
1 tsp soy sauce
1 tbsp fresh lime juice
1 medium carrot, shredded
Toasted sesame seeds

Directions and Total Time: 20 minutes

Preheat oven to 360 F.

Coat the wonton with some sesame oil and arrange on a baking sheet. Put in the oven and bake for 5 minutes until golden brown and crispy. Set aside.

Warm the olive oil in a skillet over medium heat. Place the mushrooms and sir-fry for 5 minutes, until soften. Add in green beans and soy sauce and cook for 2-3 minute; reserve.

In a bowl, whisk the lime juice and the remaining sesame oil. Stir in carrot and mushroom mixture. Divide the mixture between the wontons and sprinkle with sesame seeds. Serve.

French Mushroom Tarts

Ingredients for 4 servings

12 thin slices whole-grain bread
1 tbsp olive oil + more for brushing
2 spring onions, chopped
2 garlic cloves, minced
12 oz white mushrooms, chopped
¼ cup chopped fresh cilantro
1 tsp dried thyme
1 tbsp soy sauce

Directions and Total Time: 20 minutes

Preheat oven to 390 F.

Using a small round tin, make circles from the bread slices. Coat the circles with oil and press at the bottom of a muffin tin. Bake for 10 minutes, until toasted.

Heat 1 tbsp of oil in a skillet over medium heat. Place in spring onions, garlic and mushrooms and cook for 5 minutes, until tender. Add in cilantro, thyme and soy sauce and cook for 2-3 minutes more, until liquid has absorbed. Divide the mixture between the muffin cups and bake for 3-5 minutes. Serve.

Maple-Pumpkin Cookies

Ingredients for 12 servings

2-pound pumpkin, sliced
3 tbsp melted coconut oil, divided
1 tbsp maple syrup
1 cup whole-wheat flour
2 tsp baking powder Sea salt to taste

Directions and Total Time: 70 minutes

Preheat oven to 360 F.

Place the pumpkin in a greased tray and bake for 45 minutes until tender. Let cool before mashing it.

Mix the mashed pumpkin, 1 ½ tbsp of coconut oil and maple syrup in a bowl.

Combine the flour and baking powder in another bowl. Fold in the pumpkin mixture and whisk with a fork until smooth.

Divide the mixture into balls. Arrange spaced out on a lined with parchment paper baking sheet; flatten the balls until a cookie shape is formed. Brush with the remaining melted coconut oil. Bake for 10 minutes, until they rise and become gold. Serve cooled.

Middle Eastern Onion Phyllo

Ingredients for 8 servings

2 tbsp olive oil
2 medium onions, thinly sliced
1 garlic clove, minced
1 tsp chopped fresh rosemary
Salt and black pepper to taste
1 tbsp chopped dill pickles
1 sheet vegan puff pastry, thawed
18 pitted black olives, quartered

Directions and Total Time: 25 minutes

Warm the oil in a skillet over medium heat. Place in onions, garlic, rosemary, salt, and pepper and sauté for 5 minutes. Add in dill pickles, stir and set aside.

Preheat oven to 390 F. Roll out the pastry and using a small bowl, cut into 3-inch circles. Arrange the circles on a greased baking sheet and top with onion mixture. Scatter the olives over. Bake for 15 minutes until golden brown. Serve warm.

Arugula & Hummus Pitas

Ingredients for 4 servings

1 garlic clove, chopped
¾ cup tahini
2 tbsp fresh lemon juice
Salt to taste
⅛ tsp ground cayenne
¼ cup water
1 (15.5-oz) can chickpeas
2 medium carrots, grated
4 pita breads, whole wheat, halved
1 large ripe tomato, sliced
2 cups arugula

Directions and Total Time: 15 minutes

In a food processor, add in garlic, tahini, lemon juice, salt, cayenne pepper, and water. Pulse until smooth. In a bowl, mash the chickpeas with a fork. Stir in carrots and tahini mixture; reserve. Spread the hummus over the pitas and top with a tomato slice and arugula. Serve immediately.

Roman Balsamic Tomato Bruschetta

Ingredients for 12 servings

3 tomatoes, chopped
¼ cup chopped fresh basil
1 tbsp olive oil
1 whole-wheat baguette, sliced
1 garlic clove, halved
Balsamic vinegar for garnish

Directions and Total Time: 20 minutes

Preheat oven to 420 F.

Mix the tomatoes, basil, olive oil, and salt in a bowl. Set aside. Arrange baguette slices on a baking sheet and toast for 6 minutes on both sides until brown. Spread the garlic over the bread and top with the tomato mixture. Serve right away.

Authentic Guacamole

Ingredients for 2 servings

2 ripe avocados
2 garlic cloves, pressed
Zest and juice of 1 lime
1 tsp ground cumin
1 tomato, chopped
1 tbsp cilantro, chopped

Directions and Total Time: 10 minutes

Place the avocados in a bowl and mash them. Stir in garlic, lime juice, lime zest, cumin, tomato, cilantro, salt, and pepper. Serve immediately.

Cucumber Stuffed Tomatoes

Ingredients for 6 servings

6 tomatoes, whole
2 cucumbers, chopped
Juice of 1 lemon
½ red bell pepper, minced
2 green onions, finely minced
1 tbsp minced fresh tarragon

Directions and Total Time: 15 minutes

Remove the tops of the tomatoes. Using a tablespoon, scoop out the seeds and pulp. Arrange them on a platter. Combine the cucumbers, lemon juice, bell pepper, scallions, tarragon, and salt in a bowl. Stir to combine. Divide the mixture between the tomatoes and serve.

Garbanzo Quesadillas with Salsa

Ingredients for 4 servings

1 (15.5-oz) can garbanzo beans, mashed
2 tbsp canola oil
1 tsp chili powder
8 whole-wheat flour tortilla wraps
1 cup tomato salsa
½ cup minced red onion

Directions and Total Time: 15 minutes

Warm the canola oil in a pot over medium heat. Place in mashed garbanzo and chili powder, cook for 5 minutes, stirring often. Set aside.

Heat a pan over medium heat. Put one tortilla in the pan and top with ¼ each of the garbanzo spread, tomato salsa and onion. Cover with other tortilla and cook for 2 minutes, flip the quesadilla and cook for another 2 minutes until crispy. Repeat the process with the remaining tortillas. Slice and serve.

Coconut & Parsley Wraps

Ingredients for 8 servings

½ cup fresh parsley, chopped
1 cup sprouts
1 garlic clove, pressed
2 tbsp ground hazelnuts
2 tbsp flaked coconut
1 tbsp coconut oil
1 tsp cayenne pepper
Salt and black pepper to taste
Zest and juice of 1 lime
2 tbsp ground flaxseed
2 tbsp water
2 whole-wheat wraps

Directions and Total Time: 60 minutes

Pulse parsley, sprouts, garlic, hazelnuts, coconut flakes, coconut oil, cayenne, salt, pepper, lime juice, lime zest, flaxseed, and water in a food processor until well blended.

Divide the mixture between the wraps and roll up. Let chill in the fridge for 30 minutes. Slice into 8 pieces and serve.

Tamari Lentil Dip

Ingredients for 2 servings

1 (14-oz) can lentils, drained
Zest and juice of 1 lime
1 tbsp tamari sauce
¼ cup fresh cilantro, chopped
1 tsp ground cumin
1 tsp cayenne pepper

Directions and Total Time: 10 minutes

In a blender, put the lentils, lime zest, lime juice, tamari sauce, and ¼ cup of water. Pulse until smooth. Transfer to a bowl and stir in cilantro, cumin and cayenne pepper. Serve.

Chili Roasted Hazelnuts

Ingredients for 8 servings

1 pound raw hazelnuts
3 tbsp tamari sauce
2 tbsp extra-virgin olive oil
1 tbsp nutritional yeast
2 tsp chili powder

Directions and Total Time: 20 minutes

Preheat oven to 390 F.

Combine the hazelnuts, tamari and oil in a bowl. Toss to coat. Spread the mixture on a parchment-lined baking pan and roast for 10-15 minutes, until browned. Let cool for e few minutes. Sprinkle with yeast and chili powder.

Balsamic Roasted Red Pepper & Pecan Crostini

Ingredients for 16 servings

2 jarred roasted red peppers
1 cup unsalted pecans
¼ cup water
1 tbsp soy sauce
2 tbsp chopped green onions
¼ cup nutritional yeast
2 tbsp balsamic vinegar
2 tbsp olive oil

Directions and Total Time: 15 minutes

Cut 1 red pepper and set aside. Slice the remaining pepper into strips, reserve for garnish. Pulse the pecans in a food processor until a fine powder forms. Pour in water, chopped red pepper, and soy sauce. Pulse until smooth. Put in green onions, yeast, balsamic vinegar, and oil. Blend until well mixed. Serve the mixture onto a toasted bread slice garnished with pepper strips.

Tarragon Potato Chips

Ingredients for 4 servings

1 pound potato, peeled and sliced
1 tsp smoked paprika
½ tsp garlic powder
1 tbsp tarragon
¼ tsp onion powder
¼ tsp chili powder
⅛ tsp ground mustard
1 tsp canola oil
⅛ tsp liquid smoke

Directions and Total Time: 40 minutes

Preheat oven to 390 F.

Combine the paprika, garlic powder, tarragon, onion powder, chili powder, salt, and mustard in a bowl. Mix the potatoes, canola oil, liquid smoke and tarragon mixture in another bowl; toss to coat. Spread the potatoes on a lined with parchment paper baking tray and bake for 30 minutes, flipping once halfway through cooking until golden. Serve.

Kale & Hummus Pinwheels

Ingredients for 4 servings

3 whole-grain flour tortillas
1 cup kale, chopped
¾ cup hummus
¾ cup shredded carrots

Directions and Total Time: 10 minutes

Spread hummus over tortillas and top with kale and carrots. Fold the edges over the filling and roll up to make burritos. Cut into pinwheels and serve.

Chickpea & Pecan Balls

Ingredients for 6 servings

1 (15.5-oz) can chickpeas
½ cup chopped pecans
¼ cup minced green onions
1 garlic clove, minced
3 tbsp whole-wheat flour
3 tbsp breadcrumbs
4 tbsp hot sauce ¼ tsp salt
⅛ tsp ground cayenne pepper
¼ cup plant butter, melted

Directions and Total Time: 35 minutes

Preheat oven to 350 F.

In a food processor, put the chickpeas, pecans, green onions, garlic, flour, breadcrumbs, 2 tbsp of hot sauce, salt, and cayenne pepper. Pulse until chunky texture is formed.

Shape the mixture into 1-inch balls. Arrange on a greased baking pan and bake for 25-30 minutes, turning halfway through, to ensure they cook evenly. In a bowl, whisk the remaining hot sauce with melted plant butter. Remove the balls to a serving plate and pour the hot butter all over, and serve.

Swiss Chard & Pecan Stuffed Mushrooms

Ingredients for 4 servings

8 oz white mushrooms, stems chopped and reserved
2 tbsp olive oil
1 garlic clove, minced
1 cup cooked Swiss chard
1 cup finely chopped pecans
½ cup breadcrumbs
Salt and black pepper to taste

Directions and Total Time: 20 minutes

Preheat oven to 390 F.

Warm oil in a skillet over medium heat, add the mushroom stems and garlic and sauté for 3 minutes. Mix in chard, pecans, breadcrumbs, salt, and pepper. Cook for another 2 minutes, stirring occasionally.

Divide the resulting mixture between the mushroom caps and arrange on a greased baking dish. Bake for 15 minutes, until golden. Serve immediately.

Vegetable & Rice Vermicelli Lettuce Rolls

Ingredients for 4 servings

2 green onions
2 tbsp sesame oil
2 tbsp soy sauce
2 tbsp balsamic vinegar
1 tsp pure date sugar
⅛ tsp crushed red pepper
3 oz rice vermicelli
6 soft green leaf lettuce leaves
1 medium carrot, shredded
½ cucumber, sliced lengthwise
½ red bell pepper, cut into strips
1 cup fresh cilantro leaves

Directions and Total Time: 15 minutes

Separate the white part of the green onions, chop and transfer to a bowl. Stir in soy sauce, balsamic vinegar, date sugar, red pepper, and 3 tbsp water. Set aside.

Slice the green part diagonally and set aside.

Submerge the vermicelli in a bowl with hot water for 4 minutes. Drain and mix in the sesame oil; allow to cool. Put the lettuce leaves on a flat surface.

Divide the rice noodles between each leaf, in the middle, add green onion slices, carrot, cucumber, bell pepper, and cilantro. Roll the leaves up from the smaller edges. Arrange the rolls seam facing down in a plate. Serve with the dipping sauce.

Green Salsa

Ingredients for 4 servings

3 large heirloom tomatoes, chopped
1 green onion, finely chopped
½ bunch parsley, chopped
2 garlic cloves, minced
1 Jalapeño pepper, minced
Juice of 1 lime
¼ cup olive oil Salt to taste
Whole-grain tortilla chips

Directions and Total Time: 15 minutes

Combine the tomatoes, green onion, parsley, garlic, jalapeño pepper, lime juice, olive oil, and salt in a bowl. Let it rest for 10 minutes at room temperature. Serve with tortilla chips.

Primavera Lettuce Rolls

Ingredients for 4 servings

1 tbsp olive oil
2 oz rice noodles
2 tbsp chopped thai basil
2 tbsp chopped cilantro
1 garlic clove, minced
1 tbsp minced fresh ginger
Juice of ½ lime
2 tbsp soy sauce
1 avocado, sliced
2 carrots, peeled and julienned
8 leaves butter lettuce

Directions and Total Time: 20 minutes

In a bowl, place the noodles in hot water and let them sit for 4 minutes. Drain and mix with the olive oil. Allow to cool.

Combine the basil, cilantro, garlic, ginger, lime juice, and soy sauce in a another bowl. Add in cooked noodles, avocado, and carrots. Divide the mixture between the lettuce leaves. Fold in and secure with toothpicks. Serve right away.

Citrus-Parsley Mushrooms

Ingredients for 4 servings

3 tbsp plant butter
3 tbsp fresh lime juice
2 garlic cloves, crushed
1 tsp dried marjoram
½ tsp ground fennel seed
Salt and black pepper to taste
8 oz white mushrooms, stemmed
1 tbsp minced fresh parsley

Directions and Total Time: 15 minutes

Mix the butter, lime juice, garlic, marjoram, fennel seed, salt, and pepper in a bowl. Stir in mushrooms and parsley to coat. Marinate covered in the fridge for at least 2 hours. Stir to serve.

Minty Berry Cocktail

Ingredients for 4 servings

2 tbsp pineapple juice
1 tbsp fresh lime juice
1 tbsp agave nectar
2 tsp minced fresh mint
2 cups pitted fresh prunes
1 cup fresh blueberries
1 cup fresh strawberries, halved
½ cup fresh raspberries

Directions and Total Time: 15 minutes

Whisk the pineapple juice, lime juice, agave nectar, and mint in a bowl. Set aside.

In another bowl, combine the prunes, blueberries, strawberries, and raspberries. Pour over the dressing and toss to coat. Serve right away.

Bell Peppers Stuffed with Spinach & Tofu

Ingredients for 4 servings

2 tbsp olive oil
1 onion, chopped
2 garlic cloves, minced
1 (14-oz) block tofu, crumbled
1 (5-oz) package baby spinach
2 tsp Italian seasoning
Salt and black pepper to taste
4 large bell peppers, top removed

Directions and Total Time: 35 minutes

Preheat oven to 450 F.

Heat the oil in a skillet over medium heat. Place onion and garlic and cook for 3 minutes. Put in tofu and spinach and cook for 3 minutes until the spinach wilts. Stir in Italian seasoning, salt, and pepper.

Fill the bell peppers with the spinach mixture and arrange them on a greased baking sheet. Bake in the oven for 25 minutes.

Mustard Mac & Cheese

Ingredients for 4 servings

8 oz elbow macaroni
2 tbsp olive oil
½ tsp dry mustard powder
2 cups almond milk
2 cups plant-based cheddar, grated
Salt and black pepper to taste
¼ cup flour
2 tbsp parsley, chopped

Directions and Total Time: 35 minutes

Cook elbow macaroni in boiling water for 8-10 minutes until al dente. Drain.

Heat olive oil in a skillet over medium heat. Place flour, mustard powder, salt, and pepper and stir for about 3-5 minutes. Gradually pour in almond milk while stirring constantly with a spatula for another 5 minites until the mixture is smooth. Turn off the heat and mix in cheddar cheese. When the cheese is melted, fold in macaroni and toss to coat. Sprinkle with parsley to serve.

Grilled Vegetables with Romesco Dip

Ingredients for 4 servings

1 (12-oz) jar roasted peppers, drained
½ cup toasted almonds
1 garlic clove, minced
1 tbsp red wine vingar
1 tsp crushed red chilli flakes
2 slices toasted bread, chopped
½ tsp sweet paprika
1 tbsp tomato paste
½ cup olive oil + 2 tbsp for brushing
Salt and black pepper to taste
1 green bell pepper, julienned
1 yellow bell pepper, julienned
1 bunch of asparagus, trimmed

Directions and Total Time: 35 minutes

In a food processor, place roasted peppers, almonds, garlic, vinegar, toasted bread, paprika, and tomato paste; pulse, pouring slowly ½ cup of olive oil until until the desired consistency is reached. Season with salt and black pepper and set aside.

Heat a grill pan over medium heat. Toss the vegetables in the remaining olive oil, season with salt and pepper and cook in the pan for 3-5 minutes per side. Serve with the dip.

DESSERTS & SWEET TREATS

Vanilla Brownies

Ingredients for 4 servings

2 tbsp flax seed powder
¼ cup cocoa powder
½ cup almond flour
½ tsp baking powder
½ cup erythritol
10 tablespoons plant butter
2 oz dairy-free dark chocolate
½ teaspoon vanilla extract

Directions and Total Time: 30 minutes + chilling time

Preheat oven to 375 F and line a baking sheet with parchment paper. Mix the flax seed powder with 6 tbsp water in a bowl and allow thickening for 5 minutes. In a separate bowl, mix cocoa powder, almond flour, baking powder, and erythritol until no lumps from the erythritol remain. In another bowl, add the plant butter and dark chocolate and melt both in the microwave for 30 seconds to 1 minute.

Whisk the flax egg and vanilla into the chocolate mixture, then pour the mixture into the dry ingredients. Combine evenly. Pour the batter onto the paper-lined baking sheet and bake for 20 minutes. Cool completely and refrigerate for 30 minutes to 2 hours. When ready, slice into squares, and serve.

Vegan Cheesecake with Blueberries

Ingredients for 6 servings

2 oz plant butter
1 ¼ cups almond flour
3 tbsp Swerve sugar
1 tsp vanilla extract
3 tbsp flax seed powder
2 cups cashew cream cheese
½ cup coconut cream
1 tsp lemon zest
2 oz fresh blueberries

Directions and Total Time: 1 hour 30 minutes + chilling time

Preheat oven to 350 F and grease a springform pan with cooking spray. Line with parchment paper.

To make the crust, melt the plant butter in a skillet over low heat until nutty in flavor. Turn the heat off and stir in almond flour, 2 tbsp of Swerve sugar, and half of the vanilla until a dough forms. Press the mixture into the springform pan and bake for 8 minutes.

Mix the flax seed powder with 9 tbsp water and allow sitting for 5 minutes to thicken. In a bowl, evenly combine cashew cream cheese, coconut cream, remaining Swerve sugar, lemon zest, remaining vanilla extract, and flax egg. Remove the crust from the oven and pour the mixture on top. Use a spatula to layer evenly. Bake the cake for 15 minutes at 400 F. Then, reduce the heat to 230 F and bake for 45-60 minutes. Remove to cool completely. Refrigerate overnight and scatter the blueberries on top. Serve.

Lime Avocado Ice Cream

Ingredients for 4 servings

2 large avocados, pitted
Juice and zest of 3 limes
1/3 cup erythritol
1 ¾ cups coconut cream
¼ tsp vanilla extract

Directions and Total Time: 10 minutes

In a blender, combine the avocado pulp, lime juice and zest, erythritol, coconut cream, and vanilla extract. Process until the mixture is smooth. Pour the mixture into your ice cream maker and freeze based on the manufacturer's instructions. When ready, remove and scoop the ice cream into bowls. Serve immediately.

Berries, Nuts & Cream Bowl

Ingredients for 6 servings

5 tbsp flax seed powder
1 cup dairy-free dark chocolate
1 cup plant butter
2 tsp vanilla extract
2 cups fresh blueberries
4 tbsp lemon juice
2 cups coconut cream
4 oz walnuts, chopped
½ cup roasted coconut chips

Directions and Total Time: 30 minutes

Preheat oven to 320 F. Grease a springform pan with cooking spray and line with parchment paper. In a bowl, mix the flax seed powder with 2/3 cup water and allow thickening for 5 minutes. Break the chocolate and butter into a bowl and melt in the microwave for 1-2 minutes.

Share the flax egg into two bowls; whisk 1 pinch of salt into one portion and then, 1 teaspoon of vanilla into the other. Pour the chocolate mixture into the vanilla mixture and combine well. Fold into the other flax egg mixture. Pour the batter into the springform pan and bake for 15-20 minutes. When ready, slice the cake into squares and share into serving bowls. Set aside.

Pour blueberries, lemon juice, and the remaining vanilla into a bowl. Break blueberries and allow sitting for a few minutes. Whip coconut cream with a whisk until a soft peak forms. Spoon the cream on the cakes, top with the blueberry mixture, and sprinkle with walnuts and coconut flakes. Serve.

Vanilla White Chocolate Pudding

Ingredients for 4 servings

3 tbsp flax seed + 9 tbsp water
3 tbsp cornstarch
1 cup cashew cream
2 ½ cups almond milk
½ pure date sugar
1 tbsp vanilla caviar
6 oz white chocolate chips
Whipped coconut cream
Sliced bananas and raspberries

Directions and Total Time: 20 minutes+ cooling time

In a small bowl, mix the flax seed powder with water and allow thickening for 5 minutes to make the flax egg. In a large bowl, whisk the cornstarch and cashew cream until smooth. Beat in the flax egg until well combined.

Pour the almond milk into a pot and whisk in the date sugar. Cook over medium heat while frequently stirring until the sugar dissolves. Reduce the heat to low and simmer until steamy and bubbly around the edges.

Pour half of the almond milk mixture into the flax egg mix, whisk well and pour this mixture into the remaining milk content in the pot. Whisk continuously until well combined.

Bring the new mixture to a boil over medium heat while still frequently stirring and scraping all the corners of the pot, 2 minutes.

Turn the heat off, stir in the vanilla caviar, then the white chocolate chips until melted. Spoon the mixture into a bowl, allow cooling for 2 minutes, cover with plastic wraps making sure to press the plastic onto the surface of the pudding, and refrigerate for 4 hours. Remove the pudding from the fridge, take off the plastic wrap and whip for about a minute.

Spoon the dessert into serving cups, swirl some coconut whipping cream on top, and top with the bananas and raspberries. Enjoy immediately.

Mint Ice Cream

Ingredients for 4 servings

2 avocados, pitted
1 ¼ cups coconut cream
½ tsp vanilla extract
2 tbsp erythritol
2 tsp chopped mint leaves

Directions and Total Time: 10 minutes + chilling time

Into a blender, spoon the avocado pulps, pour in the coconut cream, vanilla extract, erythritol, and mint leaves. Process until smooth. Pour the mixture into your ice cream maker and freeze according to the manufacturer's instructions. When ready, remove and scoop the ice cream into bowls. Serve.

Cardamom Coconut Fat Bombs

Ingredients for 6 servings

½ cup grated coconut
3 oz plant butter, softened
¼ tsp green cardamom powder
½ tsp vanilla extract
¼ tsp cinnamon powder

Directions and Total Time: 10 minutes

Pour the grated coconut into a skillet and roast until lightly brown. Set aside to cool. In a bowl, combine butter, half of the coconut, cardamom, vanilla, and cinnamon. Form balls from the mixture and roll each in the remaining coconut. Refrigerate until ready to serve.

Chocolate Peppermint Mousse

Ingredients for 4 servings

¼ cup Swerve sugar, divided
4 oz cashew cream cheese, softened
3 tbsp cocoa powder
¾ tsp peppermint extract
½ tsp vanilla extract
1/3 cup coconut cream

Directions and Total Time: 10 minutes + chilling time

Put 2 tablespoons of Swerve sugar, cashew cream cheese, and cocoa powder in a blender. Add the peppermint extract, ¼ cup warm water, and process until smooth. In a bowl, whip vanilla extract, coconut cream, and the remaining Swerve sugar using a whisk. Fetch out 5-6 tablespoons for garnishing. Fold in the cocoa mixture until thoroughly combined. Spoon the mousse into serving cups and chill in the fridge for 30 minutes. Garnish with the reserved whipped cream and serve immediately.

Walnut Chocolate Squares

Ingredients for 6 servings

3½ oz dairy-free dark chocolate
4 tbsp plant butter
1 pinch salt
¼ cup walnut butter
½ tsp vanilla extract
¼ cup chopped walnuts to garnish

Directions and Total Time: 10 minutes

Pour the chocolate and plant butter in a safe microwave bowl and melt in the microwave for about 1 to 2 minutes. Remove the bowl from the microwave and mix in the salt, walnut butter, and vanilla.

Grease a small baking sheet with cooking spray and line with parchment paper. Pour in the batter and use a spatula to spread out into a 4 x 6-inch rectangle. Top with the chopped walnuts and chill in the refrigerator. Once set, cut into 1 x 1-inch squares. Serve while firming.

Raspberries Turmeric Panna Cotta

Ingredients for 6 servings

½ tbsp powdered vegetarian gelatin
2 cups coconut cream
¼ tsp vanilla extract
1 pinch turmeric powder
1 tbsp erythritol
1 tbsp chopped toasted pecans
12 fresh raspberries

Directions and Total Time: 10 minutes + chilling time

Mix gelatin and ½ tsp water and allow sitting to dissolve. Pour coconut cream, vanilla extract, turmeric, and erythritol into a saucepan and bring to a boil over medium heat, then, simmer for 2 minutes. Turn the heat off. Stir in the gelatin until dissolved. Pour the mixture into 6 glasses, cover with a plastic wrap, and refrigerate for 2 hours or more. Top with the pecans and raspberries and serve.

Cinnamon Faux Rice Pudding

Ingredients for 6 servings

1 ¼ cups coconut cream
1 tsp vanilla extract
1 tsp cinnamon powder
1 cup mashed tofu
2 oz fresh strawberries

Directions and Total Time: 25 minutes

Pour the coconut cream into a bowl and whisk until a soft peak forms. Mix in the vanilla and cinnamon. Lightly fold in the vegan cottage cheese and refrigerate for 10 to 15 minutes to set. Spoon into serving glasses, top with the strawberries and serve immediately.

White Chocolate Fudge

Ingredients for 6 servings

2 cups coconut cream
1 tsp vanilla extract
3 oz plant butter
3 oz unsweetened white chocolate
Swerve sugar for sprinkling

Directions and Total Time: 20 minutes + chilling time

Pour coconut cream and vanilla into a saucepan and bring to a boil over medium heat, then simmer until reduced by half, about 15 minutes. Stir in plant butter until the batter is smooth. Chop white chocolate into bits and stir in the cream until melted. Pour the mixture into a baking sheet; chill in the fridge for 3 hours. Cut into squares, sprinkle with swerve sugar, and serve.

Macedonia Salad with Coconut & Pecans

Ingredients for 4 servings

1 cup pure coconut cream
½ tsp vanilla extract
2 bananas, cut into chunks
1 ½ cups coconut flakes
4 tbsp toasted pecans, chopped
1 cup pineapple tidbits, drained
1 (11 oz) can mandarin oranges
¾ cup maraschino cherries, stems removed

Directions and Total Time: 15 minutes + cooling time

In medium bowl, mix the coconut cream and vanilla extract until well combined.

In a larger bowl, combine the bananas, coconut flakes, pecans, pineapple, oranges, and cherries until evenly distributed. Pour on the coconut cream mixture and fold well into the salad. Chill in the refrigerator for 1 hour and serve afterwards.

Berry Hazelnut Trifle

Ingredients for 4 servings

1 ½ ripe avocados
¾ cup coconut cream
Zest and juice of ½ a lemon
1 tbsp vanilla extract
3 oz fresh strawberries
2 oz toasted hazelnuts

Directions and Total Time: 10 minutes

In a bowl, add avocado pulp, coconut cream, lemon zest and juice, and half of the vanilla extract. Mix with an immersion blender. Put the strawberries and remaining vanilla in another bowl and use a fork to mash the fruits. In a tall glass, alternate layering the cream and strawberry mixtures. Drop a few hazelnuts on each and serve the dessert immediately.

Cacao Nut Bites

Ingredients for 4 servings

3 ½ oz dairy-free dark chocolate
½ cup mixed nuts
2 tbsp roasted coconut chips
1 tbsp sunflower seeds
Sea salt

Directions and Total Time: 5 minutes

Pour the chocolate into a safe microwave bowl and melt in the microwave for 1 to 2 minutes.

Into 10 small cupcake liners (2-inches in diameters), share the chocolate. Drop in the nuts, coconut chips, sunflower seeds and sprinkle with some salt. Chill in the refrigerator until firm.

Avocado Truffles with Chocolate Coating

Ingredients for 6 servings

1 ripe avocado, pitted
½ tsp vanilla extract
½ tsp lemon zest
5 oz dairy-free dark chocolate
1 tbsp coconut oil
1 tbsp unsweetened cocoa powder

Directions and Total Time: 5 minutes

Scoop the pulp of the avocado into a bowl and mix with the vanilla using an immersion blender. Stir in the lemon zest and a pinch of salt. Pour the chocolate and coconut oil into a safe microwave bowl and melt in the microwave for 1 minute. Add to the avocado mixture and stir. Allow cooling to firm up a bit. Form balls out of the mix. Roll each ball in the cocoa powder and serve immediately.

Summer Banana Pudding

Ingredients for 4 servings

1 cup unsweetened almond milk
2 cups cashew cream
¾ cup + 1 tbsp pure date sugar
¼ tsp salt
3 tbsp cornstarch
2 tbsb plant butter, cut into 4 pieces
1 tsp vanilla extract
2 banana, sliced

Directions and Total Time: 25 minutes + cooling time

In a medium pot, mix almond milk, cashew cream, date sugar, and salt. Cook over medium heat until slightly thickened, 10-15 minutes. Stir in the cornstarch, plant butter, vanilla extract, and banana extract. Cook further for 1 to 2 minutes or until the pudding thickens. Dish the pudding into 4 serving bowls and chill in the refrigerator for at least 1 hour. To serve, top with the bananas and enjoy!

Vanilla Berry Tarts

Ingredients for 4 servings

4 tbsp flax seed powder
1/3 cup whole-wheat flour
½ tsp salt

¼ cup plant butter, crumbled
3 tbsp pure malt syrup
6 oz cashew cream

6 tbsp pure date sugar
¾ tsp vanilla extract
1 cup mixed frozen berries

Directions and Total Time: 35 minutes + cooling time

Preheat oven to 350 F and grease a mini pie pans with cooking spray. In a bowl, mix the flax seed powder with 12 tbsp water and allow soaking for 5 minutes. In a large bowl, combine flour and salt. Add in butter and whisk until crumbly. Pour in the flax egg and malt syrup and mix until smooth dough forms. Flatten the dough on a flat surface, cover with plastic wrap, and refrigerate for 1 hour.

Dust a working surface with some flour, remove the dough onto the surface, and using a rolling pin, flatten the dough into a 1-inch diameter circle. Use a large cookie cutter, cut out rounds of the dough and fit into the pie pans. Use a knife to trim the edges of the pan. Lay a parchment paper on the dough cups, pour on some baking beans and bake in the oven until golden brown, 15-20 minutes. Remove the pans from the oven, pour out the baking beans, and allow cooling. In a bowl, mix cashew cream, date sugar, and vanilla extract. Divide the mixture into the tart cups and top with berries. Serve.

Southern Apple Cobbler with Raspberries

Ingredients for 4 servings

3 apples, chopped
2 tbsp pure date sugar
1 cup fresh raspberries

2 tbsp unsalted plant butter
½ cup whole-wheat flour
1 cup toasted rolled oats

2 tbsp pure date sugar
1 tsp cinnamon powder

Directions and Total Time: 50 minutes

Preheat the oven to 350 F and grease a baking dish with some plant butter.

Add the apples, date sugar, and 3 tbsp of water to a medium pot. Cook over low heat until the date sugar melts and then, mix in the raspberries. Cook until the fruits soften, 10 minutes. Pour and spread the fruit mixture into the baking dish and set aside.

In a blender, add the plant butter, flour, oats, date sugar, and cinnamon powder. Pulse a few times until crumbly. Spoon and spread the mixture on the fruit mix until evenly layered. Bake in the oven for 25 to 30 minutes or until golden brown on top. Remove the dessert, allow cooling for 2 minutes, and serve.

Chocolate Fudge with Nuts

Ingredients for 4 servings

3 cups chocolate chips
¼ cup thick coconut milk

1 ½ tsp vanilla extract
A pinch salt

1 cup chopped mixed nuts

Directions and Total Time: 10 minutes + cooling time

Line a square pan with baking paper. Melt the chocolate chips, coconut milk, and vanilla in a medium pot over low heat. Mix in the salt and nuts until well distributed and pour the mixture into the square pan. Refrigerate for at least for at least 2 hours. Remove from the fridge, cut into squares and serve.

Aunt´s Apricot Tarte Tatin

Ingredients for 4 servings

4 tbsp flax seed powder
¼ cup almond flour
3 tbsp whole-wheat flour
½ tsp salt
¼ cup cold plant butter, crumbled

3 tbsp pure maple syrup
4 tbsp melted plant butter
3 tsp pure maple syrup
1 tsp vanilla extract
1 lemon, juiced

12 apricots, halved and pitted
½ cup coconut cream
4 fresh basil leaves

Directions and Total Time: 30 minutes+ cooling time

Preheat the oven to 350 F and grease a large pie pan with cooking spray.

In a medium bowl, mix the flax seed powder with 12 tbsp water and allow thickening for 5 minutes.

In a large bowl, combine the flours and salt. Add the plant butter and using an electric hand mixer, whisk until crumbly. Pour in the flax egg and maple syrup and mix until smooth dough forms. Flatten the dough on a flat surface, cover with plastic wrap, and refrigerate for 1 hour.

Dust a working surface with almond flour, remove the dough onto the surface, and using a rolling pin, flatten the dough into a 1-inch diameter circle. Set aside. In a large bowl, mix the plant butter, maple syrup, vanilla, and lemon juice. Add the apricots to the mixture and coat well.

Arrange the apricots (open side down) in the pie pan and lay the dough on top. Press to fit and cut off the dough hanging on the edges. Brush the top with more plant butter and bake in the oven for 35 to 40 minutes or until golden brown, and puffed up.

Remove the pie pan from the oven, allow cooling for 5 minutes, and run a butter knife around the edges of the pastry. Invert the dessert onto a large plate, spread the coconut cream on top, and garnish with the basil leaves. Slice and serve.

Chocolate & Peanut Butter Cookies

Ingredients for 4 servings

1 tbsp flax seed powder
1 cup pure date sugar + for dusting
½ cup unsalted butter, softened

½ cup creamy peanut butter
1 tsp vanilla extract
1 ¾ cup whole-wheat flour

1 tsp baking soda
¼ tsp salt
¼ cup unsweetened chocolate chips

Directions and Total Time: 15 minutes + cooling time

In a small bowl, mix the flax seed powder with 3 tbsp water and allow thickening for 5 minutes to make the flax egg. In a medium bowl, whisk the date sugar, plant butter, and peanut butter until light and fluffy. Mix in the flax egg and vanilla until well combined. Add the flour, baking soda, salt, and whisk well again. Fold in the chocolate chips, cover the bowl with a plastic wrap, and refrigerate for 1 hour.

Preheat oven to 375 F and line a baking sheet with parchment paper. Use a cookie sheet to scoop mounds of the batter onto the sheet with 1-inch intervals. Bake for 10 minutes. Remove the cookies from the oven, cool for 3 minutes, roll in some date sugar, and serve.

Mixed Berry Yogurt Ice Pops

Ingredients for 6 servings

2/3 cup avocado, halved and pitted
2/3 cup frozen berries, thawed

1 cup dairy-free yogurt
½ cup coconut cream

1 tsp vanilla extract

Directions and Total Time: 5 minutes + chilling time

Pour the avocado pulp, berries, dairy-free yogurt, coconut cream, and vanilla extract. Process until smooth. Pour into ice pop sleeves and freeze for 8 or more hours. Enjoy the ice pops when ready.

Coconut Chocolate Barks

Ingredients for 4 servings

1/3 cup coconut oil, melted	2 tbsp unsweetened coconut flakes.	A pinch ground rock salt
¼ cup almond butter, melted	1 tsp pure maple syrup	¼ cup unsweetened cocoa nibs

Directions and Total Time: 35 minutes

Line a baking tray with baking paper and set aside. In a medium bowl, mix the coconut oil, almond butter, coconut flakes, maple syrup, and then fold in the rock salt and cocoa nibs. Pour and spread the mixture on the baking sheet, chill in the refrigerator for 20 minutes or until firm. Remove the dessert, break into shards and enjoy immediately. Preserve extras in the refrigerator.

Nutty Date Cake

Ingredients for 4 servings

½ cup cold plant butter, cut in pieces	1 tsp baking powder	1/3 cup pitted dates, chopped
1 tbsp flax seed powder	1 tsp baking soda	½ cup pure date sugar
½ cup whole-wheat flour	1 tsp cinnamon powder	1 tsp vanilla extract
¼ cup chopped pecans and walnuts	1 tsp salt	¼ cup pure date syrup for drizzling.

Directions and Total Time: 1 hour 30 minutes

Preheat oven to 350 F and lightly grease a round baking dish with some plant butter. In a small bowl, mix the flax seed powder with 3 tbsp water and allow thickening for 5 minutes to make the flax egg.

In a food processor, add the flour, nuts, baking powder, baking soda, cinnamon powder, and salt. Blend until well combined. Add 1/3 cup of water, dates, date sugar, and vanilla. Process until smooth with tiny pieces of dates evident.

Pour the batter into the baking dish and bake in the oven for 1 hour and 10 minutes or until a toothpick inserted comes out clean. Remove the dish from the oven, invert the cake onto a serving platter to cool, drizzle with the date syrup, slice, and serve.

Baked Apples Filled with Nuts

Ingredients for 4 servings

4 gala apples	4 tbsp almond flour	6 tbsp plant butter, cold and cubed
3 tbsp pure maple syrup	6 tbsp pure date sugar	1 cup chopped mixed nuts

Directions and Total Time: 35 minutes + cooling time

Preheat the oven the 400 F.

Slice off the top of the apples and use a melon baller or spoon to scoop out the cores of the apples. In a bowl, mix the maple syrup, almond flour, date sugar, butter, and nuts. Spoon the mixture into the apples and then bake in the oven for 25 minutes or until the nuts are golden brown on top and the apples soft. Remove the apples from the oven, allow cooling, and serve.

Coconut & Chocolate Cake

Ingredients for 4 servings

2/3 cup toasted almond flour
¼ cup unsalted plant butter, melted

2 cups chocolate bars, cubed
2 ½ cups coconut cream

Fresh berries for topping

Directions and Total Time: 40 minutes + cooling time

Lightly grease a 9-inch springform pan with some plant butter and set aside.

Mix the almond flour and plant butter in a medium bowl and pour the mixture into the springform pan. Use the spoon to spread and press the mixture into the bottom of the pan. Place in the refrigerator to firm for 30 minutes.

Meanwhile, pour the chocolate in a safe microwave bowl and melt for 1 minute stirring every 30 seconds. Remove from the microwave and mix in the coconut cream and maple syrup.

Remove the cake pan from the oven, pour the chocolate mixture on top making to sure to shake the pan and even the layer. Chill further for 4 to 6 hours. Take out the pan from the fridge, release the cake and garnish with the raspberries or strawberries. Slice and serve.

Berry Macedonia with Mint

Ingredients for 4 servings

¼ cup lemon juice
4 tsp agave syrup

2 cups chopped pears
2 cups chopped strawberries

3 cups mixed berries
8 fresh mint leaves

Directions and Total Time: 20 minutes

Chop half of the mint leaves; reserve.

In a large bowl, combine together pears, strawberries, raspberries, blackberries, and half of the mint leaves. Divide the Macedonia salad between 4 small cups. Top with lemon juice, agave syrup, and mint leaves and serve chilled.

Berry Cupcakes with Cashew Cheese Icing

Ingredients for 4 servings

2 cups whole-wheat flour
¼ cup cornstarch
2 ½ tsp baking powder
1 ½ cups pure date sugar
½ tsp salt

¾ cup plant butter, softened
3 tsp vanilla extract
1 cup strawberries, pureed
1 cup oat milk, room temperature
¾ cup cashew cream

2 tbsp coconut oil, melted
3 tbsp pure maple syrup
1 tsp vanilla extract
1 tsp freshly squeezed lemon juice

Directions and Total Time: 35 minutes + cooling time

Preheat the oven to 350 F and line a 12-holed muffin tray with cupcake liners. Set aside.

In a bowl, mix flour, cornstarch, baking powder, date sugar, and salt. Whisk in plant butter, vanilla extract, strawberries, and oat milk until well combined. Divide the mixture into the muffin cups two-thirds way up and bake for 20-25 minutes. Allow cooling while you make the frosting.

In a blender, add cashew cream, coconut oil, maple syrup, vanilla, and lemon juice. Process until smooth. Pour the frosting into medium bowl and chill for 30 minutes. Transfer the mixture into a piping bag and swirl mounds of the frosting onto the cupcakes. Serve immediately.

Holiday Pecan Tart

Ingredients for 4 servings

4 tbsp flax seed powder
1/3 cup whole-wheat flour

½ tsp salt
¼ cup cold plant butter, crumbled

3 tbsp pure malt syrup

For the filling:

3 tbsp flax seed powder + 9 tbsp water
2 cups toasted pecans, chopped
1 cup light corn syrup

½ cup pure date sugar
1 tbsp pure pomegranate molasses
4 tbsp plant butter, melted

½ tsp salt
2 tsp vanilla extract

Directions and Total Time: 50 minutes + cooling time

Preheat the oven to 350 F. In a bowl, mix the flax seed powder with 12 tbsp water and allow thickening for 5 minutes. Do this for the filling's flax egg too in a separate bowl. In a large bowl, combine flour and salt. Add in plant butter and whisk until crumbly. Pour in the crust's flax egg and maple syrup and mix until smooth dough forms. Flatten the dough on a flat surface, cover with plastic wrap, and refrigerate for 1 hour. Dust a working surface with flour, remove the dough onto the surface, and using a rolling pin, flatten the dough into a 1-inch diameter circle. Lay the dough on a greased pie pan and press to fit the shape of the pan. Trim the edges of the pan. Lay a parchment paper on the dough, pour on some baking beans and bake for 20 minutes. Remove the pan, pour out the baking beans, and allow cooling.

In a bowl, mix the filling's flax egg, pecans, corn syrup, date sugar, pomegranate molasses, plant butter, salt, and vanilla. Pour and spread the mixture on the piecrust. Bake further for 20 minutes or until the filling sets. Remove from the oven, decorate with more pecans, slice, and cool. Slice and serve.

Cinnamon Pumpkin Pie

Ingredients for 4 servings

For the piecrust:

4 tbsp flax seed powder
1/3 cup whole-wheat flour

½ tsp salt
¼ cup cold plant butter, crumbled

3 tbsp pure malt syrup

For the filling:

2 tbsp flax seed powder + 6 tbsp water
4 tbsp plant butter
¼ cup pure maple syrup

¼ cup pure date sugar
1 tsp cinnamon powder
½ tsp ginger powder

1/8 tsp cloves powder
1 (15 oz) can pumpkin purée
1 cup almond milk

Directions and Total Time: 1 hr 10 min + cooling time

Preheat oven to 350 F. In a bowl, mix flax seed powder with 12 tbsp water and allow thickening for 5 minutes. Do this for the filling's flax egg too in a separate bowl. In a bowl, combine flour and salt. Add in plant butter and whisk until crumbly. Pour in the crust's flax egg, maple syrup, vanilla, and mix until smooth dough forms. Flatten the dough, cover with plastic wrap, and refrigerate for 1 hour.

Dust a working surface with flour, remove the dough onto the surface, and flatten it into a 1-inch diameter circle. Lay the dough on a greased pie pan and press to fit the shape of the pan. Use a knife to trim the edges of the pan. Lay a parchment paper on the dough, pour on some baking beans and bake for 15-20 minutes. Remove, pour out the baking beans, and allow cooling. In a bowl, whisk filling's flax seed, butter, maple syrup, date sugar, cinnamon powder, ginger powder, cloves powder, pumpkin puree, and almond milk. Pour the mixture onto the piecrust and bake for 35-40 minutes.

Cashew & Cranberry Truffles

Ingredients for 4 servings

2 cups fresh cranberries
2 tbsp pure date syrup
1 tsp vanilla extract

16 oz cashew cream
4 tbsp plant butter
3 tbsp unsweetened cocoa powder

2 tbsp pure date sugar

Directions and Total Time: 15 minutes

Set a silicone egg tray aside.

Puree the cranberries, date syrup, and vanilla in a blender until smooth.

Add the cashew cream and plant butter to a medium pot. Heat over medium heat until the mixture is well combined. Turn the heat off. Mix in the cranberry mixture and divide the mixture into the muffin holes. Refrigerate for 40 minutes or until firm. Remove the tray and pop out the truffles.

Meanwhile, mix the cocoa powder and date sugar on a plate. Roll the truffles in the mixture until well dusted and serve.

Tropical Cheesecake

Ingredients for 4 servings

2/3 cup toasted rolled oats
¼ cup plant butter, melted
3 tbsp pure date sugar

6 oz cashew cream cheese
¼ cup coconut milk
1 lemon, zested and lemon juiced

¼ cup just-boiled water
3 tsp agar agar powder
1 ripe mangoes, chopped

Directions and Total Time: 20 minutes + cooling time

Process the oats, butter, and date sugar in a blender until smooth.

Pour the mixture into a greased 9-inch springform pan and press the mixture onto the bottom of the pan. Refrigerate for 30 minutes until firm while you make the filling.

In a large bowl, using an electric mixer, whisk the cashew cream cheese until smooth. Beat in the coconut milk, lemon zest, and lemon juice. Mix the boiled water and agar agar powder until dissolved and whisk this mixture into the creamy mix. Fold in the mangoes.

Remove the cake pan from the fridge and pour in the mango mixture. Shake the pan to ensure a smooth layering on top. Refrigerate further for at least 3 hours. Remove the cheesecake from the fridge, release the cake pan, slice, and serve.

Raisin Oatmeal Biscuits

Ingredients for 8 servings

½ cup plant butter
1 cup date sugar
¼ cup pineapple juice
1 cup whole-grain flour

1 tsp baking powder
½ tsp salt
1 tsp pure vanilla extract
1 cup old-fashioned oats

½ cup vegan chocolate chips
½ cup raisins

Directions and Total Time: 20 minutes

Preheat oven to 370 F. Beat the butter and sugar in a bowl, until creamy and fluffy. Pour in the juice and blend. Mix in flour, baking powder, salt, and vanilla. Stir in oats, chocolate chips and raisins. Spread the dough on a baking sheet and bake for 15 minutes. Let completely cool on a rack.

Pistachios & Chocolate Popsicles

Ingredients for 4 servings

½ cup chocolate chips, melted
1 ½ cups oat milk
1 tbsp unsweetened cocoa powder
3 tbsp pure date syrup
1 tsp vanilla extract
A handful pistachios, chopped

Directions and Total Time: 5 minutes + cooling time

In a blender, add chocolate, oat milk, cocoa powder, date syrup, vanilla, pistachios, and process until smooth. Divide the mixture into popsicle molds and freeze for 3 hours. Dip the popsicle molds in warm water to loosen the popsicles and pull out the popsicles.

Cashew & Plum Cheesecake

Ingredients for 4 servings

2/3 cup toasted rolled oats
¼ cup plant butter, melted
3 tbsp pure date sugar
6 oz cashew cream cheese
¼ cup oats milk
¼ cup just-boiled water
3 tsp agar agar powder
4 plums, cored and finely diced
2 tbsp toasted cashew, chopped

Directions and Total Time: 20 minutes + cooling time

Process the oats, butter, and date sugar in a blender until smooth.

Pour the mixture into a greased 9-inch springform pan and press the mixture onto the bottom of the pan. Refrigerate for 30 minutes until firm while you make the filling.

In a large bowl, using an electric mixer, whisk the cashew cream cheese until smooth. Beat in the oats milk.Mix the boiled water and agar agar powder until dissolved and whisk this mixture into the creamy mix. Fold in the plums.

Remove the cake pan from the fridge and pour in the plum mixture. Shake the pan to ensure a smooth layering on top. Refrigerate further for at least 3 hours. Take out the cake pan, release the cake, and garnish with the cashew nuts. Slice and serve.

Party Matcha & Hazelnut Cheesecake

Ingredients for 4 servings

2/3 cup toasted rolled oats
¼ cup plant butter, melted
3 tbsp pure date sugar
6 oz cashew cream cheese
¼ cup almond milk
1 tbsp matcha powder
¼ cup just-boiled water
3 tsp agar agar powder
2 tbsp toasted hazelnuts, chopped

Directions and Total Time: 20 minutes + cooling time

Process the oats, butter, and date sugar in a blender until smooth.

Pour the mixture into a greased 9-inch springform pan and press the mixture onto the bottom of the pan. Refrigerate for 30 minutes until firm while you make the filling.

In a large bowl, using an electric mixer, whisk the cashew cream cheese until smooth. Beat in the almond milk and mix in the matcha powder until smooth.

Mix the boiled water and agar agar until dissolved and whisk this mixture into the creamy mix. Fold in the hazelnuts until well distributed. Remove the cake pan from the fridge and pour in the cream mixture. Shake the pan to ensure a smooth layering on top. Refrigerate further for at least 3 hours. Take out the cake pan, release the cake, slice, and serve.

Oatmeal Cookies with Hazelnuts

Ingredients for 2 servings

1 ½ cups whole-grain flour
1 tsp baking powder
⅛ tsp salt
1 tsp ground cinnamon
¼ tsp ground nutmeg
1 ½ cups old-fashioned oats
1 cup chopped hazelnuts
½ cup plant butter, melted
½ cup pure maple syrup
¼ cup pure date sugar
2 tsp pure vanilla extract

Directions and Total Time: 15 minutes

Preheat oven to 360 F.

Combine the flour, baking powder, salt, cinnamon, and nutmeg in a bowl. Add in oats and hazelnuts. In another bowl, whisk the butter, maple syrup, sugar, and vanilla. Pour over the flour mixture. Mix well. Spoon a small ball of cookie dough on a baking sheet and press down with a fork. Bake for 10-12 minutes, until browned. Let completely cool on a rack.

Coconut Chocolate Truffles

Ingredients for 12 servings TRUFFLES

1 cup raw cashews, soaked overnight
¾ cup pitted cherries
2 tbsp coconut oil
1 cup shredded coconut
2 tbsp cocoa powder

Directions and Total Time: 1 hour 15 minutes

Line a baking sheet with parchment paper and set aside.

Blend the cashews, cherries, coconut oil, half of the shredded coconut, and cocoa powder in a food processor until ingredients are evenly mixed. Spread the remaining shredded coconut on a dish. Mould the mixture into 12 truffle shapes. Roll the truffles in the coconut dish, shaking off any excess, then arrange on the prepared baking sheet. Refrigerate for 1 hour.

Coconut Peach Tart

Ingredients for 8 servings

½ cup rolled oats
1 cup cashews
1 cup soft pitted dates
1 cup canned coconut milk
2 large peaches, chopped
½ cup shredded coconut

Directions and Total Time: 10 minutes

In a food processor, pulse the oats, cashews and dates, until a dough-like mixture forms. Press down into a greased baking pan.

Pulse the coconut milk, ½ cup water, peaches, and shredded coconut in the food processor until smooth. Pour this mixture over the crust and spread evenly. Freeze for 30 minutes. Soften 15 minutes before serving. Top with whipped coconut cream and shredded coconut.

Layered Raspberry & Tofu Cups

Ingredients for 4 servings

½ cup unsalted raw cashews
3 tbsp pure date sugar
½ cup soy milk
¾ cup firm silken tofu, drained
1 tsp vanilla extract
2 cups sliced raspberries
1 tsp fresh lemon juice
Fresh mint leaves

Directions and Total Time: 60 minutes

Grind the cashews and 3 tbsp of date sugar, in a blender until a fine powder is obtained. Pour in soy milk and blitz until smooth. Add in tofu and vanilla and pulse until creamy. Remove to a bowl and refrigerate covered for 30 minutes.

In a bowl, mix the raspberries, lemon juice and remaining date sugar. Let sit for 20 minutes. Assemble by alternating into small cups one layer of raspberries and one layer of cashew cream, ending with the cashew cream. Serve garnished with mint leaves.

Mango Muffins with Chocolate Chips

Ingredients for 12 servings

- 2 medium mangoes, chopped
- 1 cup non-dairy milk
- 2 tbsp almond butter
- 1 tsp apple cider vinegar
- 1 tsp pure vanilla extract
- 1 ¼ cups whole-wheat flour
- ½ cup rolled oats
- ¼ cup coconut sugar
- 1 tsp baking powder
- ½ tsp baking soda
- ½ cup unsweetened cocoa powder
- ¼ cup sesame seeds
- A pinch of salt
- ¼ cup dark chocolate chips

Directions and Total Time: 40 minutes

Preheat oven to 360 F.

In a food processor, put the mangoes, milk, almond butter, vinegar, and vanilla. Blend until smooth.

In a bowl, combine the flour, oats, sugar, baking powder, baking soda, cocoa powder, sesame seeds, salt, and chocolate chips. Pour into the mango mixture and mix. Scoop into a greased muffin cups and bake for 20-25 minutes. Let cool completely before removing from the cups.

Vanilla Cookies with Poppy Seeds

Ingredients for 3 servings

- ¾ cup plant butter, softened
- ½ cup pure date sugar
- 1 tsp pure vanilla extract
- 2 tbsp pure maple syrup
- 2 cups whole-grain flour
- ¾ cup poppy seeds, lightly toasted

Directions and Total Time: 15 minutes

Beat the butter and sugar in a bowl, until creamy and fluffy. Add in vanilla, and maple syrup, blend. Stir in flour and poppy seeds. Wrap the dough in a cylinder and cover with plastic. Let chill in the fridge.

Preheat oven to 330 F. Cut the dough into thin circles and arrange on a baking sheet. Bake for 12 minutes, until light brown. Let completely cool before serving.

Kiwi & Peanut Bars

Ingredients for 9 servings

- 2 kiwis, mashed
- 1 tbsp maple syrup
- ½ tsp vanilla extract
- 2 cups old-fashioned rolled oats
- ½ tsp salt
- ¼ cup chopped peanuts

Directions and Total Time: 5 minutes

Preheat oven to 360 F.

In a bowl, add kiwi, maple syrup, and vanilla and stir. Mix in oats, salt, and peanuts. Pour into a greased baking dish and bake for 25-30 minutes, until crisp. Let completely cool and slice into bars to serve.

Easy Maple Rice Pudding

Ingredients for 4 servings

1 cup short-grain brown rice
1 ¾ cups nondairy milk
4 tbsp pure maple syrup
1 tsp vanilla extract
A pinch of salt
¼ cup dates, pitted and chopped

Directions and Total Time: 30 minutes

In a pot over medium heat, place the rice, milk, 1 ½ cups water, maple, vanilla, and salt. Bring to a boil, then reduce the heat. Cook for 20 minutes, stirring occasionally. Mix in dates and cook another 5 minutes. Serve chilled in cups.

Coconut & Chocolate Brownies

Ingredients for 4 servings

1 cup whole-grain flour
½ cup unsweetened cocoa powder
1 tsp baking powder
½ tsp salt
1 cup pure date sugar
½ cup canola oil
¾ cup almond milk
1 tsp pure vanilla extract
1 tsp coconut extract
½ cup vegan chocolate chips
½ cup sweetened shredded coconut

Directions and Total Time: 40 minutes

Preheat oven to 360 F.

In a bowl, combine the flour, cocoa, baking powder, and salt.

In another bowl, whisk the date sugar and oil until creamy. Add in almond milk, vanilla extract and coconut extract. Mix until smooth. Pour into the flour mixture and stir to combine. Fold in the coconut and chocolate chips.

Pour the batter into a greased baking pan and bake for 35-40 minutes. Let cool before serving.

Coconut Chia Pudding

Ingredients for 4 servings

Zest and juice of 1 orange
1 (14-oz) can coconut milk
2 dates, pitted and chopped
1 tbsp chia seeds

Directions and Total Time: 30 minutes

In a blender, put the orange juice, orange zest, coconut milk, dates, and chia seeds. Blitz until smooth. Transfer to a bowl and put in the fridge for 20 minutes. Top with berries, whipped cream or toasted coconut and serve.

Homemade Goji Berry Chocolate Granita

Ingredients for 4 servings

1 pear, chopped
1 tbsp almond butter
2 tbsp fresh mint, minced
¼ cup non-dairy milk
3 tbsp non-dairy chocolate chips
2 tbsp goji berries

Directions and Total Time: 5 minutes

In a food processor, place the almond butter, pear, and mint. Pulse until smooth. Pour in milk, while keep blending. Add in chocolate chips and berries. Transfer to a glass and serve.

Maple Fruit Crumble

Ingredients for 4 servings

3 cups chopped apricots
3 cups chopped mangoes
4 tbsp pure maple syrup
1 cup gluten-free rolled oats
½ cup shredded coconut
2 tbsp coconut oil

Directions and Total Time: 25 minutes

Preheat oven to 360 F.

Place the apricots, mangoes and 2 tbsp of maple syrup in a round baking dish.

In a food processor, put the oats, coconut, coconut oil, and remaining maple syrup. Blend until combined. Pour over the fruit. Bake for 20-25 minutes. Allow to cool before slicing and serving.

Peanut Chocolate Brownies

Ingredients for 12 servings

1 ¾ cups whole-grain flour
1 tsp baking powder
½ tsp salt
1 tbsp ground nutmeg
½ tsp ground cinnamon
3 tbsp unsweetened cocoa powder
½ cup vegan chocolate chips
½ cup chopped peanuts
¼ cup canola oil
½ cup dark molasses ½ cup water
⅓ cup pure date sugar
2 tsp grated fresh ginger

Directions and Total Time: 40 minutes

Preheat oven to 360 F.

Combine the flour, baking powder, salt, nutmeg, cinnamon, and cocoa in a bowl. Add in chocolate chips and peanuts and stir. Set aside.

In another bowl, mix the oil, molasses, water, sugar, and ginger. Pour into the flour mixture and stir to combine. Transfer to a greased baking pan and bake for 30-35 minutes. Let cool before slicing.

Sherry-Lime Mango Dessert

Ingredients for 4 servings

3 ripe mangoes, cubed
⅓ cup pure date sugar
2 tbsp fresh lime juice
½ cup Sherry
Fresh mint sprigs

Directions and Total Time: 15 minutes

Arrange the mango cubes on a baking sheet. Sprinkle with some date and let sit covered for 30 minutes. Sprinkle with lime juice and sherry. Refrigerate covered for 1 hour. Remove from the fridge and let sit for a few minutes at room temperature. Serve in glasses topped with mint.

Almond & Chia Bites with Cherries

Ingredients for 2 servings4

1 cup cherries, pitted
1 cup shredded coconut
¼ cup chia seeds
¾ cup ground almonds
¼ cup cocoa nibs

Directions and Total Time: 20 minutes

Blend cherries, coconut, chia seeds, almonds, and cocoa nibs in a food processor until crumbly. Shape the mixture into 24 balls and arrange on a lined baking sheet. Let sit in the fridge for 15 minutes.

Vanilla Cranberry & Almond Balls

Ingredients for 12 servings

2 tbsp almond butter
2 tbsp maple syrup
¾ cup cooked millet

¼ cup sesame seeds, toasted
1 tbsp chia seeds
½ tsp almond extract

Zest of 1 orange
1 tbsp dried cranberries
¼ cup ground almonds

Directions and Total Time: 25 minutes

Whisk the almond butter and syrup in a bowl, until creamy. Mix in millet, sesame seeds, chia seeds, almond extract, orange zest, cranberries, and almonds. Shape the mixture into balls and arrange on a parchment paper lined baking sheet. Let chill in the fridge for 15 minutes.

Chocolate Campanelle with Hazelnuts

Ingredients for 4 servings

½ cup chopped toasted hazelnuts
¼ cup vegan semisweet chocolate

pieces
8 oz campanelle pasta

3 tbsp vegan margarine
¼ cup maple syrup

Directions and Total Time: 10 minutes

Pulse the hazelnuts and chocolate pieces in a food processor until crumbly. Set aside.

Place the campanelle pasta in a pot with boiling salted water. Cook for 8-10 minutes until al dente, stirring often. Drain and back to the pot. Stir in almond butter and syrup and stir until the butter is melted. Remove to a plate and serve garnished with the chocolate-hazelnut mixture.

Pressure Cooker Apple Cupcakes

Ingredients for 4 servings

1 cup canned applesauce
1 cup non-dairy milk

6 tbsp maple syrup + for sprinkling
¼ cup spelt flour

½ tsp apple pie spice
A pinch of salt

Directions and Total Time: 25 minutes

In a bowl, combine the applesauce, milk, maple syrup, flour, apple pie spice, and salt. Scoop into 4 heat-proof ramekins. Drizzle with more syrup.

Pour 1 cup of water in the IP and fit in a trivet. Place the ramekins on the trivet. Lock lid in place; set the time to 6 minutes on High. Once ready, perform a quick pressure release. Unlock the lid and let cool for a few minutes take out the ramekins. Allow to cool for 10 minutes and serve.

Coconut & Date Truffles with Walnuts

Ingredients for 8 servings

1 cup pitted dates
1 cup walnuts
½ cup sweetened cocoa powder,

plus extra for coating
½ cup shredded coconut
¼ cup pure maple syrup

1 tsp vanilla extract
¼ tsp salt

Directions and Total Time: 15 minutes

Blend the dates, walnuts, cocoa powder, maple syrup, vanilla extract, and salt in a food processor until smooth. Let chill in the fridge for 1 hour. Shape the mixture into balls and roll up the truffles in cocoa powder. Serve chilled.

Roasted Apples Stuffed with Pecans & Dates

Ingredients for 4 servings

4 apples, cored, halved lengthwise
½ cup finely chopped pecans
4 dates, pitted and chopped
1 tbsp plant butter
1 tbsp pure maple syrup
¼ tsp ground cinnamon

Directions and Total Time: 40 minutes

Preheat oven to 360 F.

Mix the pecans, dates, butter, maple syrup, and cinnamon in a bowl. Arrange the apple on a greased baking pan and fill them with the pecan mixture. Pour 1 tbsp of water in the baking pan. Bake for 30-40 minutes, until soft and lightly browned. Serve immediately.

Pumpkin Brownie

Ingredients for 4 servings

3 oz dairy-free dark chocolate
1 tbsp coconut oil
½ cup pumpkin puree
2 tbsp pure date sugar
⅓ cup whole-wheat flour
½ tsp baking powder
A pinch of salt

Directions and Total Time: 20 minutes

Microwave chocolate and coconut oil for 90 seconds. Mix in pumpkin purée and sugar. Stir in flour, baking powder and salt. Pour the batter into ramekins. Arrange on a baking dish and pour in 2 cups of water. Bake for 20 minutes at 360 F. Let cool for a few minutes. Serve topped with raspberries.

Mango Chocolate Fudge

Ingredients for 3 servings6

1 mango
¾ cup vegan chocolate chips
4 cups pure date sugar
1 tsp pure vanilla extract

Directions and Total Time: 10 minutes + chilling time

In a food processor, blend the mango until smooth.

Microwave the chocolate until melted. Add in the pureed mango, sugar and vanilla, stir to combine. Spread on a lined with waxed paper baking pan and chill in the fridge for 2 hours. Once chilled, take out the fudge and lay on a cutting board. Discard the waxed paper. Slice into small pieces and serve.

Coconut & Chocolate Macaroons

Ingredients for 4 servings

1 cup shredded coconut
2 tbsp cocoa powder
1 tbsp vanilla extract
⅔ cup coconut milk
¼ cup maple syrup
A pinch of salt

Directions and Total Time: 25 minutes

Preheat oven to 360 F.

In a pot, place the shredded coconut, cocoa powder, vanilla extract, coconut milk, maple syrup, and salt. Cook until a firm dough is formed. Shape balls out of the mixture. Arrange the balls on a lined with parchment paper baking sheet. Bake for 15 minutes. Allow to cool before serving.

Melon Chocolate Pudding

Ingredients for 4 servings

1 cup cubed melon
4 tbsp non-dairy milk
2 tbsp unsweetened cocoa powder
2 tbsp pure date sugar
½ ripe avocado

Directions and Total Time: 25 minutes

Blitz the milk, cocoa powder, sugar, and avocado in a blender until smooth. Mash the melon with a fork in a bowl. Mix in the cocoa mixture and serve.

Sicilian Papaya Sorbet

Ingredients for 4 servings

8 cups papaya chunks
Juice of 2 limes
½ cup pure date sugar
Lime zest

Directions and Total Time: 5 minutes freezing time

Blend the papaya, lime juice and sugar in a food processor until smooth. Transfer the mixture to a glass dish. Freeze for 2 hours. Take out from the freezer and scrape the top ice layer with a fork. Back to the freezer for 1 hour. Repeat the process a few more times, until all the ice is scraped up. Serve frozen garnished with lime zest strips.

Poppy-Granola Balls with Chocolate

Ingredients for 8 servings

½ cup granola
¼ cup pure date sugar
½ cup golden raisins
½ cup shelled sunflower seeds
¼ cup poppy seeds
1 ½ cups creamy almond butter
2 cups vegan chocolate chips

Directions and Total Time: 25 minutes

Blend the granola, sugar, raisins, sunflower seeds, and poppy seeds in a food processor. Stir in the almond butter and pulse until a smooth dough is formed. Leave in the fridge overnight. Shape small balls out of the mixture. Set aside. Melt the chocolate in the microwave oven. Dip the balls into the melted chocolate and place on a baking sheet. Chill in the fridge for 30 minutes, until firm. Serve.

Caribbean Pudding

Ingredients for 4 servings

3 kiwis, divided
1 (13.5-oz) can coconut milk
¼ cup organic cane sugar
1 tbsp cornstarch
1 tsp vanilla extract
2 pinches of salt
1 tbsp turmeric
Ground cinnamon

Directions and Total Time: 10 minutes + chilling time

In a blender, place the 2 kiwis, coconut milk, sugar, cornstarch, vanilla, and salt. Blitz until smooth. Stir in turmeric. Pour into a pot. Bring to a boil, lower the heat and simmer for 3 minutes, until pudding consistency is achieved. Remove to a bowl and let cool. Refrigerate covered overnight to set.

Before serving, cut the remaining kiwi into slices. In small glasses, put a layer of pudding, a layer of kiwi slices, a layer of pudding, and finish with kiwi slices. Serve sprinkled with cinnamon.

Balsamic Glazed Caramelized Quinces

Ingredients for 4 servings

1 cup balsamic vinegar
¼ cup + 3 tbsp pure date sugar
¼ tsp grated nutmeg
A pinch of salt
¼ cup coconut oil
2 quinces, cored and cut into slices

Directions and Total Time: 20 minutes

Heat a saucepan over medium heat and add in the balsamic vinegar, ¼ cup of date sugar, nutmeg, and salt. Cook for 10-15 minutes, stirring occasionally until the liquid has reduced by half.

Melt the coconut oil in a skillet over medium heat and in place in the quinces; cook for 5 minutes until golden. Stir in 3 tbsp of date sugar and cook for another 5 minutes until caramelized.

Serve in a plate drizzled with the balsamic glaze.

Glazed Chili Chocolate Cake

Ingredients for 4 servings

1 ¾ cups whole-grain flour
1 cup pure date sugar
¼ cup unsweetened cocoa powder
1 tsp baking soda
½ tsp baking powder
1 ½ tsp ground cinnamon
¼ tsp ground chili
⅓ cup olive oil
1 tbsp apple cider vinegar
1 ½ tsp pure vanilla extract
2 (1-oz) squares vegan chocolate
¼ cup soy milk
½ cup pure date sugar
3 tbsp plant butter
½ tsp pure vanilla extract

Directions and Total Time: 45 minutes

Preheat oven to 360 F.

In a bowl, mix the flour, sugar, baking soda, baking powder, cinnamon, and chili.

In another bowl, whisk the oil, vinegar, vanilla, and 1 cup cold water. Pour into the flour mixture, stir to combine. Pour the batter into a greased baking pan. Bake for 30 minutes. Let cool for 10-15 minutes. Take out the cake inverted onto a wire rack and allow to completely cool.

Place the chocolate and soy milk in a pot. Cook until the chocolate is melted. Add in sugar, cook for 5 minutes. Turn the heat off and mix in butter and vanilla. Cover the cake with the glaze. Refrigerate until the glaze set. Serve.

Cinnamon Tropical Cobbler

Ingredients for 6 servings

3 apples, shredded
2 ripe pineapples, chopped
2 tsp lemon juice
½ cup + 2 tbsp pure date sugar
2 tbsp cornstarch
1 tsp ground cinnamon
½ tsp ground allspice
1 cup whole-grain flour
1 ½ tsp baking powder
¼ tsp salt
2 tbsp peanut butter, softened
½ cup soy milk

Directions and Total Time: 45 minutes

Preheat oven to 390 F. Arrange the apples and pineapples on a greased baking pan. Drizzle with lemon juice and toss to coat. Mix in ½ cup of sugar, cornstarch, cinnamon, and allspice.

In a bowl, combine the flour, remaining sugar, baking powder, and salt. Stir in the peanut butter with a fork until the batter resembles crumbs. Pour in soy milk and mix. Spread the mixture over the fruit and bake for 30 minutes until golden. Serve immediately.

Lemon Blackberry Cake

Ingredients for 4 servings

4 peaches, peeled, and sliced
2 cups fresh blackberries
1 tbsp cornstarch
¾ cup pure date sugar
2 tsp fresh lemon juice
1 tsp ground cinnamon
½ cup whole-grain flour
½ cup old-fashioned oats
3 tbsp plant butter

Directions and Total Time: 45 minutes

Preheat oven to 370 F.

In a bowl, mix the peaches, blackberries, cornstarch, ¼ cup of sugar, lemon juice, and ½ tsp of cinnamon. Pour the batter into the pan. Set aside. In a bowl, stir the flour, oats, butter, remaining cup of sugar, and remaining cinnamon. Blend until crumbly. Drizzle the topping over the fruit. Bake for 30-40 minutes, until browned. Serve hot.

Hazelnut Topped Coconut Caramelized Bananas

Ingredients for 4 servings

2 bananas, peeled, halved cross-wise and then lengthwise
2 tbsp coconut oil
2 tbsp coconut sugar
2 tbsp spiced apple cider
Chopped hazelnuts, for topping

Directions and Total Time: 15 minutes

In a skillet over medium heat, melt the coconut oil. Place in bananas, cook for 2 minutes. Turn them, cook for another 2 minutes. Pour the sugar and cider around the bananas, cook for 2-3 minutes, until thickens and caramelize. Serve into bowls topped with remaining liquid and hazelnuts.

Apple & Cashew Quiche

Ingredients for 6 servings

5 apples, peeled and cut into slices
½ cup pure maple syrup
1 tbsp fresh orange juice
1 tsp ground cinnamon
½ cup whole-grain flour
½ cup old-fashioned oats
½ cup finely chopped cashew
⅔ cup pure date sugar
½ cup plant butter, softened

Directions and Total Time: 55 minutes

Preheat oven to 360 F. Place apples in a greased baking pan. Stir in maple syrup and orange juice. Sprinkle with ½ tsp of cinnamon. In a bowl, combine the flour, oats, cashew, sugar, and remaining cinnamon. Blend in the butter until the mixture crumbs. Pour over the apples and bake for 45 minutes.

Tofu & Almond Pancakes

Ingredients for 10 servings

1 ⅓ cups almond milk
1 cup almond flour
⅓ cup firm tofu, crumbled
3 tbsp plant butter, melted
2 tbsp pure date sugar
1 ½ tsp pure vanilla extract
½ tsp baking powder
⅛ tsp salt

Directions and Total Time: 15 minutes

Blitz almond milk, tofu, butter, sugar, vanilla, baking powder, and salt in a blender until smooth. Heat a pan and coat with oil. Scoop a ladle of batter at the centre and spread all over. Cook for 3-4 minutes until golden, turning once. Transfer to a plate and repeat the process until no batter is left. Serve.

Almond Berry Cream

Ingredients for 4 servings

3 (15-oz) cans almond milk
3 tbsp maple syrup
½ tsp almond extract
1 cup blueberries
1 cup raspberries
1 cup strawberries, sliced

Directions and Total Time: 10 minutes

Place almond milk in the fridge overnight. Open the can and reserve the liquid. In a bowl, mix almond solids, maple syrup and almond extract. Share berries into 4 bowls. Serve topped with almond cream.

Pumpkin & Mango Lemon Cake

Ingredients for 8 servings

1 ½ cups whole-grain flour
¾ cup pure date sugar
¼ cup yellow cornmeal
1 tsp baking soda
½ tsp salt
½ tsp baking powder
½ tsp ground cinnamon
½ tsp ground allspice
½ tsp ground ginger
1 cup pumpkin puree
⅓ cup canola oil
2 tsp grated lemon zest
2 tbsp water
1 mango, chopped

Directions and Total Time: 60 minutes

Preheat oven to 360 F.

In a bowl, mix the flour, sugar, cornmeal, baking soda, salt, baking powder, cinnamon, allspice, and ginger. In another bowl, whisk the pumpkin puree, oil, lemon zest, and water, until blend. Add in the mango. Pour the flour mixture into the pumpkin mixture and toss to coat. Pour the batter into a greased baking pan and bake for 45-50 minutes. Let completely cool before slicing. Serve.

Blueberry Lime Granizado

Ingredients for 1 servings

½ cup pure date sugar
2 cups blueberries
2 tsp fresh lemon juice

Directions and Total Time: 15 minutes

Place the sugar and ½ cup water in a pot. Cook for 3 minutes on low, until the sugar is dissolved. Remove to a heatproof bowl and chill for 2 hours in the fridge. Blitz the blueberries and lemon juice in a blender until smooth. Add in cooled sugar and pulse until smooth. Place in an ice cream maker and follow the directions. Once ready, serve immediately or freeze another 1-2 hours for a firm texture.

Coconut Bars with Chocolate Chips

Ingredients for 16 servings

¼ cup coconut oil
1 cups shredded coconut
¼ cup pure date sugar
2 tbsp agave syrup
1 cup vegan chocolate chips

Directions and Total Time: 45 minutes

Grease a dish with coconut oil. Set aside. In a bowl, mix the coconut, sugar, agave syrup, and coconut oil. Spread the mixture onto the dish, pressing down. Place the chocolate chips in a heatproof bowl and microwave for 1 minute. Stir and heat 30 seconds more until the chocolate is melted. Pour over the coconut and let harden for 20 minutes. Chop into 16 bars. Store in a container for up to 1 week.

Made in the USA
Monee, IL
15 March 2020